Now featuring three additional essays, and with an original afterword by bestselling author Jason Reynolds, this new edition of *They Can't Kill Us Until They Kill Us* is a celebration of the lyricism, brilliance, and endearing voice of a breakout writer.

Whether he's attending a Bruce Springsteen concert the day after visiting Michael Brown's grave, or considering public displays of affection at a Carly Rae Jepsen show, Abdurraqib writes with a poignancy and magnetism that resonates profoundly. In the wake of the 2015 Paris nightclub attacks, Abdurraqib recalls how he sought refuge as a teenager in music, at punk shows, and wonders whether the next generation of young Muslims will be afforded that same opportunity. While discussing the everyday threat to the lives of Black Americans, Abdurraqib recounts the first time he was ordered to the ground by police officers.

Described as "a collection of death-defying protest songs for the Black Lives Matter era*," in these searing, unforgettable essays, Abdurraqib reflects on everything from Chance The Rapper and Nina Simone to Allen Iverson and Serena Williams, from summer crushes to the thrill of common joys in children. In his thoughtful consideration of music, culture, and daily life as a lens through which to view our world, Abdurraqib proves himself a bellwether for our times.

*Walton Muyumba, *Chicago Tribune*

"By turns incisive, exciting, and insightful. It is a musical inventory of America's past, present, and future... Abdurraqib writes about things we know in ways we don't, and readers are sure to learn something if they stop and listen to this vital voice."
—**REBECCA VALLEY,** *DRIZZLE REVIEW*

"One of the most vital books on music I read this year... which spoke so eloquently to the importance of making space for dreaming, laughing, and, of course, listening to joyful music in troubled times."
—**LINDSAY ZOLADZ,** *SLATE*

"This tome stands as a bold statement for a great writer and a complete breath of life from a rare thinker."
ERICK MERTZ, *NEW NOISE MAGAZINE*

"As powerful and touching as anything I've read this year, and Abdurraqib has emerged as the Ta-Nehisi Coates of popular culture." —**JAMES MANN,** *THE BIG TAKEOVER*

"Abdurraqib writes about the music he holds dear, and the experiences which have embedded this music in his life, with such lyricism that the writing nears music itself—and his love of the subject is palpable." —**ARIANNA REBOLINI,** *BUZZFEED*

"Abdurraqib will make you think critically about music and the culture it influences, and his thoughts will stay with you."
—**GABRIELA TULLY CLAYMORE,** *STEREOGUM*

"Magnetic and poignant, and tinged with heartache."
—**NIKESH SHUKLA,** *THE GUARDIAN*

"Poignant and important. Abdurraqib offers a perspective that connects music, art, and memory, with the political realities of our time." —**ANGELA LEDGERWOOD,** *ESQUIRE*

"A collection of death-defying protest songs for the Black Lives Matter era." —**WALTON MUYUMBA,** *CHICAGO TRIBUNE*

"[Abdurraqib] invites us to acknowledge the unbridgeable gaps formed by centuries of history, to observe with respect the moments that don't include us all, and to cherish all the more the opportunities we have for empathy, which bring us as close as we can get to harmony." —**AIDA AMOAKO,** *PROSPECT*

"A much-needed collection for our time. [Abdurraqib] has proven to be one of the most essential voices of his generation." —**JUAN VIDAL, NPR**

"Abdurraqib is unflaggingly curious about the salvation that music brings, and the, intentional or not, consequences of listening." —**LESLEY JENIKE,** *PLOUGHSHARES*

"There are times where Abdurraqib's writing seems to physically overflow with emotion and urgency." —**KYLIE MASLEN,** *KILL YOUR DARLINGS*

"Challenging and lyrical, his writing delivers compelling observations in bite-sized pieces, allowing you to digest the deeper ramifications of his insights." —**FRANNIE JACKSON,** *PASTE*

"Hanif Abdurraqib doesn't promise us anything beyond brilliant flashes of light in a dark and complicated world, but he does it with such generosity, such grace that we might not deserve it." —**JAIME FOUNTAINE,** *FANZINE*

"To say Hanif Abdurraqib writes about the music that's the soundtrack to our lives is an understatement... Abdurraqib is taking the music many already enjoy and asking us to consider its more profound implications." —**MANDY SHUNNARAH,** *PANK MAGAZINE*

"There are few critics alive today that can talk about music and culture with the same level of adoration and encyclopedic knowledge." —**GINA MEI,** *SHONDALAND*

"A joyful requiem—emphasis on joyful. Abdurraqib has written a guide for the living as well as a memorial for those we have lost." —**DAVID BREITHAUPT,** *LOS ANGELES REVIEW OF BOOKS*

"Abdurraqib is concerned with life, with actuality and experience: he's an artist in troubled times; may his writing shine some light on our own paths."
—**EMILIO JESÚS TAIVEAHO,** *CAROLINA QUARTERLY*

"There is something precious in how Abdurraqib's writing transcends changes in emotion and in tone to flow so seamlessly from one topic to the next... In his writing, there is no separation between art and life. Each informs and intertwines with the other." —**ALLISON J. SCHARMANN,** *THE HARVARD CRIMSON*

"As expansive in scope as it is rich in content... His writing is alive and breathing, criticism infused with stories, lived experience and emotion. For Abdurraqib, it's never just a song, never just an artist; music is a lens through which he sees the whole world." —**ASIF BECHER,** *THE MICHIGAN DAILY*

"A penetrating and profoundly timely collection of essays. It is music writing at its sharpest, most perceptive, and most urgent... Most remarkable, perhaps, is Abdurraqib's ability to perceive and define connections between his subjects, himself, and the fractured, complicated culture in which we live."
—*FOREWORD REVIEWS* (**STARRED**)

"Abdurraqib's essay collection is mesmerizing and deeply perceptive... filled with honesty, providing the reader with the sensation of seeing the world through fresh eyes."
—*PUBLISHERS WEEKLY* (**STARRED**)

"Highly recommended." —*LIBRARY JOURNAL* (**STARRED**)

"Abdurraqib writes with uninhibited curiosity and insight about music and its ties to culture and memory, life and death, on levels personal, political, and universal." —*BOOKLIST* (**STARRED**)

Also by Hanif Abdurraqib

The Crown Ain't Worth Much

Go Ahead in the Rain:
Notes to A Tribe Called Quest

A Fortune for Your Disaster

A Little Devil in America:
Notes in Praise of Black Performance

They Can't Kill Us Until They Kill Us

Essays

HANIF ABDURRAQIB

Introduction by
EVE L. EWING

Afterword by
JASON REYNOLDS

Two Dollar Radio
Books too loud to Ignore

Two Dollar Radio
Books too loud to Ignore

WHO WE ARE Two Dollar Radio is a family-run outfit dedicated to reaffirming the cultural and artistic spirit of the publishing industry. We aim to do this by presenting bold works of literary merit, each book, individually and collectively, providing a sonic progression that we believe to be too loud to ignore.

TwoDollarRadio.com

Proudly based in
Columbus
OHIO

 @TwoDollarRadio

 @TwoDollarRadio

 /TwoDollarRadio

Printed in **The United States of America**

SOME RECOMMENDED LOCATIONS FOR READING: Grandpa's Cheesebarn in Ashland, Ohio; The back row of a Punk Rock show where all of the parents are; On the road, in between the place you want to be and the place you're going; Or, pretty much anywhere because books are portable and the perfect technology!

COVER→ Wolf, cropped: Lynn_Bystrom/iStock; **Jacket**, cropped: Tim Parker, https://flic.kr/p/9NMoCt; **Necklace**, cropped: sookie, https://flic.kr/p/2swfHX.

The following essays have appeared in slightly different forms in the following publications:

Sections I, II, II, IV, V, VI in *Pacific Standard* (as "In the Morning, I'll Be All Right: Marvin Gaye and the Unlikely Patriotism of Resistance"); "I Wasn't Brought Here, I Was Born: Surviving Punk Rock Long Enough to Find Afropunk" in *Pitchfork*; "On Paris" in *Splinter*; "My First Police Stop" in *The New York Times*; "Serena Williams and The Policing of Imagined Arrogance" in *Blavity*; the following have appeared in in *MTV News*: "Chance The Rapper's Golden Year" (as "Chance The Rapper: Artist of the Year"), "A Night In Bruce Springsteen's America," "Carly Rae Jepsen Loves You Back (as "Carly Rae Jepsen's Public Displays of Affection"), "The Night Prince Walked On Water," "Under Half Lit Fluorescents: The Wonder Years And The Great Suburban Narrative," "Searching For A New Kind Of Optimism," "Death Becomes You: My Chemical Romance And Ten Years Of The Black Parade," "Black Life On Film," "Tell 'Em All To Come And Get Me, "Burning That Which Will Not Save You: Wipe Me Down And The Ballad Of Baton Rouge (as "Lil Boosie, 'Wipe Me Down,' and the Ballad of Baton Rouge"), "Rumours And The Currency Of Heartbreak (as "Fleetwood Mac's Rumours at 40: Heartbreak and Magic"), "Nina Simone Was Very Black," "The Obama White House, A Brief Home For Rappers (as "Saying Goodbye to a White House that Welcomed Hip-Hop"), "Surviving On Small Joys."

CONTENTS

Introduction, by Eve L. Ewing

I.

Chance The Rapper's Golden Year

A Night In Bruce Springsteen's America

Carly Rae Jepsen Loves You Back

The Night Prince Walked On Water

ScHoolboy Q Wants White People To Say The Word

The Weeknd And The Future Of Loveless Sex

II.

I Wasn't Brought Here, I Was Born:
Surviving Punk Rock Long Enough To Find Afropunk

Under Half-Lit Fluorescents: The Wonder Years
And The Great Suburban Narrative

All Our Friends Are Famous

The Return Of The Loneliest Boys In Town

Brief Notes On Staying // No One Is Making
Their Best Work When They Want To Die

Searching For A New Kind Of Optimism

Death Becomes You: My Chemical Romance And
Ten Years Of The Black Parade

Defiance, Ohio Is The Name Of A Band

III.

    Fall Out Boy Forever

IV.

    Ric Flair, Best Rapper Alive

    It Rained In Ohio On The Night Allen Iverson Hit Michael Jordan With A Crossover

    There Is The Picture Of Michael Jackson Kissing Whitney Houston On The Cheek

    Black Life On Film

    Tell 'Em All To Come And Get Me

    Burning That Which Will Not Save You: Wipe Me Down And The Ballad Of Baton Rouge

    Rumours And The Currency Of Heartbreak

V.

    February 26, 2012

    On Kindness

    In The Summer Of 1997, Everyone Took To The Streets In Shiny Suits

    Nina Simone Was Very Black

    Blood Summer, In Three Parts.

    August 9, 2014

    Fear In Two Winters

On Paris

My First Police Stop

Serena Williams And The Policing
Of Imagined Arrogance

They Will Speak Loudest Of You After You've Gone

Johnny Cash Never Shot A Man In Reno. Or, The Migos:
Nice Kids From The Suburbs

The Obama White House, A Brief Home For Rappers

The White Rapper Joke

On Future And Working Through What Hurts

November 22, 2014

Surviving On Small Joys

VI.

Bonus Tracks:

On Summer Crushing

Carly Rae Jepsen And The Kingdom Of Desire

On Seatbelts And Sunsets

Afterword, by Jason Reynolds

Acknowledgments

I wish to live because life has within it that which is good, that which is beautiful, and that which is love. Therefore, since I have known all of these things, I have found them to be reason enough and I wish to live. Moreover, because this is so, I wish others to live for generations and generations and generations and generations.

Lorraine Hansberry

I cannot die because this is my universe

Lil Uzi Vert

Introduction

I was probably a little over-eager when I asked Hanif Abdurraqib to form a Death Cab for Cutie cover band with me. "It could be called Movie Script Ending," I said. Ever generous, his reply skirted the need for a yes or a no. "You strike me as someone who could front a band," he said.

Probably a little much. After all, we had only met in person once. We were mostly internet friends, part of the interwoven network of old buddies and mutual Twitter followers and quiet rivals that comprises a loose community of Black poets of our generation. We had just, a little over a month prior, connected in person for the first time at a Memorial Day barbecue, where he told me quietly that he had an idea for an essay about how "Trap Queen" was an important love song and I told him that that sounded awfully good.

So maybe I was overzealous with the cover band thing. But I was just so excited to feel a little less alone in the world, so enthused by his Facebook posts about the music I had loved so fiercely during my teen and college years, music that seemed to speak to the very center of my heart while it also made me feel impossibly lonely in rock venues and divey bars packed to the gills with white people. This is what I told him via voice text as I careened down the interstate one night, alone, euphoric to the point of delusion, listening to songs that made me feel full and feeling like he might understand that in a way others might not. I was sad, and I desired a chance to pivot my sadness into something like dancing, something like making people sing along. "This, too, is a response to grief," he tells us. "Covering yourself in the spoils of your survival."

Because, you see, Hanif Abdurraqib is something between an empath and an illusionist. Among the thousands who have read his work, I am confident that I am not alone when I say that Hanif lured me in with a magic trick—by apparently knowing the textures of my relationship to songs and athletes and places that I love. He knows our secrets. He has an uncanny ability to write about music and the world around it as though he was sitting there on the couch with you in your grandma's basement, listening to her old vinyl, or he was in that car with you and your high school friend who would later become your boyfriend, singing until you were hoarse, or he was on the bus with you when you sat in the back with your headphones on trying to look a lot harder and meaner than you really were. He seems to know all about that summer, that breakup, that mix she made you that you lost when someone broke into your car later that year.

> *It is an album of return and escape and return and escape again. It feels, in tone and tension, like coming home for a summer after your first year of college, having tasted another existence and wanting more, but instead sleeping in your childhood room. Home is where the heart begins, but not where the heart stays. The heart scatters across states, and has nothing left after what home takes from it.*

—

> *At moments in the show, I felt like I was exiting my current body and watching myself from through my younger eyes, wondering if this is what it was always*

going to come to. Returning to the balm for an old
wound, ashamed that I once decided to wear it.

—

Kendrick Lamar says "God got Us" and the Us crawls
out of the speaker and wraps its arms around the Black
people in the room. The way a good preacher might say
"We" in a Black church and the congregation hums.
The way I say "My people" and My People know who
they are even if we've never met, or even if we've never
spoken, or even if all we have is the shared lineage of
coming from a people who came from a people who
came from a people who didn't intend to come here but
built the here once they arrived

But then, like any good magician, he pivots. Sure, he found
the card you chose and that's impressive, but then you realize
he's turned the whole deck into the queen of hearts and that's
so much more remarkable. And all of a sudden you're drawn
into an irresistible account of some artist whose work you never
cared about, maybe someone whose work you even hated or
always thought was kinda stupid, or just ignored altogether, and
you realize how foolish you've been. A while ago we showed
up for lunch with a group of friends, and our fellow poet Jose
Olivarez invited his brother to join us. Pedro showed up proudly
sporting a Carly Rae Jepsen shirt paired with a chain and crisp
Nikes, and explained that Hanif had been the one to put him
on. Indeed, his passion for CRJ is legion, and I confess that for
a while I thought it was an ornate joke (because People Like Me,
People Like Us, don't listen to Carly Rae Jepsen) until I actually
put on *E•MO•TION* and when it was over, found myself putting
it on again, and hitting repeat.

We've run out of ways to weaponize sadness, and so it becomes an actual weapon. A buffet of sad and bitter songs rains down from the pop charts for years, keeping us tethered to whatever sadness we could dress ourselves in when nothing else fit. Jepsen is trying to unlock the hard door, the one with all of the other feelings behind it.

This is what he does. His work asks not, as much criticism does, *what is happening here*, but rather, *what does this work mean?* What is it doing in the world?

This is a book about life and death—in particular, though not exclusively, about Black life, and Black death. In our era, the election of the first Black president this gruesome nation had ever seen, and the unavoidable broadcasts of Black people murdered have twisted into a sick double helix such that they all decided to pay attention to us again. That means that we have been living and reading and writing in an era when Blackness and the spectacle of our irreconcilable, uncomfortable, formative presence in this country, and all the implications of that spectacle, is in full view in a way that is by no means unprecedented but sure is awfully loud. There is lots to say and lots of people are saying it, some distinctly and some less so. Amidst it all, it can be hard for those of us who are having our second coming of age within the din of a violent country to determine where our voices fit. In that context, *They Can't Kill Us Until They Kill Us*—in its very title honoring death and life regarding each other in inward-facing mirrors, a memorial of a memorial of our brother slain—manages against all odds to be really something special. Consider this moment, when Hanif retells the tale of Jordan and Iverson in a way that is really the tale of the constraints placed on the Black body, on who is allowed to move freely and who is allowed to mourn, and how—narrated,

in the end, through a boy attempting an Iversonian crossover
alone on a wet court.

You will believe that I once wore baggy jeans that
dragged the ground until the bottoms of them split into
small white flags of surrender and you will also believe
that I dreamed of having enough money to buy my way
into the kind of infamy that came with surviving any
kind of proximity to poverty. You will believe, then, that
I remember all of this by the way the ball felt in my
hands as I stood on the court alone the next day, pulling
the wet ball from one hand to the next and feeling the
water spin off of it. You will believe that I only imagined
the defender I was breezing past, and pushing my way
to the foul line. And even as I missed shot after shot
after shot, I still cheered. Alone in the wet aftermath of
a night where I first saw the player I imagined myself
becoming. A shot, finally finding the bottom of the net,
and my hand, still extended, to an audience of no one.

Freedom. And its inverse (as David Stern made us see
when Iverson's cornrows became a minor crime), constraint.
Abdurraqib indicts the country doing the police work of this
constraint—not through a direct admonition, but through the
kind of quietly damning observation we Midwesterners so excel
at.

The daughter of a Black man murdered on camera
by police records an ad for a presidential candidate
and the white people who support the candidate are
so moved by her retelling of a life without her father.
And I do imagine that it must be something, to be able
to decide at what volume, tone, and tenor you will

allow Black people to enter your life, for praise or for scolding.

In many of the essays in this book, the crowd—whether the crowd at a tiny punk club or the crowd gathered in protest at JFK airport—also becomes a character, an audience, an imagined chorus to the comedy or tragedy Abdurraqib is witnessing. Implicitly, he reminds us of the magic of live music and human interaction in an era when on-demand streaming means that many of us lack any physicality whatsoever in our listening lives. I think it was 2010 when I sold all my CDs to a store I'm pretty sure is closed on a street that is now unrecognizable to me. For a writer who came of age in small Midwestern punk, emo, and hardcore shows, bodies are paramount—the ambitious and the listless alike packed in a room, sweating on each other, the safety pin from someone's ripped jeans come undone and stabbing you in the back of the shoulder, your bigger or taller friend keeping you from getting your head stomped in the pit. Bodies and the glory and inconvenience of bodies. Music, Abdurraqib reminds us, is something that is not only received but *happens*, takes place in a place where people are.

Our parents' generation of Black folks are known to greet each other with the koan-like tautology *everything is everything.* "How you doin brother?" "Man, listen. Everything is everything." "Everything is everything." In *They Can't Kill Us Until They Kill Us*, everything is quite literally everything. Race is music is love is America is death is rebirth is brotherhood is growing up is a mother is music is music is music is music. Everything is everything. Abdurraqib makes you realize that the music you listen to isn't about People Like Us, because it turns out all of us are People Like Us. All of us are frightened and heartbroken and ecstatic and mourning and in love and driving fast down the interstate, and we are blessed enough to live in a time when there are plenty of artists adept to holding that mirror. Last month when I sat on the floor with my seven-year-old cousin, playing checkers, she started singing a Carly Rae Jepsen song to herself in an earnest voice I'd never heard before: *I really really really really like you.* I pulled the song up and we sang it together, and for the moment that was our highway.

Hanif would probably laugh at this because I don't think he counts himself as any sort of optimist, but this book makes me almost believe in things I thought I'd given up on. I might even dance again, daring to move my legs across this wasted land.

—Eve L. Ewing,
November 2017

They Can't Kill Us Until They Kill Us

I can't afford love.

The Weeknd

I.

When Marvin Gaye sang the National Anthem at the 1983 NBA All-Star Game, he knew he was going to die soon.

If you are in Columbus, Ohio, on July 3rd of any year, you will likely drag yourself downtown with a blanket in the middle of the day, when the sun is still at its highest and most hungry. If you're lucky, you'll get a space at Huntington Park, where our beloved Triple-A baseball team, the Columbus Clippers, delivered back-to-back titles in 2010 and 2011. When night comes, you'll fall back into someone's arms, or be the arms that someone falls back into. And you'll roll your eyes when "Born in the U.S.A." plays while fireworks fly screaming into the sky, tucking all its darkness into their pockets.

There are days when the places we're from turn into every other place in America. I still go to watch fireworks, or I still go to watch the brief burst of brightness glow on the faces of Black children, some of them have made it downtown, miles away from the forgotten corners of the city they've been pushed to. Some of them smiling and pointing upwards, still too young to know of America's hunt for their flesh. How it wears the blood of their ancestors on its teeth.

Chance The Rapper's Golden Year

THIS, MORE THAN ANYTHING, IS ABOUT EVERY-
thing and everyone that didn't get swallowed by the vicious and
yawning maw of 2016, and all that it consumed upon its violent
rattling which echoed into the year after it and will surely echo
into the year after that one. This, more than anything, is about
how there is sometimes only one single clear and clean surface
on which to dance, and sometimes it only fits you and no one
else. This is about hope, sure, but not in the way that it is often
packaged as an antithesis to that which is burning. It was an
endless year that was sometimes hot and sometimes unbearable,
and I sometimes threw open my windows and let music flood
into the streets and I sometimes watched people glance up with
a knowing smile, the way we do when a sermon calls us home,
or calls us back to something better or away from somewhere
worse.

I haven't been to church in years but I am of a people who
know how to preach. Chance The Rapper has probably been to
church more recently than I have, or at least he understands the
gospel better than I ever will. By which I mean the gospel is, in
many ways, whatever gets people into the door to receive whatever blessings you have to offer. Everyone I knew needed blessings in 2016. The world, it seemed, was reaching yet another
breaking point in a long line of breaking points. An endless election barreled forward, a xenophobic bigot leading the charge.

Deadly attacks seemed to be a monthly occurrence, anchored by the Pulse nightclub massacre—the deadliest attack in our country's history. There were funerals I missed, and funerals I didn't. People I loved walked out of doors they didn't walk back through. The summer was cloaked in blood and fear, with more in the fall. If you believe, as I do, that a blessing is a brief breath to take in that doesn't taste of whatever is holding you under; say I Speak To God In Public and mean more than just in his house, or mean more than just next to people who also might speak to God in public, or say God and mean whatever has kept you alive when so many other things have failed to.

It isn't hard to sell people on optimism, but it's hard to keep them sold on it, especially in a cynical year. Yet when it was all said and done, Chance The Rapper stood as 2016's greatest optimist. His *Coloring Book* was one of the albums that wouldn't go away, no matter what came after it. First, it was the perfect summer album. Then summer passed, and I was still kicking up dead leaves in my neighborhood and listening to cars roll by with their windows slightly cracked listening to "Smoke Break" or "Mixtape." Chance made the only thing in 2016 that fit unconditionally. There is something about his joy that makes it stretch longer—perhaps that it demands nothing immediate from a listener or observer, except to take it in and let it be a brief and necessary bandage over anything that hurts.

Joy, or the concept of joy, is often toothless and vague because it needs to be. It is both hollow and touchable, in part because it is something that can't be explained as well as it can be visualized and experienced. For this, Chance benefits greatly. He has made joy into a brand, particularly coming to light in the middle of 2015, when he released the grinning, dancing, bright video for "Sunday Candy," an infectious ode to old Black people and church music.

Chance The Rapper is always smiling, or seems like he always could be on the verge of smiling. It is, kind of, just how his face is. He is mostly teeth, and carries an expressive nature that pushes and pulls his brow in various directions while he raps or speaks, but his mouth is often pushing the edges of a smile. A lot of white people love Chance The Rapper, which makes me reluctant to paint him as some smiling and dancing young Black artist, appealing to the white masses. There is a lot to be made out of Chance's relationship to white rap fans, and how he, as an artist, manages to maintain that relationship while not straying from his reliance on the roots of Black church music, and the spirit of Black preaching. I think, though, that a natural reaction to Black people being murdered on camera is the notion that living Black joy becomes a commodity—something that everyone feels like they should be able to consume as a type of relief point. I may not come down on the same side of that as everyone who listens to Chance, but I think what Chance does is what the best artists of color manage to do in this setting: makes music facing his people while also leaving the door open for everyone else to try and work their way in. Yes, this Black grandmother being praised isn't a universal grandmother for all who are living, but there is praise in the living hand of someone who raised the person that raised you, pressed against your face.

For months of 2016, I wondered, sometimes out loud, if this could still have been The Year of Chance had he come out of any other city. If Chance had been someone who hailed from the coasts, I imagine that the sound of *Coloring Book*—a joyous mess of voices and harmony, with the self as the most reliable instrument—would have moved us just the same. But what of everything else that came with it? What about the feel-good aspects of Chance's story, the Midwest kid made good? And it's not as though he rose from the cornfields of central Iowa. Unlike any other city in its region, Chicago sits at the center of the national conversation, taking up space in exciting, uncomfortable ways. Its name is deployed by politicians who imagine any place Black people live as a war zone. Black people live and die in Chicago; they create and thrive in Chicago. This year, in particular, the city has been a driving force behind art, sound, writing, and a movement of young Black creatives claiming a space of their own—SABA and Noname and Mick Jenkins and Jamila Woods and Vic Mensa, to name a few. Chance, though, was the one who tapped into exactly what this year needed. The soundtrack to grief isn't always as dark as the grief itself. Sometimes what we need is something to make the grief seem small, even when you know it's a lie.

I went to Chicago in late May of 2016. I found myself crammed into a seat on a school bus driving through the city to an undisclosed location. Chance carried me here, strictly on the promise of something spectacular. It was the first time in years that an artist had made me believe in their capacity for the unbelievable in such a way that I got on a plane and flew toward something unknown. The school bus eventually pulled up to a warehouse, where I settled into a long and snaking line. Once inside, Chance's voice rang out over the loudspeakers, inviting everyone to Magnificent Coloring World: an interactive event and funhouse for all ages to be experienced while *Coloring Book* played through in its entirety. It was, in many ways, like watching a visual album playing out, created in real time by random participants. Teenagers colored, twentysomethings rapped to every word of every song while leaning into glowing church pews, young children broke out in dance wherever there was a clear bit of floor—first a handful, and then others, and others. There were bowls of candy, coolers of cold drinks, and the entire set from the music video for "Sunday Candy" pushed back against a wall. It was a brilliant creation, in both scope and execution. When the album died down, the final handclaps of "Blessings (Reprise)" echoing off of the warehouse's brick, a silence fell over the room, and then it quickly became everything but silence, as Chance himself rose from a riser. He was smiling, a Chicago Bulls jersey nearly down to his knees. He stood for a moment, waiting for the cheers to die down. And then he stayed for a moment longer, and a moment longer, until he seemed to realize that the cheers weren't going to stop.

There's something about the way Chance takes up space that causes these types of intense reactions. It's a rock-star-like quality, like The Beatles stepping off the Boeing 707 in New York back in 1964. Because he seems too good to be true, witnessing Chance in person, even in stillness and silence, can prompt a type of thrilling madness. It's also in the energy he gives off, particularly in Chicago. By the time he arrived to the people at Magnificent Coloring World, he was nearly vibrating, radiant. Eventually he spoke, briefly: "Hi. Thanks for coming to Magnificent Coloring World. I hope you had a good time, and please be sure to try to clean up a little for the next group coming in." He smiled as someone in the back yelled, "Thank YOU, Chance!" And then he was gone, waving as the riser took him back underneath the wonderland he'd created. The air was still buzzing as the masses walked back outside into the sun.

It is one thing to be good at what you do, and it is another thing to be good and bold enough to have fun while doing it. It keeps us on that thin edge of annoyance and adulation. When Steph Curry shoots a three-pointer and turns to run back down the court before it even goes in, there is a second where I tell myself that I'd love for the ball to spin around the rim and fall out, that no one should get to be both good and confident in a time when it's hard enough to be either. But when the ball inevitably falls through the net, I cheer like I always do. I rewind the play and watch again. Chance has the nerve to have fun, which has to be hard on the rap fan who wants something more urgent out of these urgent times, or who imagines that Chance being from a city like Chicago means that he has to commit to only a single narrative. In interviews, he's still excited to talk about his own work, sometimes rapidly burning through cigarettes and bouncing up and down in his seat. In live performances, he's still able to come across as genuinely in love with the people he performs with, staring with admiration at Lil Wayne during a performance of "No Problem" on The Ellen DeGeneres Show.

At the end of the long and bloody summer, I sat with friends in New York and wondered how we survived it all. In June, a gunman massacred 49 people at a gay nightclub in Orlando. In July, three Black men were shot and killed by police officers over the course of just three days in Brooklyn, Baton Rouge, and Saint Paul. In August, the protests spreading through every city, in the face of something that seemed like it was going to swallow us all. I thought back to Magnificent Coloring World then, or at least I considered what it might be like to live inside of an album, and if there would be any pain there if we did. The truth is that I, like so many of you, spent 2016 trying to hold on to what joy I could. I, like so many of you, am now looking to get my joy back, after it ran away to a more deserving land than this one. And maybe this is what it's like to live in these times: the happiness is fleeting, and so we search for more while the world burns around us. There is optimism in that, too, in knowing that more happiness is possible. *Coloring Book*'s childlike aspects can feel a bit overwhelming at times for the more grown of us, but in watching what those seeds produce in young people, I am, again, energized. Watching people younger and more carefree than I am now spill toward any space Chance is standing in unlocks the part of me that once did the same thing for Kanye West or Lupe Fiasco. When you watch hope closely enough, manifested in enough people, you can start to feel it too.

What Chicago poet Gwendolyn Brooks was most aiming toward, I think, was freedom. Freedom for herself, of course, but also freedom for her people—or at least knowing that one can't come without the other. She was a poet for the ordinary Black Chicagoan, writing of their triumphs and failures, and understanding that a whole and complete life sat at the intersection of both. And perhaps that is freedom, more than anything.

To turn your eye back on the community you love and articulate it for an entire world that may not understand it as you do. That feels like freedom because you are the one who controls the language of your time and your people, especially if there are outside forces looking to control and commodify both. Though we don't see the comparison often, Chance fits directly in the lineage of Brooks, more an archivist and community griot than the high-wire gospel act that sells tickets and makes him fit comfortably on suburban playlists. We all do what we gotta do to sell what we gotta sell, and I'll never begrudge that, for Chance or anyone else. But there's history that he's facing, too. Whether he knows it or not.

Chance's biggest strength is his remarkable ability to pull emotion out of people and extend those feelings into a wide space. But he is also a skilled writer, one who you can tell was molded through Chicago's poetry and open-mic scene. He is the type of writer I love most: one who thinks out loud and allows me to imagine the process of the writing. He stacks rhymes in exciting and unique ways; his delivery is the type that seems entirely unrestrained but is, truly, deeply controlled. In "How Great," he sets a hard act for Jay Electronica to follow in one of the album's finest verses, spitting, "Electrify the enemy like Hedwig till he petrified / Any petty Peter Pettigrew could get the pesticide" and, later in the verse, "Exalt, exalt, glorify / Descend upon the Earth with swords and fortify the borders where your shortage lie." His breath control allows for a cadence that seamlessly dances between rapping and singing. There is an urgency in his writing, the idea that he truly believes that this is more than just rap. The leap between 2013's *Acid Rap* and *Coloring Book* is massive, largely in lyrical direction rather than technical ability. It's the distance from "Trippy shit to watch / Drugs while on the clock / Acid on the face / That's a work of art" to "Clean up the streets so my daughter can have a place to play." On *Coloring Book*, "Smoke Break" seems like a smoking anthem from a distance, but up close, it's a song about cherishing silent and stolen moments in the face of new parenthood. In "Same Drugs," Chance meditates on clinging to youth, even as it slips through your fingers. When he softly sings, "Don't forget the happy thoughts," it is an anchor, a reminder that hangs over many of us, even in the year's worst moments.

Another thing that Chance showed on *Coloring Book* is that he's one of rap's great collaborators. He is capable of bowing to anyone he is sharing a track with, without it coming off as forced—like the aforementioned "Mixtape," when he finds a way to meet Lil Yachty and Young Thug where they're at, delivering a verse that sounds right at home, and then, two tracks later, sliding on the airy and mellow "Juke Jam" and lighting a path for Justin Bieber to follow. There is something very Chicago about this, too, like when I call my friends from Chicago who are artists, and we only get five minutes into conversation before they want to know what I'm working on, or how they can help. It is fitting that Chance comes from a city that never lets you walk alone.

He's also young, and an activist learning to be an activist in these times, as we all are. It's thrilling, sure, to see so many artists and athletes figuring out how to navigate their role in the political landscape. But with Chance, it feels even more urgent that he "get it right"—a deeply unfair expectation, but one that he seems up to. National attention is shined on things like his Parade to the Polls on November 7, when he performed a concert and then led thousands to an early-voting site in Chicago. But there is also Open Mike, a series for young Chicago writers and performers, founded by Chance and his friends. Last spring, Chance surprised high school students there with guest appearances by Kanye West and Vic Mensa. There is global activism, but there is also the work of turning and facing your people, which has to become harder with the more distance put between you and those people. I don't know what the future holds, but

Chance's commitment to Chicago is truly pushing the needle forward. This isn't without its flaws; a wide, far-reaching community is always going to be failed by its heroes from time to time. But when all else fails, you have to be able to go home again and have people call your name in a way that is familiar to only them. Regardless of how wide your wings stretch, they were still born from a single place. For those of us with an eye always facing toward home, Chance inspires.

The truth is, if we don't write our own stories, there is someone else waiting to do it for us. And those people, waiting with their pens, often don't look like we do and don't have our best interests in mind. With rap in the midst of what may become its greatest generational shift, geography has taken on a new importance. Chance and his peers are looking at gentrification as a generational issue, looking at place and seeing memories unfold that have to be archived somewhere. I hear that in Vince Staples, in Kamaiyah, of course in Kendrick Lamar, and even in Drake's *Views*, a sprawling love letter to Toronto. Chance, at his best, is half rapper, half tour guide. The demand is simple: no one gets to speak the name of my city without first knowing it as I have. The interior of the land is always layered. Yes, sometimes with blood, but sometimes with bodies marching, with bodies moving, with bodies flooded into the streets chanting or dancing at the roller rink. There is no singular version of any place, but particularly not Chicago. Everyone, turn your eyes to the city you are told to imagine on the news and, instead, listen to the actual voices inside of it. There is nothing on *Coloring Book* that I haven't felt on the streets of Chicago in any season. It is the album that puts a hand inside of a city's back and makes it speak, makes it sing.

So many people want to talk about church when they talk about Chance. I understand this, in the same way that I understand my hands clapping, almost against their will, when a choir swells into a single, unmistakable voice. I understand it in the way that I understand gospel in its simplest terms, despite not being raised in the church. But here is what I also know: we stomp our feet in my church. In my church, we yell the names of those who will never be able to hear us. We curse in my church, the way our grandmothers did, loud and defiant, anchored by a life. My church is Black, yes, but you might be able to get in if you can stay on beat long enough. My church sits high on a hill, away from a world on fire below it. And all of our time in it is brief, far too brief, but we get free there. We do it at the feet of musicians like Chance The Rapper, and the people who love him. If this year was bad, next year might be even worse, or at the very least it might be harder. We are nothing without our quick and simple blessings, without those willing to drag optimism by its neck to the gates of grief and ask to be let in, an entire choir of voices singing at their back.

And so, this is about the choir and about those who might be bold enough to join it before another wretched year arrives to erase another handful of us. This is, more than anything, about those still interested in singing. Say a prayer before you take off. Say a prayer when you land.

A Night In Bruce Springsteen's America

TO WATCH BRUCE SPRINGSTEEN STEP ONTO A stage in New Jersey is to watch Moses walk to the edge of the Red Sea, so confident in his ability to perform a miracle, to carry his people to the Promised Land. I believe in the magic of seeing a musician perform in the place they once called home. The Jersey air felt different, lighter than usual, as I walked into the massive Prudential Center and made my way to my seat.

Having seen Springsteen before, I wasn't surprised by the aesthetics of the arena. I imagine, though, that this could be overwhelming for someone who has never seen Springsteen live. The chanting and relentless fist-pumping beforehand while the stage is being set up, the American flags wrapped around foreheads or hanging off of backs. From another angle, this may feel like a strange political rally. On its face, it matches the tone, passion, and volume of political theater at its base form.

Whether or not the preacher himself intends this, in the church of Bruce Springsteen, it is understood that there is a singular America, one where there is a dream to be had for all who enter, and everyone emerges, hours later, closer to that dream.

I found my seat next to an older man who, despite our fairly close proximity to the stage, was still using binoculars to scan the rapidly growing crowd around us. Without looking away from his binoculars, he told me that he saw Bruce back in 1980, when *The River* was first released. He explained that he saw Bruce play on December 8, 1980. I thought on this for a moment, before it came together. "Lennon," I said. "The night Lennon was murdered." He finally put down his binoculars, nodded lightly, looked at the exit, toward the outside world, and said, "I hope no one gets killed out there during the show this time."

The day before I crossed into New Jersey to watch Bruce Springsteen play, I found myself in Ferguson, Missouri, standing over Michael Brown's memorial plaque. There was no notable reason for this trip. I'm not sure what I wanted to feel, other than closer to a sadness and rage that had become a very real part of my life. I was in St. Louis, and I think I wanted to return to a place where a city was still fighting to pull itself back together, against the backdrop of suffocating injustice that still hangs above it. The air feels different in Ferguson, too. Unlike New Jersey on the night of Bruce Springsteen's homecoming, the air in Ferguson still feels heavy, thick with grief. Yet it is still a town of people who take their joy where they can get it, living because they must.

There is a part of me that has always understood *The River* to be about this. Staring down the life you have left and claiming it as your own, living it to the best of your ability before the clock runs out. In "Jackson Cage," a man dreams of a life more fulfilling than the one he has with the woman he loves in a New Jersey town, but he settles. He gives himself over to the fact that what he has will do, until he has nothing else. This, too, is the promise that has always been sold in Bruce Springsteen's music. The ability to make the most out of your life, because it's the only life you have.

The technician in me has always loved watching how deftly Bruce Springsteen commands the E Street Band, and this night in New Jersey was no different. During "Sherry Darling," it takes a mere turn of his head and a slight nod to pull sax player Jake Clemons to the front of the stage for a solo. During "Two Hearts," Bruce leaves the stage to walk among the crowd, and Stevie Van Zandt slides directly into the hole Bruce left onstage. Not a note was missed, even as Bruce crowd-surfed and danced with members of the audience.

What has always fascinated me most about *The River* is the start of Side 2. The way "Hungry Heart" bleeds into "Out in the Street," two of the most upbeat songs on the album, but the two that I have always found the saddest, both explicitly and implicitly. In one, a man, overcome by dissatisfaction with the perceived American Dream, leaves his wife and children, never to return. In the other, there is a celebration of freedom from what we are to believe is a soul-crushing job. During "Out in the Street," while most of the audience danced and clapped along to the lyrics about going in to work at a job you don't love on Monday and dreaming of stripping out of your work clothes on Friday, I thought, as I do every time I hear the song, about living the Tuesday, Wednesday, and Thursday. The machinery of a mundane week that wears one down until it becomes normal. The sharpness of an alarm rupturing the silence of sleep. The bagged lunch and forced joy with co-workers who are not-quite-friends. How that all feels different on a Friday, at the edge of a weekend, when anything is possible. During the second chorus of the song, a woman behind me tapped my shoulder, smiled, and yelled, "Come on! You gotta want to dance to this!"

Here is where I tell you that this was a sold-out show, and as I looked around the swelling arena when I arrived, the only other Black people I saw were performing labor in some capacity. The fact that I noticed this, I'm sure, would potentially seem absurd to many of the other people attending the concert. As the band launched into a killer extended version of "Cadillac Ranch," I looked over to the steps and saw a young Black man who had been vending popcorn and candy. He was sitting on a step, covered in sweat, and rubbing his right ankle. A man, presumably attempting to get back to his seat, yelled at him to move.

In Bruce Springsteen's music, not just in *The River*, I think about the romanticization of work and how that is reflected in America. Rather, for whom work is romantic, and for whom work is a necessary and sometimes painful burden of survival. One that comes with the shame of time spent away from loved ones, and a country that insists you aren't working hard enough. In New Jersey, Springsteen's songs are the same anthemic introspective paintings of a singular America: men do labor that is often hard, loading crates or working on a dock, and there is often a promised reward at the end of it all. A loving woman always waiting to run away with you, a dance with your name on it, a son who will grow up and take pride in the beautiful, sanctifying joy of work.

I do not know what side of work the employees in the Prudential Center came down on that night, or any night. I know that I understand being Black in America, and I have understood being poor in America. What I know comes with both of those things, often together, is work that is always present, the promise of more to come. Even in my decade-plus of loving Bruce Springsteen's music, I have always known and accepted that the idea of hard, beautiful, romantic work is a dream sold a lot easier by someone who currently knows where their next meal will come from.

I have been thinking a lot about the question of who gets to revel in their present with an eye still on their future, and who gets discussed as though nothing about them could be promising. *The River*, stripped down to its base, is a romantic story about a guy who has nothing, trying to make his life and loves work in a world that doesn't always give him the breaks he thinks he deserves. Hanging above Mike Brown's memorial was a small paper sign. It read, in all capital letters: "THEY CAN'T KILL US UNTIL THEY KILL US."

It seemed odd, at first, to see this statement over the memorial of a person who had been murdered and long buried. I think the consideration, though, was that when you come from a people born of a true oral tradition, you live lives even after you are no longer living a life. Mike Brown was flawed, but young enough to be romanticized in the way Springsteen's romantics bleed all throughout *The River*, where mistakes are large and beautiful, and pointing to some much more spectacular end.

What I understand about *The River* now that I didn't before I saw it in New Jersey is that this is an album about coming to terms with the fact that you are going to eventually die, written by someone who seemed to have an understanding of the fact that he was going to live for a long time. It is an album of a specific type of optimism—one not afforded to everyone who listens to it. It is an album of men and women and families and the grand idea of surviving to enjoy it all. It is often fearless and forward-looking in its talk of both love and loss. There's a conflict between dreams and reality, of course, but the reality is still always one of survival.

As the final saxophone solo in "Drive All Night" kissed every corner of the Prudential Center and hundreds of cell phone flashlights cut through the dark of the arena, I realized that I am now the age Bruce Springsteen was when *The River* was released in 1980. I once thought that I saw the same version of adulthood that *The River* speaks of. One with conflict and cele-bration, but always living. It is 2016, and not watching the videos of Black people murdered doesn't mean that Black people aren't still being murdered. I try not to think about death—my own, or that of anyone I love—but I don't consider the future in the way that *The River* seems to consider the future. I don't fear what the future holds as much as I fear not being alive long enough to see it. It could have been the ghosts of Ferguson that I carried with me to New Jersey, or the sheer emotional exhaustion I felt as the last notes of "Wreck on the Highway" died out, but I felt like I fell in a different type of love with *The River* after seeing it in this way. What it must feel like to write an album like this. To listen to an album like this with different eyes on the world. What it must feel like to imagine that no one in America will be killed while a man sings a song about the promise of living.

Carly Rae Jepsen Loves You Back

"IS THAT WEED? WHO THE FUCK BRINGS WEED TO a Carly Rae Jepsen concert?"

This question is almost certainly rhetorical, yelled in my general direction during an in-between song silence by a man in a yellow polo shirt with the words "EVENT STAFF" plastered across the chest. He tilts his nose to the thick and hot air (which does carry with it the strong and unmistakable smell of weed), twists his face the way a child does when forcing down cough medicine, and shakes his head. He turns to me and again asks, "Seriously. Who brings weed to a show like this?" I shrug and laugh nervously, trying to gauge his interest in an actual answer. "A show like this" is an interesting measuring stick, as there's no real way that an outsider would be able to look at the crowd and pinpoint exactly what type of act is playing. There are teenagers here, but there are also early-30s hipsters and Black people in their 20s. I notice that the event staff person is still looking at me, searching my eyes for an answer, so I consider one. As I fix my mouth to respond with "pretty much everyone," a playful synth drowns the silence. The thin silhouette of Carly Rae Jepsen cuts through the blue light of the stage. "All right," she says, the light illuminating half of her face. "Let's get lost."

Watching Carly Rae Jepsen play *E•MO•TION* live is an hourlong clinic in vulnerability. It is a public display of affection, for the artist more than anyone in the audience. Jepsen is the most honest pop musician working, and for this, she may never be a star. But to dismiss her as a one-hit wonder is unfair: *E•MO•TION*, with its 1980s nostalgia and hazy shine, was never asking for hits. I have been in rooms where one-hit wonders have played, the ones who had a big single and spent an entire lifetime chasing another one. Semisonic, in a small bar, over a mumbling crowd, played "Closing Time" three times in the same set. Marcy Playground, slouching with disinterest to an encore, so that the bored crowd could finally hear them play "Sex and Candy."

This show is bigger than that. This is not Carly Rae Jepsen's room. When I see her play a sold-out show at New York's Terminal 5, no one is suffering through all the other songs in order to get to the one they heard on the radio. By the time Jepsen plays "Call Me Maybe" at the end of the night, it feels like it doesn't fit—like a sweet dessert after we're already full.

Intimacy is generally not something that a concertgoer can opt out of at Terminal 5. A difficult venue to navigate, with limited quality views of the stage, the room quickly becomes a mass of bodies funneling to the same few spots before spending hours jostling for space. Drinks are spilled on pants, elbows are pressed into the soft spaces on other bodies—by accident at first, and then perhaps with a little more purpose. Everyone apologizes for their manipulation of space before settling into discomfort, pushed into a wall or the back of a stranger. It is, perhaps counterintuitively, the perfect venue for Jepsen to play through *E•MO•TION*, an album obsessed with the physical space we take up when we're forced next to each other, both in romance and friendship. The feeling barrels toward you as the lights go down and the signature saxophone part from "Run Away With Me" blankets the eager crowd: anything is possible. Even in a city that makes you feel small, there is someone waiting to fall in love with you.

Some will say that Jepsen's appeal is that she seems like she could be one of your friends—someone who you could sit down with and truly open up to, someone who will laugh honestly at your jokes and sit through your Netflix marathons. She is often packaged this way: Carly Rae Jepsen, your friend with boy problems and big dreams. Your friend with two dance moves at her disposal, milking them so energetically to every beat that it becomes endearing, until there is no such thing as a "bad dancer" or a "good dancer," just a set of unchained limbs answering a higher calling.

All of this seems really great on the surface—a pop musician only an arm's reach away. *E•MO•TION* has been critically adored, despite disappointing sales totals. None of its songs has lit the Billboard charts on fire. It occurs to me that maybe no one actually wants a pop star who could be their friend. It erases the boundary of spectacle. That's what keeps so many of us drinking from the pop music well: the star who stops a room when they walk in, someone we can't access, in a life that looks nothing like ours. *E•MO•TION* is too honest an album to pretend to be interested in spectacle. With her band behind her, Jepsen gets through three songs before speaking to the audience. When she finally speaks, it's a rushed sentence or two before she launches into another song. In a white blazer and a head of messy dark hair, she looks like a modern artist's vision of Pat Benatar, somehow both awkward and entirely at ease. Some musicians don't carry on much interaction with their audience because they have no interest in it. With Jepsen, you get the sense that she is just so excited to play these songs that nothing else matters. She is the person handing you a gift at Christmas, tearing into the wrapping paper before you can start to, with an eagerness that says, "I made this gift for you, for all of you. And I want you to have it, while there's still time to enjoy it." It is hard for me to imagine anyone wanting an actual friend this close to them, asking them to feel everything.

From a metaphorical standpoint, one of the worst things we do is compare love to war. We do this in times of actual war, without a thought about what it actually means. Mothers bury their children while a pop musician calls the bedroom a war zone and romance a field of battle—as if there is a graveyard for heartbreak alone. We've run out of ways to weaponize sadness, and so it becomes an actual weapon. A buffet of sad and bitter songs rains down from the pop charts for years, keeping us tethered to whatever sadness we could dress ourselves in when nothing else fit. Jepsen is trying to unlock the hard door, the one with all of the other feelings behind it. It's evident tonight, as she bounces along the stage, smiling while pulling off her two dance moves to every note of every song; as she abandons her blazer for a sleeveless tee, and then a cape, only for a song, before throwing it to the side; as her voice trembles with nervous excitement before bringing out Dev Hynes to play "All That" with her, both of them basking in the audience's voracious response.

This is the difficult work: convincing a room full of people to set their sadness aside and, for a night, bring out whatever joy remains underneath—in a world where there is so much grief to be had, leading the people to water and letting them drink from your cupped hands. Inside Terminal 5, under the spell of Carly Rae Jepsen, love is simply love. It is not war. It is not something you are thrown into and forced to survive. It is something you experience, and if you're lucky enough, time slows down. It is not as fashionable as our precious American anguish, our feelings that eclipse all else. But, then again, there is a time to throw all else aside and see if maybe dancing will bring us back to life, packed so tightly in a room of strangers that everyone becomes one whole body, shaking free whatever is holding it down.

Sometime around the third song of Jepsen's set, I started to notice people kissing. One couple first, and then another, and then another. This continued for the remainder of the show. I never looked long, usually just a glance after nearby movement caught my eye. A couple directly in front of me, occupying the same small bit of wall that I was forced to occupy, began kissing each other passionately during "Warm Blood," while Jepsen held the microphone stand with both hands and whispered, "I would throw in the towel for you, boy / 'Cause you lift me up and catch me when I'm falling for you," into the mic. The couple pushed back into me, one of them stepping on my shoes. They broke their embrace long enough for one of them to mouth the words "Sorry, dude" to me.

I smiled and gave an understanding nod that was not seen, as they were already falling back into each other. I considered how often there is shame attached to loving anyone publicly. The shame, of course, comes on a sliding scale, depending on who you are and who you love. How often I hear people complain about things like engagement photos, couples being tender with each other in public, or someone who can't stop talking about someone they love. How often I first think of who may be watching before I lean in to give someone I love a really good kiss in a crowded store. Here, that shame falls to dust. It is something beyond the smoke that lingers above our heads that does this—turning a person's face to the face of someone they love, and kissing the way we do in our homes, with the curtains drawn.

The Night Prince Walked On Water

"I remember [broadcast producer] Don [Mischer] said, 'Put me on the phone with Prince.' Don says, 'Now, I want you to know it's raining.' And Prince is like, 'Yes, it's raining.' [Don said], 'And are you okay?' and Prince is like, 'Can you make it rain harder?'"

—Bruce Rodgers, production designer of the Super Bowl XLI Halftime Show

AND OF COURSE THERE WAS RAIN, AS IF SUMMONED by the man himself. The elements favor some of us more than others. When we speak of Prince in Miami, at halftime of Super Bowl XLI, let us first speak of how nothing that fell from the sky appeared to touch him. How his hair stayed as perfect as it was upon his arrival, wrapped tight in a bandanna. All of my friends leaned close to the TV on that night and wondered how someone could play that hard, that furiously, in the midst of a storm. This was Prince, on a stage slick with rain, walking on actual water. There are moments when those we believe to be immortal show us why that belief exists. I will only remember Super Bowl XLI by what happened at halftime. Nothing before, and nothing after.

Prince is gone now, and nothing seems fair. He seemed magic and permanent—the one who would outlive each of us, floating on immortality as a small gift for what he'd given for so long. Prince didn't just arrive one time, but many. His career was that of endless arrivals and re-arrivals, and so it makes sense, upon the news of his death, that he would once again return. That seems unlikely as I write this now, reminiscing on another moment where he arrived, several times in one night, to deliver a show inside of a show. To, once again, eclipse something seemingly greater than himself.

Many of us accept football's violence, and the culture it breeds, because the game itself promises great rewards—a spectacular play, or the sight of men performing supreme acts of athleticism, at the very edge of impossible. Before Super Bowl XLI, it never occurred to me that a halftime show could exist that would upstage the spectacle on the field. There had been attempts, but often clumsy ones: the awkward cluster of Jessica Simpson, P. Diddy, Justin Timberlake, Nelly, and Kid Rock in 2004; The Rolling Stones, in 2006, looking like they were fulfilling a long-held-off errand, like going to the DMV. Griping about the Super Bowl halftime show had become a sport itself, a bit of glee that could be had by everyone, even casual football watchers.

Then, out of the Miami rain in 2007, rose Prince. He could have played through a list of his hits that night, and we would have all been satisfied. He did play some, of course: a rendition of "Baby, I'm a Star" where he steps to the edge of the stage, pauses, and tells the crowd, "Somebody take my picture with all this rain." But the surprise at the bottom of the box—the unexpected bonus tacked onto a paycheck—was the way "All Along the Watchtower" bled into the Foo Fighters's "Best of You" right after that. The true joy in this for me, both at the time and every time I've watched it since, is the mastery and confidence with which he played these songs. Even when Prince wasn't explicitly telling them, "I can do this shit better than you," I imagine that most other musicians had to know it was entirely true. And there, for a moment, he reminded us. Prince, for all of his stoic mystery, never gave up on the element of surprise.

The crown jewel, of course, is what ended the performance: a glowing, towering performance of "Purple Rain." That moment forced me to imagine a world in which this was the Super Bowl itself. I saw all of the players, coaches, and cheerleaders bowing at the feet of Prince and going home, letting football take the rest of the night off in a show of respect. There are times when the night pushes against the clock and time slows down: when you lock eyes across the room with someone who you think you could love. When a football is thrown down a field and into an end zone where a mass of bodies await its descent. When Prince leans into a microphone and generously asks, "Can I play this guitar?" as if there could be anything other than one million affirmative answers. A sheet blowing up from the front of the stage until Prince is only a silhouette making beautiful noise. There is no moment like this one in any other halftime show, before it or since. Prince, only a shadow, putting his hands to an instrument and coaxing out a song within a song. And of course there was still rain, beads of it covering the camera lens from every angle, drops of it covering the faces of people in the front row, and still none of it visible on Prince himself. And of course there were two doves scattering themselves above Prince's head when the sheet came down and he was whole, in front of us again, walking back to the mic and asking, "Y'all wanna sing tonight?"

Yes, Prince. This is the one we know all of the words to. Throw the microphone to the ground and walk away. We don't need you now like we did in that moment, but we will remember it always. Dearly beloved, we are gathered here today to get through this thing called life. Dearly beloved, we are gathered here today to cast away another hero on the face of a flood that began on a Miami night in 2007 and never stopped. Dearly beloved, when the sky opens up, anywhere, I will think of how Prince made a storm bend to his will. How the rain never touches those who it knows were sent into it for a higher purpose. Dearly beloved, I will walk into the next storm and leave my umbrella hanging on the door. Please join me.

ScHoolboy Q Wants White People To Say The Word

"NIGGA" AT HIS CONCERTS. HIS DESIRE IS NOT PAS-
sive, either. It isn't that he doesn't mind if white people say it,
he wants to witness the word spoken into existence. "When the
beat drops, I'll expect y'all to say it," he says in a radio interview.
"It's not like I'm asking them to go out in the world and say it,
but if they paid for a show and put food on my family's table,
I'm not going to be up there saying the word alone."

It's interesting, when framed this way. It's an exchange for
him, it seems. If you can afford entry to his shows, and you've
offered him a way to work himself into a distance from that
which he raps about, you have earned a pass, in his eyes, to fit
his language over your tongue. No matter what it is.

In the fall of 2013 in California, ScHoolboy Q has instructed
his DJ to stop the music before going into his last two songs. He
leans over the stage, looking a bit exhausted. He takes this time
to directly speak to the crowd, much of it white, encouraging
them to say "nigga" during his last two songs. He assures them

that they don't need to be uncomfortable, as he'd noticed them being earlier in the show. Ain't nobody here gonna get in your face about the shit, he promises. It's all about having a good time. And so he launches into "Yay Yay," the first single from his third album, *Oxymoron*. The song is, more or less, a detailed accounting of Q growing up on Figg Street. When he gets to the lyrics "I'm a drug dealing nigga / cause them grades ain't get me paid" the silence that would normally sit at the utterance of the word was filled in by one hundred eager voices.

The problem is that everyone wants to talk about language entirely independent of any violence that the existence of that language has accumulated over time. If, for example, a word can be hurled through the air while a boot comes down on a face, that part of the word's lineage has to be accounted for. Any language that is a potential precursor to bloodletting has a small history that it can't be pulled apart from. All Black parents I know, particularly those of some Southern origin, have a story about the first time they were called a nigger, deliberately, and with some measure of anger behind the word. There is often running involved, or at least the story has a tone of the teller of it understanding that they might not have lived to do the telling if not for some stroke of luck.

For all of the debate over it, these stories make the reclaiming of the slightly modified "nigger" a political act. This is also, I imagine, why so many white people have an obsession with who can say it, when they can say it, and all of the circumstances in today's America where it might be all right to say it. It is one thing to watch a people take a weapon out of your hands, but it is another to fashion it into something else entirely, something that doesn't resemble a weapon at all. And it is even another thing to then see the newly-fashioned once-weapon scattered into a lexicon that denies you immediate access. I think of this when, on the news, there is another long debate about who can say any variation of "nigger" and when. The argument is often one of equality: no one should be able to utter a word that all people cannot utter. People who are not Black often cite the word's ugly history as the reason why *no one* should say it, but also in a defense of non-Black people being able to say the word without repercussions, or in defense of why a Black person who speaks the word shouldn't be taken seriously by any establishment they are trying to live safely within.

My mother thought it to be an ugly word with an ugly history, and so I grew up imagining the word as only ugly. When singing along to rap music, snuck into headphones, I would self-censor the word, feeling my mother over my shoulder. It never felt right coming out of my mouth, because all I associated it with were stories of violence, and then debates around how it could be used to do harm, or offer someone even more space than they already had. It was impossible, then, for me to imagine it as a word of love, or a word speaking to a unique bond.

In a 1995 interview, Wu-Tang Clan member Raekwon is asked about why the Wu-Tang Clan has been able to succeed as a group where other groups have failed. He responds, "It's about love. Love the niggas you're rolling with. Love them."

In '02 me and my nigga Troy were the only two Black people on the floor of our college dorm & we used to kick it but not all like that because wasn't too many other niggas on campus & we didn't all like being seen together at once because someone would inevitably have some jokes about the NAACP of Bexley, Ohio, or some shit & we would have to pretend to laugh because wasn't none of us trying to get kicked out of some college that we were all there to play sports for & Troy was the first one in his family to finish high school & one night he told me his daddy used to play football in Mississippi before he got kicked off the team for fighting some fans that called him a nigger & Troy said the coaches told his daddy that he was *too much of a liability to the team* & so now Troy was at this school playing football & living out his daddy's dreams & on the anniversary of Biggie's death we was playing Biggie's music real loud on the speakers in the dorm community room & we let it spill out into our dorm hallway because we both grew up rapping this shit through headphones & eventually more bodies piled into the room & they were mostly white kids who we made friends with because when you're all piled on top of each other in the same building there ain't much else to do & the song "Niggas Bleed" came on the playlist & Biggie raps "N****s bleed just like us" at least that's what I wanted to hear when I looked around the room but everyone who rapped it in the room filled in the blanks & then again & then again & sometimes louder & I don't know who the "us" was supposed to be in the rhyme anymore & when the song died down there was still Eric who was from Findlay, Ohio & who pitched for the baseball team & he sung the words "Niggas bleed just like us" one last time & I looked over at Troy & his hand was in a fist & it was trembling & I wonder if in that moment he was thinking about what his father couldn't survive

Most of my white friends never knew what to make out of Gym Class Heroes, and white critics didn't either. They were an odd bunch who came along at an odd time in an odd genre. Decidedly a rap group, they were fronted by Travis McCoy, a Black, lanky, tattooed art nerd with a punk rock lineage. To brand Gym Class Heroes as rap-rock isn't exactly accurate in the traditional sense: sludgy, chunky guitars and bass backing someone doing a rap-ping/screaming hybrid as vocals. They were, instead, an earlier version of what so many live rap acts look like today: subtle and live instrumentation behind an MC. McCoy was, by no means, the best rapper. In the band's early days, he was often too reliant on punchlines and bad puns, and coasted off of his charm more than any actual ability. Still, they were the official rap darlings of emo's third wave.

This, I thought, was always interesting. I saw them at one of the early Warped Tours they were on, which they entered with all of the right credentials. Pete Wentz co-signed them, and then eventually actually signed them to his record label, Decaydance. They had a catchy song, an album with decent buzz, and they looked the part. The problem was that, when they were pushed into these circles, they stood out so sorely, and in the worst ways possible. The pop punk kids who might enjoy rap as a forbidden fruit couldn't get into Gym Class Heroes. Travis McCoy was rapping about what emo singers sang about. The Four Ls: Longing, Love, Loss, Loneliness. It wasn't the rap that most of my white friends at the time were most excited about, the commercial hits with a taste of danger nestled inside. Travis McCoy, for two whole albums, never says the word "Nigga."

I am, of course, not saying that this is why white fans and critics had a hard time embracing Gym Class Heroes in 2005. I'm not saying that their lack of proximity to what these people might have seen as "traditional" rap music was their undoing, even as critics would veil their reviews in things like "something feels off" or "they just aren't speaking to what I think they should be speaking to."

But it is entirely true that an appeal that music offers us is a way to escape our understanding of the world. It is working within a food chain of sorts, particularly in rap music. A rapper boasts about a life that they may be close to living, but not entirely living, giving a listener a chance to rap along those words and briefly, even though it is not real, get closer to that image of a life separate from their own. I have done it my whole life, using lyrics that actually do not reflect my life as a signal for a life that seems briefly more exciting. I suppose no one wants to hear a rapper, of all people, rap exclusively about something that we could get from a collective of sad boys who can sound sad singing sadness.

But I imagine this as a problem with how Black people sit in the imagination of people who are not Black, and not entirely a content or genre issue. We often see Black people, more than any other demographic, restricted to what versions of themselves can be briefly loved and then discarded. The rapper with chains and a past worth a dangerous fantasy, but not worth considering as something that makes them full and human. The problem with Gym Class Heroes, and Travis McCoy particularly, is that they were outside of the current era of Black weirdness that has been accepted in more mainstream spaces as a type of visible and understood Blackness. By the time their wave came along, they had already ridden a lesser one. This, too, is a failure of imagination.

What ScHoolboy Q is doing at his shows is, in some ways, giving a permission to something that would likely occur even if a permission wasn't granted. He is allowing it to be done louder, and more comfortably. As the demographics of rap fans shift, and the things those fans have access to shifts, a thing that I have a problem with is the population of the rap show. ScHoolboy Q is not alone, but as a rap artist gets bigger, and their ticket prices become higher, their audiences become whiter. It's a question of who can afford the show, which in the case of ScHoolboy Q, becomes a question of who can afford to be comfortable saying a word that comes with a violence they'll never know. I wonder, sometimes, if the trade-off is worth it. If my desire to see young Black artists "make it" is worth my desire to watch them bowing to the comfort of others in this way. People who may, for a moment, put food on a table for their family, but would also not always fight for that family's right to not hear a word that, out of the wrong mouth, can still be a weapon.

ScHoolboy Q can certainly do whatever he wants and doesn't need my permission. When, in another interview, he says, "it's not like these white people are racist, they're at a rap show," I understand that this is all rooted in what I have convinced myself of for years: that a closeness for, or even a love for culture, puts you so far into it that you can embody all aspects without harm. That love is the great equalizer, even if there is blood underneath a word that no longer belongs to you. For this, I feel for ScHoolboy Q when he says that he is not encouraging these white fans to use the word outside of the concert venue. I feel for him, and I envy his optimism.

I consider, today, the importance of Black men loving each other in public. Of Black people, in general, loving themselves in public. I think back to the pointed response that Raekwon gave in 1995, and how it changed not only my view of the word "nigga," but also my view of how men loving each other deeply could open up an entire dialogue around the goals and emotional connectivity of a people. I am not saying that I toss the word about in every setting I am in, or even that I think of it as the only affectionate word I can attach to my people. But the truth is that I am comfortable here, under the swallowing moonlight, throwing an arm around my niggas and laughing loud into an uncontainable night, regardless of what trouble our sound might bring. This is a particular type of love. The type that has survived history and the weapons formed against the body and all of its lineage. The type that has turned the weapon back in on itself and now, that which welcomes violence can also welcome two arms, spread apart in a wide and waiting hug. I am comfortable here, shouting at my niggas across a card table with a hand full of cards during a spades game at its tense climax. I want to imagine that I can keep at least these moments to myself and not have them given back over to other mouths. I want to believe that they're still for us, even if I can see the lie every time the word jumps off of my own tongue.

The Weeknd And The Future Of Loveless Sex

PROJECTED BEHIND THE WEEKND ON STAGE IN Seattle, two women wearing smeared makeup and little else are rolling around on a bed, frantically kissing each other. It is a mess of hands and naked skin, with some soft groans sprinkled in. Being that this is an all-ages show, the parents, undoubtedly dragged here by their eager children without knowing what to expect, are either shuttling their children toward the exits or staring in shock with the rest of us, mouths open. The Weeknd, unbothered by the commotion, begins to launch into the song "Kiss Land," the title track from the album he is touring on the back of tonight. As the song goes on, the pornography projected behind him becomes increasingly graphic. He sings the lyrics to the song out over the film's sounds of passion: "This ain't nothing to relate to / even if you tried / you tried / you tried." It occurs to me, in the moment, that a lot of kids are going to have a story about how they went to a concert and ended up sitting through a pornographic film with their parents. It is both funny for me, here alone as an adult, and not funny at all, thinking back to my younger years. As the song reaches its climax, so does the film, cutting out right as one woman prepares to go down on the other. When the screen goes dark, the echoes of intimate moaning remain, shaking off of every wall in the theater. It seems exorbitant when it all ends. A pointless, uncomfortable exercise from an artist who believes vanity means no stone of excess can be left unturned.

The Weeknd, real name Abel Tesfaye, sings about sex. The kind of sex you have if you aren't interested in love, but perhaps interested in warmth. The kind of sex you have when you're lonely, or rich, or both. When the desire for a body outweighs the desire for a name. He's made a career off of this, songs about drug-fueled conquests laced with intervals of paranoid boasting and small cautionary tales. Two years before the Seattle concert, in 2011, the Toronto native released three mixtapes: *House of Balloons* in the spring, *Thursday* in the summer, and *Echoes of Silence* in the winter. It was a chilling musical onslaught. The songs were dark and claustrophobic. In the world of The Weeknd, there was rarely a woman worth trusting, unless they were high, or naked, or both. Even here, he would skirt the line between sexual exuberance and chilling inappropriateness. "The only girls that we fuck with seem to have 20 different pills in 'em," he sings on "Loft Music." In "High For This," the first song on *House of Balloons*, and the song that introduced The Weeknd to the world outside of Canada, he sings about convincing a woman to take a pill before intercourse. "It's all consensual," he said in an interview. "The tone is dark, but it's consensual. Everyone is just trying to have a good time."

He appeared to be an unimpressed student of R&B: someone who had seen so many singers get close to the line and then back away from it right when the audience was begging for something that felt like risk. This was his edge. He's a marginal singer, at best, who relies on the same wave of vocal melody to get most of his lyrics out: a low start to a line that ascends briefly before cutting out. He curses more than all of his contemporaries, and is young enough to imagine a world in which he is invincible, so his interest in nihilism doesn't feel like it's directly trimming any years off of his life.

But, more than anything, The Weeknd sings about sex. His trilogy of mixtapes landed him a major label record deal, and a debut album in *Kiss Land* that found itself hotly anticipated. It is a colder, more isolated album than his mixtape efforts. It sounds like what it is: an album made by someone who never thought that their haunted tales of debauchery would make them *this* famous. It's a subtle shift in tone, dialed a bit down in content, but with an attempted dial-up in concept, which leads to a more open and personal world that ends up falling flat.

Still, when I realized he was coming to Seattle, where I was briefly spending time with old friends, I paid way too much cash for a ticket on the street because once, about a year ago, a dark-haired girl from Toronto I was hanging out with told me, "If you ever get a chance to see The Weeknd, you have to do it. There's nothing like it."

Seattle is sitting in summer's dying moments, which makes the city's usual tone of gray seem all the more suffocating. Inside of the Paramount Theater, however, fluorescent colors splash the stage and bleed out into the crowd. Upon entry to the theater, there are *Kiss Land* condoms being handed out. Someone shoves a handful into my surprised and waiting palm, and while killing time before The Weeknd takes the stage, I flip them over in my hand, looking at the various lyrics etched on the outside of the packaging. On one: "YOU DESERVE YOUR NAME ON A CROWN" from the song "The Town." On another, from the song "Wanderlust": "GOOD GIRLS GO TO HEAVEN" on one side, "BAD GIRLS GO EVERYWHERE" on the other. As I shove them back into my pockets, the curtain on stage drops, and a bath of blue light seeps out onto the audience, so intense it forces a few people to shield their eyes as a head rises from below the stage, a mess of dreadlocks atop it.

"Can I get on top tonight, Seattle? Can I make you cum?"

These were the first words spoken to the crowd by The Weeknd, forcing a wave of screams back at him in response. It was not so much a question as it was a direct invitation, or a statement of intent. The fascinating thing about The Weeknd is that, when compared to his direct peers within his genre, he stands out. He may not personally consider himself an R&B singer, aligning himself more with the rappers he spent time around in Toronto, but there is no mistaking that the music he is creating, particularly on *Kiss Land*, is rooted in R&B tropes, sounds, and imagery. With this in mind, it bears pointing out that The Weeknd is not exactly a physical sex symbol in the way that soul and R&B has manifested physical sex symbols since the 1960s. Even now, with R&B folding aggressively into the umbrella of pop, the male R&B sex symbol is what sells. Months before this, at a Trey Songz concert, I watched Songz abandon his shirt one song in, to the delight of fans. By three songs in, he was grinding against the mic stand. By the end, he was on the ground, simulating sex with the stage floor. The Weeknd, by comparison, layers his clothes and approaches the stage with a calm, almost laziness. Tonight he wears a jacket, a vest, and then another shirt underneath, with baggy pants. He is attractive, but not in the sharply-groomed way that a traditional R&B heartthrob might be attractive. He often looks like he is trying to give off the aesthetic impression that he is only present in between breaks from being in bed, immersed in some unspeakable passion.

It is startling how well one can sell sex without doing much of the work themself. As he powers through the show, sometimes turning to conduct the band behind him, The Weeknd is not doing anything explicitly sexual. He's letting the atmosphere do the work, and folding into it. During the song "Live For This," his face is projected on monitors around the theater, overwhelming the audience with his presence. Not his face singing, or doing anything romantic. Just his face, staring, blinking occasionally. There is a tension in this, something that pulls you in and dares you to break first. The sex is sold by that which is implied after The Weeknd opens the show by making his intentions known. The way the pornographic film looping behind him cut out right before the film reached its climax, because it could. Because it didn't have to show the audience what the audience was already building to in its head. The Weeknd, even with his faulty choirboy vocals, is at his best when planting an idea in the head of those who are watching him. It's sexual inception: first leave nothing to the imagination, and then leave everything to the imagination. At the end of the song "Kiss Land," with the echoes of passion still hanging thick in the air, The Weeknd stands entirely still on stage, overly satisfied with the display he just offered the audience. When he finally moves, after the crowd goes silent, he flicks his wrist toward the mic stand. Everyone in the theater screams.

No one during the show is touching, despite the themes being sensual, at the very least. I'm interested in the physical space bodies take up at times like these. The way we fold into each other when a slow jam works its way out of the speakers. But tonight, everyone is at least performing distance. It occurs to me that this could be because there is nothing about The Weeknd that assumes love as a necessary vehicle for physical intimacy. This isn't new, in all genres of music, but for The Weeknd, there is such a clear dismissal of love as a trope in his lyrics. He isn't necessarily chasing women as much as he is chasing a feeling, which creates an audience that also sets out looking for that feeling. And, look, I am saying that I have wanted to forget the day and run into whatever allowed me to do so at night. I'm saying that I want to be in love, but sometimes I just don't want to be alone, and I don't want to do the work of balancing what that means in what hour of whatever darkness I'm sitting in. And across the theater in Seattle, I lock eyes with someone for what was mere seconds but feels like an entire small lifetime, and I wonder what it must be like to trust a stranger with your undoing in the way that The Weeknd asks us to. What it must be like to feel briefly full without considering if any emptiness might follow.

I'm unimpressed by The Weeknd. I am perhaps unimpressed by The Weeknd because I'm jealous of the way he makes that which I once believed to be complicated sound so simple. Miles away from here, in my Ohio apartment, there is still hair on a pillow from a woman who hasn't slept in my bed in two weeks, and likely never will again, after a year of doing it. Before I boarded the flight here, I pulled one of her long, black hairs off of a sweater and held it briefly to the light. When I arrived in Seattle, there was a small bottle of nail polish, from a trip we'd taken together months ago. Not enough people face the interior of separation in this way. What it is to find small pieces of a person who you know you'll never get to wholly experience again. It feels, almost always, like piecing together a road map that places you directly in the middle of nowhere.

The Weeknd closes out the night with "Wicked Games," a song about entering into a doomed one-night relationship with a woman who was, moments ago, a stranger. It is his most personal song, of the night and perhaps his young career. It's the song where he's asking for a thing greater than forgettable sex. In the final chorus, as the curtain begins to descend, he fights through the last lyrics, his already worn-down voice breaking even further on "so tell me you love me / only for tonight, only for tonight / even though you don't love me / just tell me you love me."

It is the first thing he's truly asking. The way the concert has come full circle: first, him asking if he can make an audience cum, and then, asking for someone to tell him that they love him. I suppose the lesson is that the one-night stand takes as many forms as the desires of the people inside of it. Once the curtain falls completely, the sound of women moaning push back through the speakers hanging in front of the few remaining fluorescent lights. I'm here because a woman I loved told me I had to be, months before she left her hair on my pillow for the last time, and as I scan the crowd quickly for the woman I shared brief eye contact with, I think about how much of myself I've left behind for people to gradually find, heartbroken, over the course of several months. The Weeknd tells the same tale: it's never about love but then again, how can it be about anything but love, even if the love is just the love you have for your own ravenous desires. Stepping out into the night, swallowed by gray even inside of the black, I'm not sure if I came here tonight to forget pain, or to remember thirst.

Oh, how wrong we were to think that immortality meant never dying

Gerard Way

II.

Rehearsals for his All-Star Game performance had been rocky. People feared that he wouldn't show on time to sing. He arrived late to the arena, disheveled and anxious.

There are times when I like to think that I see America the way that Marvin Gaye saw it in the spring of 1970. After he buried Tammi Terrell, and after his brother came back from a bloody war, when Marvin stared at all of our country's mess and told Smokey Robinson that he couldn't sleep because God was using him to write the album that would become *What's Going On*

What's Going On is, more than anything, an album with few solutions. We are a world obsessed with proof of work, demanding results at every turn, even when we have little hope to tie ourselves to. I always appreciate *What's Going On* as an album that asks first and holds no optimism that the answers will be what it's looking for. Even the album's most optimistic song, "God Is Love," feels like it's banking on a shaky hand at a poker table, trying to convince everyone of something it isn't certain of itself.

What I imagine to be most difficult is the exact moment when you realize that your wealth and success will still not save you. To be Black and understand that you are in a country that values these things, but will still speak of how you earned your death after you are gone far too soon. Blackness and labor have been inextricable in America for hundreds of years, but still, being reminded of that hovering truth can destroy a man who does not think of what he does as *labor*, a man who perhaps thinks *it's not "work" if I'm bringing people joy*. I think of all this reality arriving to Marvin Gaye at once in 1970, and he could not, in good conscious, continue as the same artist.

I Wasn't Brought Here, I Was Born: Surviving Punk Rock Long Enough To Find Afropunk

I DON'T REMEMBER THE FIRST TIME I HEARD A racist joke at a punk rock show. Rather, I don't remember the first time I was grabbed into a sweaty half-hug by one of the laughing white members of my Midwest punk scene and told don't worry about it. We don't think of you that way. I don't remember the first time I saw a teenage girl shoved out of the way so that a teenage boy her size, or greater, could have a better view of a stage. I don't remember the first time that I made an excuse for being a silent witness.

I don't remember the first time I noticed the small group in the back corner of a punk show at the Newport Music Hall (one of the many venues that I fell in and out of love with in my hometown of Columbus, Ohio), all of them, in some way, pushed out of the frenzied circle of bodies below, and the alleged loving violence that comes with it. I do remember the first time I became one of the members of that group in the back corner of shows. At 18, I hung in the back corner of the Newport and watched NOFX with the rest of the kids who didn't quite fit, or at least became tired of attempting to fit. I looked around and saw every version of other, as I knew it. The Black kids, the girls my age and younger, the kids most fighting with the complexities of identity. We sat back and watched while NOFX tore through an exceptionally loud version of "Don't Call Me White," and watched below, as a monochromatic sea crashed against itself.

There is nothing simple about this. What we're sold about punk rock is that anyone can pick up an instrument and go, something that we've seen proven time and time again by a wide number of awful bands. But even in a genre that prides itself on simplicity, the complexities of erasure and invisibility in punk rock go deep. It is hard to hear the word "brotherhood" without also thinking of the weight behind what it carries with it in this country, and beyond. When I still hear and read the punk rock scene referred to as a "brotherhood," I think about what it takes to build a brotherhood in any space. Who sits at the outskirts, or who sits at the bottom while the brotherhood dances oblivious and heavy at the top. In the punk landscape, we are often given imagery that reflects the most real truths of this scene: the exclusion of people of color, of women, of the queer community, and that exclusion being sometimes explicit, sometimes violent, but almost always in direct conflict with the idea of punk rock as a place for rebellion against (among other things) identity.

A friend recently posed a question to me, similar to one that Lester Bangs wrote about being posed to him (in 1979's "The White Noise Supremacists"):

Well, what makes you think the attitudes of racism and exclusion in the punk scene are any different from that of the rest of the world?

The answer, of course, is that they aren't. Or at least it is all born out of the same system. In the '70s, the answer was perhaps easier to digest. That punk rock, born in part out of a need for white escape, just wasn't prepared to consider a revolution that involved color, or involved women as anything that the scene deemed useful. That, of course, also being a reflection of the time. Today, we sit back and watch seemingly evolved artists talk about tearing down these large political structures and uniting the masses, and making safe spaces for everyone who wants to come out and enjoy music, but the actual efforts to build and create these spaces fall extremely short, as evidenced (in one example) by Jake McElfresh being allowed to play Warped Tour. McElfresh has a now admitted history of preying on underage girls, a demographic that the touring music showcase predominantly caters toward.

It is a luxury to romanticize blood, especially your own. It is a luxury to be able to fetishize violence, especially the violence that you inflict upon others. To use it as a bond, or to call it church, or to build an identity around it while knowing that everyone you can send home bloody will not come back for revenge. To walk home bloody. To walk home at night. At the time of writing this, a video is circulating of a Black man being killed by police, on camera. Before this, there was another Black man. And a Black boy. And Black women vanishing in jail. And Black trans women vanishing into the night. I do not blame punk rock for this.

I instead ask to consider the impact of continuing to glorify a very specific type of white violence and invisibility of all others in an era where there is a very real and very violent erasure of the bodies most frequently excluded from the language, culture, and visuals of punk rock. I ask myself who it serves when I see countless images showing examples of why "punk rock is a family," images with only white men. It does no good to point at a neighborhood of burning houses while also standing in a house on fire. It is true, now, the flames in the house of punk may climb up the walls more slowly than, say, the flames in the Fox News building. But the house is still on fire. Too often, the choice in punk rock and D.I.Y. spaces for non-white men is a choice between being tokenized, or being invisible. Having experienced both, I chose the latter, and then chose to stop going to as many shows altogether. Which isn't mentioned in sadness. To watch the casual packaging of a violence that impacts and affects bodies that look like yours, and to watch that violence knowing that you have no place in it, other than to take it in, feels similar to being Black every other place in America.

After reading a few poems about being Black at punk rock shows in Boston a few months ago, a Black woman came up to me. We talked about our experiences in our respective scenes, how we eventually got less excited about them, and gravitated toward the Afropunk festival. Where the music may not be rooted in the short/fast/loud assault of sound that permeated my Midwest upbringing, the dreamt-of ethos of punk is there. The idea of finding your own crew, and keeping the circle open. An idea that I think many traditional punk scenes struggle toward, or have forgotten about, in part because when you create the crew, the concept of opening a circle to those who seem different never crosses your mind.

When I left the last Afropunk festival I went to, I remembered that I wasn't alone. Afropunk by itself isn't going to save us, or dismantle a racist world, but if punk rock was born, in part, out of the need for white escape, Afropunk signals something provided for Black escape from what the actions of white escape breeds. The fantasies that it, often violently, provides its young men with, and the people who suffer beneath those fantasies, vanishing. Like all dismantling of supremacy, punk, D.I.Y., and likeminded scenes have to cut to the core, and rewire the whole operation. There has to be an urgency to this; the world demands it. There is no war, but for the one that is claiming actual casualties. It is outside. And the bodies all look the same. There is no option now but to be honest about that.

Last year, I was at a Brand New show. One where, in typical Brand New fashion, they charged through half of their set and dragged through the back half. It was a hot night, and even hotter in the venue, a closed-in brick space with few windows. I stood upstairs, looking down. Halfway through "Sic Transit Gloria... Glory Fades," I noticed the only Black kid in the pit had passed out. Likely due to heat, or the physical nature of the pit. As a few of us above pointed, to try and draw attention, I watched his peers step over him; some kicked him, in the pursuit to keep dancing. To maybe touch the edge of the stage that their heroes graced.

The prone body of this Black boy, unnoticed and consumed by noise, and moving feet. Already forgotten.

It was jarring. Another example of how expendable the Black body can be when in the way of needs that are greater than it, the range of those needs changing by the hour, or second. It was another image of Black fragility and dismissal, of course not as harsh as videos of guns firing into Black men, or the force feeding of mugshots we get when a dead victim is Black. But it was a reminder that choosing invisibility means giving yourself over to what so many systems in this country already deem you. Punk rock, as it stands now, being no different.

Eventually, as the song winded down (ironically with the line "die young and save yourself," a line that I used to have scrawled on a notebook before I got older and started to quite enjoy living, or at least stopped finding death romantic), I watched the boy sit up, shake his head, and gingerly stand up. He looked around, and slowly made his way to the back of the venue. Like I did when I was his age. After the show, I aimed to find him, to at least make eye contact. There is something powerful in someone who looks like you actually seeing you. I never caught up to him, and I don't know what I would have said if I did. I don't know how to be honest enough to say that there isn't a place for kids like us, so we need to make our own, and nothing is more punk rock than that. Nothing is more punk rock than surviving in a hungry sea of white noise.

Under Half-Lit Fluorescents: The Wonder Years And The Great Suburban Narrative

IT IS A STRANGE THING TO GROW UP POOR, OR IN any interpretation of the hood, and be in very close proximity to the suburbs—a short walk or bike ride away from a world that seems entirely unlike your own, a dream that you could be snatched from at any moment. As a curious kid, always fascinated by the idea of escape, I would sometimes meet my friends and ride our bikes to the edge of our neighborhood, into the blocks where the houses were taller. The sidewalks were more even underneath our bike tires, and the silence was a gift to a group of reckless and noisy boys, spilling in from a place where everything rattled with the bass kicking out of some car's trunk. We would ride our bikes with our dirty and torn jeans and look at the manicured lawns and grand entrances and the playgrounds with no broken glass stretched across the landscape. During the day in the summer, we were just kids there. Black, sure, but not particularly threatening or dangerous to all of the other kids who were, like us, trying to find a way to kill time while their parents were at work and school was out.

And then, with the sun setting on another hot day, we would ride back a few blocks to our neighborhood's familiar skin—the language we knew, the songs we could rap along to, and the comfort that comes with not standing out. When I say it is a strange thing to live in close proximity to a world so vastly different than your own, I mean that it creates a longing within the imagination. You long for a place that you know only by its snapshots and not by the lives moving within them. It allowed me to fantasize, imagine a world where everyone was happy and no one ever hurt.

The Wonder Years' third album, *Suburbia I've Given You All and Now I'm Nothing*, released nearly five years ago as of 2016, takes its title from the Allen Ginsberg poem, "America." The poem opens: "America I've given you all and now I'm nothing. / America two dollars and twentyseven cents January 17, 1956. / I can't stand my own mind. / America when will we end the human war?" The poem, like most Ginsberg poems of its era, is sprawling and emotionally uneven, a meditation on the unrest of war's aftermath that is equal parts angry and humorous, confused yet determined.

We meet The Wonder Years here in their truest form on the album opener, "Came Out Swinging," a song that, even now, is a high-functioning album opener, an arm that reaches from the speaker and wraps around you, pulling you gently to the speaker's mouth. We find this Pennsylvania pop-punk band as we found Ginsberg in a different time. Not lost and anxious in the aftermath of actual war, of course—only war is war—but the anxiety on the album is palpable nonetheless. It is an album of return and escape and return and escape again. It feels, in tone and tension, like coming home for a summer after your first year of college, having tasted another existence and wanting more, but instead sleeping in your childhood room.

Home is where the heart begins, but not where the heart stays. The heart scatters across states, and has nothing left after what home takes from it. I know the suburbs best by how they consumed the kids I knew in my teenage years: the punk kids, the emo kids, the soccer kids, the kids who came out to the basketball courts with the Black kids to play the way they couldn't in their backyard. So many of us, especially teenagers, strive to be something we're not. Escape is vital, in some cases, as a survival tool. Once, I never knew how anyone who lived in a beautiful home in a nice neighborhood could be sad. Sometimes, when you know so much of not having, it is easy to imagine those who do have as exceptionally worry-free.

Sadness, when you are truly being swallowed by it, can feel almost universal. Not the vehicle that drives you to the doorstep of sadness, and certainly not the way it manifests itself inside of you. But the sadness itself, the soaking feeling of it, is something that you know everyone around you has had a taste of. The kids who came to rap and punk shows in nice shoes, always fighting to stay out just a bit later, anything to keep them away from home, anything to keep them in a world unlike their own. This is the cycle we create and live through: we see the greener grass and then run to it.

The first time I lost a friend, a true friend, to the unfamiliar violence of a bottle of pills, I wondered what it must be like to not feel like you were destined for death, but still want to arrive at it. And then another friend. And then another. A rooftop, a car crash. When you go to enough funerals in summer, you learn tricks: bring a lighter jacket, something that can be carried. Wear a shirt that you don't mind sweating through. Deep pockets to stash your tie after it gets taken off and your shirt buttons are loosened. I don't remember when my friends and I stopped asking the question of "why?" around death. I understand what it is to be sad, even when everyone around you is demanding your happiness—and what are we to do with all of that pressure other than search for a song that lets us be drained of it all?

The great mission of any art that revolves around place is the mission of honesty. So many of us lean into romantics when we write of whatever place we crawled out of, perhaps because we feel like we owe it something, even when it has taken more from us than we've taken from it. The mission of honesty becomes a bit cloudy when we decide to be honest about not loving the spaces we have claimed as our own. This is the work of *Suburbia*. It isn't carried out with bitterness, but with a timeline of questions. Who is going to be brave enough to ask where home is, and seek out something else if they don't like the answer? And, yes, the songs that fall out of this process are as brilliant as any songs the pop-punk/emo genre have ever seen. "Local Man Ruins Everything" dresses up the grief in the center of the room until it becomes forgettable. "Summers in PA" could be about you and all of your friends in any summer where you all felt invincible. "Don't Let Me Cave In" is a negotiation of distance, and home, and greater distance. The band was operating at a level of greatness they hadn't reached before that point. It's a jarring, emotionally honest undertaking that chooses interrogation over nostalgia's soft and simple target. The album ends with "And Now I'm Nothing," the ultimate anchor, echoing a small plea of freedom: "Suburbia, stop pushing / I know what I'm doing / Suburbia, stop pushing / I know what I'm doing."

A lot of the people I knew who dismissed "emo" while the genre was at its peak did so because they believed emotions were things that should be sacred and unspoken, not screamed out to the listening masses. I push back against that, both in personal practice and as someone who has seen the other side of that coin, or known people completely eaten alive by the hoarding of sacred emotion. And, of course, we say the world doesn't care about your problems. We say that and we know that our problems aren't only our problems, and that there are people who need to know that their problems aren't only their problems. The glory of The Wonder Years, in *Suburbia* and everything since, is that their mission seems to be entirely unselfish in scope. This is what, to me, has separated them from their peers in the genre: a willingness to own their shitty pasts and everything they entail without also trying to cash it in for points, without trying to be the smartest or most charming band in the room. *I'm sad and I've hurt people and I'm a beautifully tortured survivor of my past* is a hard thing to say out loud (or scream on a chorus), but it is the honest thing, which means it is the thing that I would rather have sitting in the room with me on the days I miss everyone.

Suburbia is the first of a stunning trilogy of Wonder Years albums that all seem to be in conversation with each other. 2013's *The Greatest Generation* and 2015's *No Closer to Heaven* all sit in the same space. They are albums that are awash with questions, and content not providing any answers. They are all telling singular stories in their frantic urgency and emotion: *Suburbia* about the idea of home, *Greatest Generation* about the idea of growing up and leaving things behind, *No Closer to Heaven* about death and loss—all of them, particularly the first two, centered on the American suburban experience. All of them say, "I'm sad like you are, and I can't promise to fix this, but we're going to be here together."

I am still, always, a Black kid from a Black neighborhood, who once biked to the edge of the suburbs and then once loved my friends from the suburbs and then sometimes buried my friends from the suburbs. And even then, never understanding the interior of those lives beyond the angst-ridden stories that teenagers share, I never understood how a life that looked beautiful could be immensely sad. Where you live and grow up in America has very real implications, and that isn't to be ignored here. But I found myself, and still find myself, always considering the place I'm from and the pressure and expectations that come with that. I am proud to have survived where I'm from, and I happily keep it close to me. What The Wonder Years do best, first with *Suburbia*, is kick a door wide open to the rest of us who admire the imagined life from afar. I listen to The Wonder Years, and I am back on my bike again, tearing through the even sidewalks and manicured lawns. The difference is that when I close my eyes and imagine this, I can see the houses now. I can see the lives inside. I can feel the unshakable and honest grief, thick in the air, as I bike home.

All Our Friends Are Famous

MY BUDDY NICK SCREAMED IN THIS METALCORE band called Constellations because he couldn't really play an instrument and didn't want to learn, but he wanted to get laid at least close to as much as our other buddy Nick who wasn't in a band at all, but who had dark hair and boyish good looks, and a devil may care ambiance that all the girls we hung around found irresistible. Constellations wasn't that good of a band and Nick wasn't that good of a frontman but the band still got gigs because during the slow season, The Basement would let any band that can fill the place play a set and an argument can be made that when it comes to impressing a potential date, being some scene kid who knows the band might be better than actually being the scene kid *in* the band, because if you embarrass yourself, at least it won't be on a stage with everyone watching. Plus, all of our pals got drink tickets but only about half of them could drink, and so, in half full venues full of our friends, we could live like brief and generous kings. Constellations cut an EP called *Alpha* right before the summer of 2008, and all of the songs sounded the same, but we still played it in our cars like it was hot shit because when would we ever get to hear one of our own dripping out of our car speakers. Constellations never sold out a show, but they did get to play The Basement in summer once, toward the end of the band's run in 2009, before Nick got kicked out of the band for not being a good enough screamer to justify the mental headaches he caused the so-called creative process. And at that summer show, they played their song "Model T Drive By," which was maybe the only song that felt like it had real potential, or at least the one song that didn't sound like everything else. When the breakdown came, Johnny, who played guitar for the band, jumped directly into the thrashing of the pit, guitar still plugged in. Nick had, somehow, obtained a drumstick from some other band's setup, and was using it to orchestrate the violence in the pit, almost pulling the bodies from one side to the other like they were attached to a string at the drumstick's tip. For a moment, you could only hear Johnny's furious guitar playing, but you couldn't see him through the wave of arms and elbows swinging in every direction, enclosing him. The dude behind the bar at The Basement, who drank heavily on the job and never made a sound during these shows except to let out the occasional skeptical or frustrated sigh, looked up from his second beer of the night, took stock of this brief and incredible madness, put his hand on my shoulder and said, "Now this is a fucking hardcore show."

Constellations broke up a month later. Nick didn't get laid nearly as much as he thought he would. I found unused drink tickets in my pockets for months.

II. Twenty One Pilots Are Innocent! (After Lester Bangs)

This is the truth! You are only from here if you're from here! Sure, the suburbs count, but only if you're winning! Twenty One Pilots are from the suburbs! Not the suburbs like the ones my pals would skate through to score cheap weed! Tyler and Josh have never actually flown a plane! But there's only so many band names I guess! Twenty One Pilots are good Christian kids! They make music that you don't have to love God to like! Finally, a

Christian band that speaks to me! Well I guess! Relient K wasn't bad! At least they had the decency to write something more than hooks! Relient K is also from Ohio! It's called the Bible Belt for a reason! Being religiously ambiguous sells more records! Twenty One Pilots are at the top of the charts again! Some dirge about all their friends being heathens! Which friends! Tell me the clear truth! I know some of their old friends and they all seem all right to me! What's a heathen anyway! We're all innocent until our friends write songs about us! Was there at the Newport back in '11 when *Regional At Best* dropped and all the record labels packed the house! Felt like the whole city made it! Well I mean I guess it felt that way! If you count the suburbs and surrounding areas! Before that at Independents' Day they put on a real show! Dragged a whole piano in an alley! Tyler jumped on top! No one in the alley could move! He parted the crowd with just a single finger! It was biblical probably! I walked home that night thinking they'd be the biggest band in the city! I walked home thinking they'd be here forever and never make it out!

III. The Sadness of Proximity

When Twenty One Pilots won their first Grammy award, winning in the Best Pop Duo/Group Performance category, beating out far more deserving songs (Rihanna's "Work," for example), they accepted the award with their pants down. Literally, on stage, Tyler Joseph and Josh Dun pulled down their pants, going into a drawn out story from their younger days about watching the Grammy Awards without pants and dreaming of being there. It was charming, if you're into the type of charm the band has become known for: a Midwestern emotional affectation that both wins over parents and emotionally starved youth.

There's something magical about all of your friends being in shitty bands with no intention of really making it. Columbus is like any other midsize-but-close-to-big city. It overflows with talented people who don't always know where to place their talent, and sometimes there are far less talented people who just have access to a stage and enough people to watch them. In the era right before Twenty One Pilots exploded, it didn't seem like any single band would ever approach the heights they eventually would, and so most everyone I knew rolled around in some trashy hardcore outfit, trying to make the nights a little more fun. The bands barely practiced, played shows to whoever could afford the five buck cover, and sometimes took whatever change they made from the show and got everyone pizza. These people all had day jobs. Some would work waiting tables for two weeks just to afford the amp to plug a guitar into so that the band could stay together for another show or two.

I'm not making a value judgement on one versus the other, when it comes to success and simply survival. I'm saying that I celebrated Twenty One Pilots on that Grammy stage with their pants down, even though their song wasn't the best song in the category, and even though they saddled the speech with a corniness that only their Midwestern brethren could recognize underneath all of the attempted charm. I always hoped for Columbus, Ohio, to have a band make it big, and Twenty One Pilots sit as one of the biggest bands in the world. So I feel guilty when I say that I wish it could be someone other than them. Someone who didn't feel so intensely manufactured, or line-toeing. Someone who knew their way around more than just a catchy hook. I'm proud of them because I watched them from their early days, and I'm hard on them because I watched them from their early days.

The closest I'll get to knowing real rockstars were my friends in summer, before record labels came to town looking to pluck the next big thing. Constellations was a shit band, but they were a shit band that was a labor of love for a few kids I cared about deeply, in a scene full of kids that I cared about deeply, just trying to afford whatever it would take to make it into a studio and put a few tracks together. A week after Twenty One Pilots won their Grammy, I found *Alpha*, the first Constellations EP. It was in an old CD book, wasting away with the rest of the dead technology of its time. I put it on in my car on a long drive back to Columbus. When the first song hit, I remember the smile on Nick's face as he burst into our friend's apartment with the CDs for the first time. How we all listened to every track three times over. How we told ourselves that we loved it. How it didn't matter whether or not we did.

The Return Of The Loneliest Boys In Town

CUTE IS WHAT WE AIM FOR IS A BAND FROM EMO'S mid-2000s boom, when any kids who met in high school and had long hair were getting signed to Fueled By Ramen after Blink-182 and Fall Out Boy and a handful of other bands made good enough for there to be a run on groups that might be able to cash in on a hit album or two. Their name is clunky and embarrassing, but it's mostly because they listened to too many emo albums that had exhaustingly long song titles and thought they'd cut out the middleman. They weren't as endearing and fun as some of the other mid-2000s bands. Hellogoodbye also had a corny name, but at least they had the good sense to play synthesizers and bring beach balls to their concerts. That particular era of emo was all about kids who were self-aware enough to know that they were the joke. Cute Is What We Aim For pretended to think they were the joke, but they seemed to want to be taken seriously with their sprawling songs about heartbreak and distance. Their first album, 2006's *The Same Old Blood Rush with a New Touch*, had no depth and felt entirely contrived, like a band trying on a bunch of clothes that someone told them they *should* be wearing, even though all of the shirts are too big. Still, I sang along to "Curse of Curves" at enough house parties in 2006 to make the record a worthwhile purchase in the sea of emo albums that flooded the summer of 2006, but were forgotten by winter.

After another album, a handful of lineup shuffles, and a lengthy hiatus, Cute Is What We Aim For returned in the summer of 2016 to tour, playing the full *Same Old Blood Rush* album in its entirety, honoring its tenth anniversary. This was an odd choice, and felt explicitly like an attempt at a money grab. The album carried no memorable hits, peaked at a meager #75 on the charts, and was critically panned. Still, my fascination getting the best of me (and my deeply uninterested partner out of town), I made the trip to see them when they came through Hamden, Connecticut, a college town filled with early-20s kids who, in most cases, wouldn't be able to pick the band out of a lineup. The venue, which I entered about ten minutes before show time, was close to barren.

The problem with *Same Old Blood Rush* is the problem with a lot of emo albums from its era, and why most emo bands don't drag out their old albums in their entirety. One of the first lines you hear on the album is: "in every circle of friends there's a whore," courtesy of the song "Newport Living," and the album builds around a single common theme: bitterness, most commonly aimed at an imagined woman who has wronged the band in some way. This is a common trope in all music, of course, but it took on a more visceral tone in the second and third waves of emo. In the early 2000s, the first albums by bands like Taking Back Sunday, Brand New, and Fall Out Boy, while stunning in many ways, also acted as revenge fantasy. The theme, in these albums and beyond, revolved around summoning "the girl," and then wishing for ill to befall her as a punishment for heartbreak. Punishment rarely doled out by the man dreaming it up, but by some other circumstance: a car crash, choking on a meal, being attacked by an animal. It was, for me, very in the moment—something that I did myself in my teens from behind the security of a keyboard or behind a pen. It's in the spirit of male loneliness to imagine that someone has to suffer for it.

Same Old Blood Rush takes this approach, but with less direct and explicit violence, and more of an angle that feels like the band is in a high school hallway, spreading rumors about the girl who slept with them and didn't call the next day. This leads to incessant binary moral judgements based more on gender than actual judgements. The hook before the first chorus in "Newport Living" is "If you lie, you don't deserve to have friends," repeated on loop. "Curse of Curves" bemoans attractive women who just can't keep up with the band's intellect. So does "Lyrical Lies." So does "There's A Class For This," with a hint of even more boastful arrogance ("I may be ugly / but they sure love to stare"), the kind of lyrics that sound like things you tell yourself after rejection. "The Fourth Drink Instinct" is a messy narrative about a young girl being taken advantage of by a man while drunk, but quickly turns into a song blaming the girl for drinking in the first place. In the place of explicit bursts of violent fantasies, the album instead opts for a low and consistent hum of violences, the ones that seem more logical to someone who might also be sad, who might also want to turn their loneliness into a weapon without having it actually look like a weapon.

In Hamden, the crowd has filled out a bit more, but barely. The band is stalling, waiting for more bodies to get into the room. You can tell, because it is easy to see them shuffling backstage, a member poking a head out every now and then. This is, in part, no fault of their own—Hamden is not New York City or even Pittsburgh. I wouldn't have crossed state lines for this show, and was amazed to see that it was happening at all. For a 15 minute drive and a 10 dollar ticket, I could be easily convinced to see if there was any residual magic that my desire for nostalgia could drag up.

When the band finally comes out and plays through "Newport Living" and "There's A Class For This," it becomes obvious that they aren't invested. The crowd of maybe 25 tries; a guy next to me nodding along to "Risque" and trying to sing all of the words stops himself in the middle of the "Medically speaking you're adorable / and from what I hear you're quite affordable" that opens the chorus. He looks around my age, both of us at the start of our 30s. We were perhaps both heartbroken a decade ago, at the dawn of our 20s, and looking for somewhere to place our pain. I feel this, the way I've aged and the loves and losses I've suffered in that aging, hanging over the room. It makes the display of dragging this particular album back out of the closet at first fascinating and then comically uncomfortable. There are endless ways that we have found and will find to blame women for things, particularly when it prevents us from unraveling our own unhappiness. But with Cute Is What We Aim For, all of its members either in their 30s or late 20s, standing on a stage and weaponizing decade-old bitterness doesn't exactly echo to the corner of nostalgia that I thought it would. Even in the album's catchier moments, like a very sharp performance of "Curse of Curves" and a slightly warmer acoustic version of the album's best song, "Teasing to Please," watching the show feels like being a senior in college and going back to hang out in the high school parking lot. Halfway through the show, I ask myself what I expected. I think I was hoping for the band to come out and play revised versions of their old songs, less bitter, less explicit in their hatred of the women they've built out of thin air and been broken by.

Twisting anger over heartbreak into something, well, cute, is easier for some genres than others. In emo, particularly during its heyday of attractive frontmen who fancied themselves poets, the misogyny was seen more as process than problem. Who among us, regardless of gender, hasn't scrawled something in the silence of a notebook about an ex-someone? It's a part of the coping, at least to a point. The problem is one of audience, though. The problem is the one of the notebook becoming public, sung to thousands. The problem is one of men being, largely, the only ones doing the singing. And, ultimately, the problem becomes when those men don't age beyond the adolescent heartbroken temper tantrums that we all have before we learn better and start to know better. It's not a measure of being morally superior to this band on stage, or not failing in my own politics around sadness, gender, and anger. But it's the difference between trying to chip away at the emotional debt one has accrued versus piling on top of it. At moments in the show, I felt like I was exiting my current body and watching myself from through my younger eyes, wondering if this is what it was always going to come to. Returning to the balm for an old wound, ashamed that I once decided to wear it.

Though I didn't know at the time I arrived at the Cute Is What We Aim For show in Hamden, a few days earlier, lead singer Shaant Hacikyan made the news for weighing in on Brock Turner, the Stanford rapist who got a decidedly light sentence for his crime. "Rape culture isn't a thing, for real," Hacikyan wrote on Facebook. "Playing the victim seems to fit the narrative," he said. "In my 29 years I've yet to encounter a human who is looking to rape someone […] Look into the actual statistics & get back to me." It was a terrible and ill-informed take, one that came from someone who seemed to have very little understanding of the world. It was slow to pick up news, in part because it was a Facebook comment, and in part because the band's fading relevance made it so that few people cared. When I found out about it, googling the band in the dark of my office after the show, it was both stunning and not. It was a stance that directly echoed the band's entire history. By the time the story gained traction, Hacikyan already issued a toothless apology, thanking people for educating him on the topic of rape culture before taking the stage to sing a song about a young girl, drinking so much that the men around her just can't help themselves.

Before the encore, most of the crowd leaves, but I stay, the guy who gave up on singing lyrics still sticking around next to me. As the break before the encore stretches out, we look at each other, and he says the first words that he's said to me all night.

"Shit, man. I dunno. I got a wife and a daughter now. This ain't like it was when we were young, is it?"

I smile, and shake my head. No. No, it isn't.

Brief Notes On Staying // No One Is Making Their Best Work When They Want To Die

I DON'T MEAN SADNESS AS MUCH AS I MEAN THE obsession with it. Once, on the wrong edge of a bridge, a boy I knew who played songs let his feet slip off. I found a tape of his after he was gone, and the music sounded sweeter, or at least I told myself it did. What I really want to do is say that life is impossible, and the lie we tell ourselves is that it is too short. Life, if anything, is too long. We accumulate too much along the way. Too many heartbreaks, too many funerals, too many physical setbacks. It's a miracle any of us survive at all. I know that I stopped thinking about extreme grief as the sole vehicle for great art when the grief started to take people with it. And I get it. The tortured artist is the artist that gets remembered for all time, particularly if they either perish or overcome. But the truth is that so many of us are stuck in the middle. So many of us begin tortured and end tortured, with only brief bursts of light in between, and I'd rather have average art and survival than miracles that come at the cost of someone's life. There will always be something great and tragic to celebrate and I am wondering, now, if I've had enough. I am, of course, in favor of letting all grief work through the body and manifest itself creatively. But what I'm less in favor of is the celebration of pain that might encourage someone to mine deeper into that unforgiving darkness, until it is impossible for them to climb out. I'm less in favor of anything that hurts and then becomes theater, if that theater isn't also working to heal the person experiencing pain. I, too, am somewhat obsessed with watching creations that feel like work. I am less drawn to the artist who at least appears to make it look easy. But our best work is the work of ourselves, our bodies and the people who want us to keep pushing, even if the days are long and miserable and even if there are moments when the wrong side of the bridge beckons you close. All things do not pass. Sometimes, that which does not kill you sits heavy over you until all of the things that did not kill you turn into a single counterforce that might. No matter what comes out of a person in these times, the work that we make when we feel like we no longer want to be alive is not the best work if it is also not work that, little by little, is pushing us back toward perhaps staying, even if just for a moment.

What I'm mostly saying, friends, is that I've lost too much. And everything sounds good when you know it was the last thing a person would ever make. All of the words sit more perfect on the page when they are the last words. What I'm mostly saying, friends, is that I am sad today. I am sad today, and I may be sad tomorrow. But I watched a video where rappers hung out of the roof of a car and threw money in slow motion, and it made me briefly consider another type of freedom. I am sad today, but I held, in my hands, a picture of me on a day where I was not sad. In it, the sunlight leaked over my face in a city I love, and my eyes were wide and eager. I am sad yesterday, and I might be sad tomorrow, and even the day after. But I will be here, looking for a way out, every time. Staying is not always a choice, and I have lived and lost enough to know that. But the way I think about grief is that it is the great tug-of-war, and sometimes the flag is on the side you don't want it to be on. And sometimes, the game has exhausted all of its joy, and all that's left is you on your knees. But, today, even though I am sad, my hands are still on the rope. I am making my best work when my hands are on the rope, even if I'm not pulling back. Life is too long, despite the cliché. Too long, and sometimes too painful. But I imagine I have made it too far. I imagine, somewhere around some corner, the best part is still coming.

Searching For A New Kind Of Optimism

"It is so easy to be hopeful in the daytime when you can see the things you wish on. But it was night, it stayed night. Night was striding across nothingness with the whole round world in his hands."

— Zora Neale Hurston

MY FRIENDS AND I WERE WRONG ABOUT A WHOLE lot of things in 2016, and I imagine you and your friends were, too, if the concert of all our cages rattling in unison in our respective corners of the internet is any indication. I was once content with being wrong about the big things, as long as I could cloak myself in hope for something better. But at the end of a year in which I was wrong about almost everything, nothing about that felt worthy of praise, so I opted for silence. A few days before Christmas, I drove to Provincetown, Massachusetts, at the very tip of Cape Cod. A beach town consumed by tourists in the summer months, it is largely silent in the winter. You might see a few committed locals, a handful of artists, a small mass of people shifting from bar to bar and tripping down Commercial Street, swaying and drunkenly singing into the calm. It gets dark early there, on the very northeastern edge of the country. On the day I arrived, it was the winter solstice, the darkest day of the year. At 4 p.m., it was pitch black. There's a particular kind of darkness that hangs over a space that's surrounded by nothing but an ocean—a vast, swallowing darkness. It's the kind that makes the memory of light seem hopeless, impossible.

In a Cape Cod record store two days before Christmas, I picked up a copy of the 1977 Richard Hell and the Voidoids album *Blank Generation*. Richard Hell holds open a leather jacket on the album cover, the words "YOU MAKE ME _____" scrawled across his chest. I thought about the old Lester Bangs profile, from shortly after this album came out, in which Hell prattled on about how much he wanted to die. Later, rereading that profile, I found that Hell wasn't searching for death as much as he was looking for a way to halt feeling entirely. I find myself personally far removed from such longing, and I also find it worth pointing out that Hell is still alive in 2017. In his more recent writings, he seems resigned to the wisdom that can come with age. So does Pete Townshend, long after he hoped to die before he got old. But even if I don't long for destruction the way these men once did, I understand how it feels to desire that kind of longing.

All emotion, when performed genuinely and facing an audience, can be currency. Sadness and fear are, perhaps, the two biggest bills in the billfold, and what was haunting about both Townshend and Hell in their youth is that their death wishes seemed believable. They didn't sound like friends of mine joking on social media about wanting an asteroid to take us all out; theirs wasn't a hope for human extinction, just the extinction of the self, the feelings that come with having to exist in uncertain times. There is plenty of rock optimism to counter this, of course, from Bruce Springsteen's insistence on overcoming through labor to Tom Petty's slick nostalgia as a survival tool. But when you grow up with punks, the kind of kids who listened to Richard Hell records and then found more like that, it's easy to feel some distance from the kind of optimism that we're taught to lean into during difficult times. Even now, I'm not as invested in things getting better as I am in things getting honest. The week of Christmas, I drove alone into the dark, and I did that, in part, knowing that the dark was going to be there when I arrived, knowing that it would still be my work to find something small and hopeful within.

My friends say that I've gotten too cynical, and I suspect this might be true, judging by how quickly many people get exhausted when talking to me about the future. I am working on it, truly. A therapist tells me to challenge my "inner cynic," but when I do, I simply find another inner cynic behind that one. I am, it turns out, a nesting doll of cynics. There is no evidence to suggest that humans are going to become any more kind this year, or more empathetic, or more loving toward each other. If anything, with our constant exposure to all of one another's most intense moments, the bar for what we seem prepared to tolerate gets lower with every second we spend screaming into each other's open windows. Yes, without question, 2016 was a year that dragged on more heavily than most before it. It felt exhausting, and like it would never end. But all past logic was pulling us toward that breaking point: a year that finally pushed us to the edge. And all logic in this moment points to another year that might not feel quite as long but will surely be just as trying.

I have been thinking, then, about the value of optimism while cities burn, while people are fearing for their lives and the lives of their loved ones, while discourse is reduced to laughing through a chorus of anxiety. A woman in a Cape Cod diner the day after Christmas saw me eyeing the news and shaking my head. She told me that "things will get better," and I wasn't sure they would, but I nodded and said, "They surely can't get any worse," which is the lie that we all tell, the one that we want to believe, even as there are jaws opening before us.

I'm not sold on pessimism as the new optimism. I need something that allows us to hope for something greater while confronting the mess of whatever all this foolish hope has driven us to. America is not what people thought it was before, even for those of us who were already familiar with some of its many flaws. What good is endless hope in a country that never runs out of ways to drain you of it? What does it mean to claim that a president is not your own as he pushes the lives of those you love closer to the brink? What is it to avoid acknowledging the target but still come, ready, to the resistance?

The greatest song on *Blank Generation* is the title track, on which Richard Hell shouts, "It's such a gamble / When you get a face." I laughed when I heard that line in an empty room in the seeming always-darkness of the Cape in winter. In 2016, the gamble returned not only a bad face, but a hall full of mirrors turned on the faces of everyone who avoided looking deeply into those mirrors in past years in the name of hope.

The day before leaving the Cape, I ran into a man I had been seeing in the streets since the day I arrived. He was often drunk but very kind. He stopped me on my run and asked if he could make a call on my phone. I didn't have it with me, and I muttered out an awkward response, littered with too much information about not carrying it while I ran. From the open door of a coffee shop, more news about Donald Trump blared from the television, flooding out into the street where we were standing. The man looked past me to the beach, drenched in gray and threatening clouds. "We're all going to die," he said. Then he was gone.

We are all going to die. That's true, though I hope I get a few more trips on this sometimes wretched ride. I have tasted enough of its highs to know that they're worth sticking around for, though not worth worshiping as a sole survival tool in the face of its lows. I've abandoned hopeless hope, but I am not rooting for the meteor. I'm still rooting for us, my people and their people and their people beyond that. I'm rooting for us to clean off the dusty mirror and look at the bad bet staring back. This is me challenging my inner cynic the best way I know how—taking a few lazy swings and seeing if I can tire him out in time to get back to whatever the real work may be this time. It is another new year, and most of my pals made it to the other side with me. Some of us called each other and heard each other's voices. Some sent blurry pictures, drowning in fluorescent light. Some of us made sure that those who weren't alone knew that they weren't alone.

I have started other years at funerals, in hospital rooms, in studio apartments with my phone off entirely. So in spite of the newest realities that we must confront and stay uncomfortable with, I'm hoping that I get to stick around for a while. I am hoping, mostly, that we all get better at wishing on the things we need, even in darkness.

Death Becomes You: My Chemical Romance And Ten Years Of The Black Parade

So fake your death Or it's your blame
And leave the lights on When you stay
   —My Chemical Romance, "Fake Your Death"

ACT I

IN THE FALL OF 2006, I WAS IN THE MIDST OF TYPI-cal early-20s purgatory. Having struck out during my initial pass at adulthood, and cloaked in a sadness that felt directionless, I moved back in with my father—back into my childhood bed-room. This is one of the more romantic failures, the one that takes you back to the place where you started and allows you to stare directly into the memories of a time when you were young-er, with endless potential. Above my bed still hung my soccer jersey from my senior year of high school. In one of the night-stand drawers, there were still letters from high school friends, papers I'd written, pictures from the summer before college— the last summer of complete freedom that I would ever know. In this way, I was given a type of distance from the life I felt I couldn't succeed in. I wasn't a child again, but I was, certainly, re-living another life through new eyes.

A total stereotype of early-20s apathy, I spent my time work-ing a shit job at a dollar store in the neighborhood where I grew up, mostly because I could walk there and walk home with something in my headphones. When I got to the store, I would slump over the cash register, playing a CD of often inappropri-ate shopping music over the store's speakers.

In the middle of this, My Chemical Romance's *The Black Parade* arrived. A dark, deliciously overblown, theatrical concept album about that which carries us into an imaginary afterlife. It was a massive album, in both sound and scope. I first loved it because of how the actual sounds filled headphones or a room. On a day off from the dollar store, with my father away at work, I would throw the album on and turn up the surround-sound stereo, letting the chunky guitars chew at the framed and rattling photos on the wall. I insisted on falling for the music first, having never had an immense interest in concept albums, particularly ones that came out of the emo/punk scenes, so many of which were filled with sprawl for the sake of sprawl, sacrificing narrative for hard-to-track, excessively emotional lyrics. I thought even My Chemical Romance's previous album, *Three Cheers for Sweet Revenge*, failed in its pursuit of concept while succeeding in the pursuit of music. Still, I believed in *The Black Parade* more than any other My Chemical Romance project before it because I believed in their willingness to be entirely certain of their mission at a time when I was without a mission, and also without certainty. They were, always, a bit outside of the scene. They played at the typical emo festivals and were covered by all the typical alternative music magazines, but they were a little surer of the emotional dark spaces they were navigating than their peers. Even at their most performative—which *The Black Parade* definitely is—there was something about My Chemical Romance's vision that felt comfortable, touchable, genuine. It was easy to be confident on *The Black Parade*, an album that unpacks a complete certainty: that we are all going to die, and none of us know what comes next.

ACT II

I am not afraid to keep on living
I am not afraid to walk this world alone

Today, in 2016, death is a low-hovering cloud that is always present. We know the dead and how they have died. We can sometimes watch the dead be killed. We can sometimes watch the best moments of their lives be replayed after they are gone—a reminder that they were once something other than buried. In this way, we can come to know the dead more efficiently than we know some of the living who occupy the same spaces we do. Yet even with all of this, exploring the interior of death's endless rooms is a far less virtuous endeavor than continually and somberly reacting to the endless river of graves.

The Black Parade, in concept, is about a single character, "The Patient," who is suffering from cancer and facing down an inevitable death. More than simply honing in on The Patient's decay, My Chemical Romance frontman Gerard Way presents an operatic theme that revolves around The Patient's slow passing into a life after death, carried by a parade. The idea is death coming to you in the form of your first and most fond memory: a flower opening slow in your front yard, a bright and colorful sunrise, or a slow-marching parade of musicians and merry makers walking with you to the gates in their darkest regalia.

In retrospect, *The Black Parade* isn't as large of a leap for My Chemical Romance as it was billed as in 2006. It feels instead like a natural progression, the album where the band finally figured out their formula and how to cash in on it. It still has all of the musical, lyrical, and visual dramatic and aesthetic of a My Chemical Romance album; it's just turned up to a higher level. Where the sharpest growth exists is in their idea of "concept." They are a band of storytellers who simply needed to dial in on a single small story and pull the narrative along, instead of falling into the trap of trying to connect too many threads at once. *The Black Parade* doesn't insist on resolution because it doesn't deal in the resolute. Death, yes, is inevitable. But that which we see before it arrives, the things that happen after the lights go out, is pure imagination. The work of *The Black Parade* was simply to bring it to life.

And musically, visually, the life is a glorious one: the tinkling piano on "Welcome to the Black Parade" giving way to a shower of guitars ripped straight from late-'70s arena rock, Gerard Way half-growling, half-singing the same tense lyrics that dance along the lines of loneliness and desire. The video for the album's proper final song, "Famous Last Words," is perhaps the album's finest moment, where the band, so committed to putting a bow on the album's immense mission, thrash and wail in front of a wall of fire. The parade float is burning at their backs, their marching outfits are worn out and covered in dirt, and the parade itself is gone. It is only them, alone, fighting to survive. They have, on their journey, become The Patient and his fight. It is a dark video, one that speaks to sacrifice, both metaphorically and very literally: drummer Bob Bryar sustained third-degree burns on the back of his legs while filming, Gerard Way tore muscles in his foot and leg, and lead guitarist Ray Toro fractured his fingers, which were already blistered from the heat. Watching the video is as fascinating as it is agonizing. Toward the end there's a shot of rhythm guitarist Frank Iero on his knees. He lets his guitar slip out of his hands and breathes heavily while the fire rages at his back. His exhaustion, in that moment, feels real. It is brief, but it pushes through the screen and sinks into you. Even in the face of a spectacular album, this single video served as proof of a single band's commitment to something daring, as well as the cost of that commitment. To push so deep into the imagination of death that it becomes you.

ACT III

Well, I think I'm gonna burn in Hell, Everybody burn the house right down.

What I don't know, friends, is whether or not I believe in a life after this one that I've rattled around in for this brief and sometimes beautiful bunch of years. I know that I have thought about dying, like many of you likely have. When I have buried people I love and wondered if we would ever again sit across from each other at a table and laugh at an old joke. The uncertainty of an afterlife has also kept some of us here: at my youngest, most reckless and uncertain, I had moments where I thought life was done with me and I thought myself done with it. And, perhaps like some of you, I have remained here because of my comfort with the darkness I know and my fear of the darkness I do not.

The afterlife is, most times, talked about as an achievement as opposed to a full-bodied existence. A place some of us "get" to enjoy, while the rest of us languish in a more terrifying place. I imagine the afterlife, and what carries you there, like Gerard Way does. I imagine my fondest memories gathering me in their palms and taking me to a place where I can join a discussion already in progress with all my pals in a room with an endless jukebox.

And this is not groundbreaking. The great thing about an afterlife is that we've always been able to imagine it as the best possible place for us and our needs. *The Black Parade* is brilliant, though, because it complicates that. It finds small slivers of hope in the darkness of death and afterlife, yes, but the darkness is still darkness. It still sits, firmly, in the center of the experience of a slow and tedious demise. It does the work that all of our terrific afterlife fantasies don't: it reckons with the idea that a departure is most difficult because of who we leave behind. The song "Cancer" is stark, frank, and heartbreaking. The Patient is in a hospital bed, cycling through his fading appearance, wishing to have his family close so that he can bid them goodbye. This is the part of death as art that isn't always noble: the idea that the death, before it is art, is still death. There is still a person leaving, leaving us behind. *The Black Parade* works because it doesn't imagine death as romantic. The Patient goes, fighting, to the gates of whatever is on the other side. The album, for all of its wild and operatic fantasies, stays honest. When faced with all that is being left behind, even when death is inevitable, there are so many who will still fight against it.

ACT IV

To un-explain the unforgivable,
Drain all the blood and give the kids a show

Around my kitchen table this past Sunday night, in the company of some of my poet friends, we were having a stereotypical conversation, the type that people most likely imagine poets having, about what people are "owed" from our work. Who is owed our grief, and discussions of our grief, or how to carry everyone's grief within our own. If I tell a sad story, and then you, reader, tell me a sad story, and then your friend tells me a sad story, how do I take that with me and try to make something better out of it?

As the conversation wore on, my friend Nora turned to the table and said, "Why do we think of grief as a collection of individual experiences anyway? Why don't we just instead talk about grief as a thing that we're all carrying and all trying to come to terms with?"

And I know, I know that may seem like what all of our missions may be, but I tell stories of the sadness of an individual death first and the complete sadness of loss second. I have, in a lot of ways, convinced myself that more people will feel whatever I am asking them to feel if there is a name or a history to go with the body. If I can unfold a row of photos and stories and name a life worthwhile to a stranger, they might connect better with what I'm saying. And that might be true in some cases, but what I'm learning more and more as I go on is that my grief isn't special beyond the fact that it's mine, that I know the inner workings of it more than I know yours. I imagine *The Black Parade* as a conversation about grief ahead of its time, dealing in the same tensions that I find myself wrestling with at a table with poets 10 years after its release. The Patient is only The Patient. We arrive at his story as it ends and get only the details we need.

He is forever nameless, without major signifiers. It is telling that by the end, by the visuals for "Famous Last Words," The Patient is projected onto the band themselves. The message of a universal grief, yours and mine, that we can acknowledge together and briefly make lighter for each other, is in that moment. That which does not kill you may certainly kill someone else. That which does not kill you may form a fresh layer of sadness on the shoulders of someone you do not know, but who still may need to press their ear to the same thing that told you everything was going to be all right when you didn't feel like everything was going to be all right. *The Black Parade* doesn't treat the recesses of grief as a members-only party, where we show up to the door with pictures of all our dead friends and watch the gates open. It assumes, instead, that we've all seen the interior, and offers a small fantasy where the other side is promising.

ACT V

Mama, we're all gonna die. Mama, we're all gonna die.

The My Chemical Romance song that I return to the most is "Fake Your Death." It's not on *The Black Parade*; it's a random track that showed up as the opener on their 2014 greatest hits album *May Death Never Stop You*. It's a good song, sitting firmly in the *Danger Days* canon of My Chemical Romance history. Gone are the echoing and heavy guitars and the stadium howl of Gerard Way—it's a simple tune, only piano and percussion, taking on a bit of a pep-rally feel. I not only like it as a song but as a companion piece to *The Black Parade*. It's a good signifier of the band's end, equal parts heroic and reflective. On it, they sound both proud and defeated. I think, often, about what that album must've taken out of them. Gerard Way, in recent years, has said that he imagined the band being done after they finished *The Black Parade* tour. In between *The Black Parade* and the aforementioned *Danger Days: The True Lives of the Fabulous Killjoys*, released in 2010, an entire album was recorded and scrapped. *Danger Days* is a fine album—it's a bit scattered thematically, not as focused or inspired, but it's a good collection of songs that I have grown to enjoy as much as any other My Chemical Romance album.

The Black Parade celebrated its 10th anniversary in 2016 by releasing a weighty, sprawling boxset. Demos, remastered songs, the works. The album still lives, but the conclusion of it remains: The Patient is gone by the end of *The Black Parade*. We know this, and still, I think of The Patient as I would a full, breathing character in a film. He drives the way I think about the band that was My Chemical Romance, even before they inserted him into their music. I wonder how long he was living in Gerard Way's head before he lived through the brief and glorious burst of an album that was *The Black Parade*. And I wonder, always, how art can immortalize even imaginary lives.

Even though "Fake Your Death" signaled the end of the band, I think its message for an audience is one about what you can come back from. This, relying on the other definition of death, the one that does not take you from here but makes you feel like there is something weighing on you that you can't lift off. The song is, through that lens, about shedding old skin and stepping into a newer, lighter version of oneself. I listen to it now, on repeat, and I think of myself at 22, saddled with doubt in a room filled with my childhood memories, not knowing what to make of a life that hadn't gone as I'd planned. And I get it. Even if Gerard and the boys don't ever come back again, I get it all. I'm better for it. And I'm still here.

Defiance, Ohio Is The Name Of A Band

& THE THING IS THAT THEY ARE FROM COLUMBUS, Ohio, which is confusing to folks on the East Coast when I tell them about the time they played for four hours at the Newport & it was raining outside but me & everyone I knew still locked arms after the show & walked down High Street singing "Oh, Susquehanna!" at the top of our lungs till some dive bar security threatened to kick all our asses & he had 20 pounds on all of us combined & Defiance, Ohio plays folk punk which pretty much means that sometimes they let a banjo or a cello crawl into bed with the screaming & all of their shows feel like they were made just for you & Geoff Hing plays guitar for them & makes singing look effortless & I guess it is kind of because all of their fans know all of the words to their songs & they sing them so loud it's like the band doesn't even have to & their fans are often cloaked in tattoos & trucker hats & ironic hand-me-down shirts from old car garages or little league baseball teams & they jump on each other's backs at shows & scream in each other's faces & it's, like, familial I guess, or I guess it is most times & one time at a show I saw a dude with some straight edge tattoos knock out some dude who had an entire school of fish inked on his arm & so okay, it's certainly not always familial & when the guy hit the floor, someone from the band stopped the music & said "Hey, listen, don't come to a Defiance, Ohio show and fight. Cut that shit out. Hold hands with each other or some shit" which is funny to say coming from a band that put the song "I Don't Want Solidarity If It Means Holding Hands With You" on their first album, which was a fine album but it had a little too much acoustic noise for my taste & Defiance, Ohio is a real town in Ohio & the band is not from there & anyone who is from there either leaves or dies & in the summer of 1794, General Mad Anthony Wayne ordered a fort be built at the confluence of the Maumee and Auglaize rivers in Ohio & when it was done, a soldier from Kentucky named Charles Scott stood in front of the fort & said "I defy the English, Indians, and all the devils of hell to take this" & that's how the fort was called Fort Defiance & how a whole city spilled around it by 1904 & that city was also named Defiance & the site of the fort is a library now, or at least that's what I've been told & me and my pals would drive up to Defiance (town) every now & then when we were old enough for adventure but too young to properly wallow in the depths of Columbus's scene & we would go to Bud's diner & flirt with the waitresses & sometimes we would drive down the backroads screaming the words to some punk dirge out of the open windows of a car we had to have back in someone's parent's driveway by morning & sometimes we would take out mailboxes with a baseball bat & once a man ran out of a house with a confederate flag hanging from the porch & he chased us down the road calling us outside of all of our names & my buddy Derek said he swore he saw the man holding a shotgun & so we stuck to the fears of our own city from that point on & the second Defiance (band) album came out in 2006 & it was called *The Great Depression* & it nearly started an honest revolution in my little corner of heartbreak & I barely made it through 2006 cuz we had to bury Tyler & Marissa too & in the song "Condition 11:11," there are the lyrics "I remember in the kitchen when you told me your grandma died. That's when I realized it gets worse" & it does, oh it does & it is really something to really remember that you can *actually* be alone & so when the band sings "Here's to this year I never thought I'd make it through" I put my arms around someone else who did make it & swayed along as the clock swung itself past midnight at the end of December & I saw Defiance (band) in another sweaty room in '07 & everyone there was sad & so no one was into fighting that night & the band let the cello & the banjo strings sit thick & heavy in the air that night & no one seemed to mind & it's like if we all try hard enough in the same room, everyone can remember what it is to lose somebody at the same time & Defiance (town) is awash with heroin now & I see it on the news, a man nodding off in a car & two people overdosing in the same night & 27 people dragged to the town jail in a drug bust & it is the kind of town that will hold you under its tongue until it is ready to swallow you whole & they found the body of a kid who used to come up to Columbus for punk shows in an abandoned Defiance (town) apartment & his body was surrounded by spent lighters & he was at the Defiance (band) show where they played "Grandma Song" & everyone put up their cell phone lights but the true punks put up lighters & waved them when the band sang "Do you come from a dead people?" & Defiance (town) is dying off like all of Ohio's other towns that feed the bigger cities, in both food & those who escape & in the Defiance (town) paper I read a story about the heroin epidemic & the headline said "WE WILL NOT LET THIS DESTROY US" & above it is a picture of a mother pulling her young daughter's frail body close to her chest in front of a worn-down house & in her eyes is a determination & in her eyes she is daring all the devils of hell to come & take what is hers & I thought about what it must be like to name yourself after a town that has become a ghost factory & play songs about surviving all manner of haunting &

Defiance (band) hasn't made a record in six years & the last one sounded like they were trying to get out of each other's way & I heard they played in some Indiana dive last spring & I heard the pit was wicked & later that week there was another drug bust in Defiance (town) & there are times when destruction is not as much of a choice as we think it is & man, I barely made it out of 2006 alive & in the Defiance (band) song "Oh, Susquehanna!" the chorus that everyone sings goes "and I wonder / what do they do with the bodies / and I wonder / what do they do with the bodies / and I wonder."

This story never really had a point. It's just a lull—a skip in the record. We are addresses in ghost towns. We are old wishes that never came true. We are hand grenades. We are all gods, we are all monsters.

Pete Wentz

III.

He wore a dark suit and oversized sunglasses to cover his eyes. His voice trembled when singing the first line.

Though an album of little solutions, *What's Going On* is, at its most literal and perhaps most difficult to process, an album that presents a small series of inquiries that weave into a much larger and rhetorical narrative: what are we doing to each other, and what will the world look like if we don't change?

To be Black and still alive in America is to know urgency. What Marvin Gaye knew, even as a man of God, was that Heaven might not be open for him, or for any of us. He knew then what so many of us know now: we have to dance, and fight, and make love, and fight, and live, and fight, all with the same ferocity. There are no half measures to be had. It is true, yes, that joy in a violent world can be rebellion. Sex can be rebellion. Turning off the news and watching two hours of a mindless action film can be rebellion. But without being coupled with any actual HARD rebellion, without reaching our hands into revolutionary action, all you've done is had a pretty fun day of joy, sex, and a movie. There is no moment in America when I do not feel like I am fighting. When I do not feel like I'm pushing back against a machine that asks me to prove that I belong here. It is almost a second language, and one that I take pride in, though I wish I did not need to be so fluent in it. I know what it is to feel that urge to build a small heaven, or many small heavens. Ones that you cannot take with you, but ones that cannot be taken from you. A place where you still have a name. I believe, at one point, that Marvin Gaye looked at a country on fire, and wanted that for us all.

Fall Out Boy Forever

Chicago, 2008

"Thanks to the city for letting us play here… I feel like last time there were pyrotechnics in here, it nearly burned the city down."

Fall Out Boy bassist Pete Wentz, on stage at the Chicago Theatre, is pushing his dark bangs out of his eyes while the band's lead singer, Patrick Stump, re-tunes his guitar. The fire that Pete is talking about is one that happened in 1903, and he's technically wrong. The fire didn't happen at this theater, but at what was once the Iroquois Theater, a bit down the road from here. The fire was in December, the same month of this concert, with people packed to the walls, testing the limits of the modern fire code. The fire in 1903 was caused by a spark from an arc light falling onto a muslin curtain, starting a blaze that spilled onto the highly flammable flats that held scenery paintings. The theater had no sprinklers, alarms, or telephones. The Chicago Fire Department insisted that it delay its performances until it was fire-ready. The theater charged on, imagining that there were no dangers that could not be survived. When the fire started to spread, there was no way to contact the fire department quickly. A stagehand had to run from the theater and find the nearest fire house. By that time, the fire had spilled into the seats, wiping out nearly half of the building. 575 people were killed, their bodies piled ten high around the doors and windows. People, in an attempt to escape, tried crawling over the already dead bodies to reach the windows, before falling victim to the gas themselves, making a wall of dead who were once almost free.

Pete Wentz and Patrick Stump are having a bad night. If you've seen enough Fall Out Boy shows, you can tell by how little they play off of each other during a set, or how often Patrick tries to rush Pete through an in-between song monologue. During the song "This Ain't A Scene, It's An Arms Race," Pete attempts to scream into the microphone that Patrick is singing in, not unusual for their on-stage partnership. Tonight, Patrick leans away from Pete, cutting a sideways glare at him from underneath his low hat. By this time in the band's evolution, Pete is an attention vacuum, racking up weekly tabloid covers and paragraphs of speculation on internet blogs. As Pete goes, so goes the band. And as he's become more hated, so has the band. It's wearing on them, and you can see it tonight, in all of them. Even at home, they look like they would rather be anywhere else.

Fall Out Boy's newest album, *Folie à Deux*, is set to be released in two weeks. That is the reason we've all gathered here, skipping a few meals and trips to the movies along the way in order to afford the tickets. I can hear my friend Tyler's voice as I sink into a spot in the crowd and shake my head. "In fucking Chicago, of all places," he'd say. And then, likely, "We used to be able to see these guys here for two bucks and some cash for gas." He'd be right, of course. And I'd punch his shoulder and tell him to quit complaining. That tonight was *important*. I almost turn to say this to him, as if I've imagined him here with me, to my right, as he always was. But there's only a short kid with purple hair there, and I'm snapped back to reality.

Folie à Deux is French for "a madness shared by two," which feels prophetic for a band that has operated as a translating service as much as anything, Patrick giving a life and entire body to Pete's words for the better part of a decade. It has drained them both by this point, Pete weary of fame and addicted to pills. And Patrick, weary of the way Pete's fame had moved into a world where he imagined himself less in the spotlight. No one tonight knows that ten months from now, Fall Out Boy will be broken up, on a four-year hiatus. That this is their last big show in their hometown, where they played in basements and dives and pool halls and broke their instruments against brick walls in houses with 30 punk kids packed to the walls.

During "Saturday," the band's traditional final song, Pete always abandons his bass and strips off a layer of clothing to bring home the song's closing moments by screaming close into the mic while Patrick sings the lyrics "I read about the afterlife / but I've never really lived." It's a nod to Pete's hardcore roots, even though they are, by now, flimsy at best. Tonight, perhaps because it was in Chicago, or perhaps because a mood of finality was in the air, the crowd takes on a heightened excitement when Pete tosses his sweatshirt to the masses. It falls somewhere just behind me and the memory of Tyler, and I can feel the people crawling over each other for it. Jumping on each other's backs while a pile collapses around us, searching for a small piece of fabric. A lifeline out of some imagined fire.

Los Angeles California, 2005

On the VH1 "Big In '05" special, Pete Wentz takes off his bass guitar and launches it into the drumset behind him. It narrowly misses the head of Andy Hurley. The band had just gotten done playing the song that made them a household name this year, "Sugar, We're Goin Down." In the audience, celebrities like Paris Hilton sing along to every word. The band isn't in Midwest basements playing to kids who scraped together gas money anymore—they're actually famous now, bordering on pop stardom. Pete is beginning his great moral conflict: the desire for fame pushing back against the desire to be famous. While his bass guitar crashes into the drumset, sending a cymbal up in the air and knocking off Andy's glasses, he storms off stage defiant, while the crowd cheers. To them, it seems like they are witnessing a true rock star moment and not an artist struggling with his disdain for the process. Fall Out Boy was never supposed to be *this* famous, after all. Not playing to stars and socialites on national television, at the end of a year where they covered major music magazines. It has been said before, for decades prior to this one, that no band can live this fast for this long. While the drumset collapses, Joe Trohman slings his guitar across the stage floor. Patrick, while walking off the stage, gently places his guitar on the drum riser, Pete's bass spearing a snare drum on the edge of falling.

Columbus, Ohio, 2007

When it's a funeral for a suicide, the air feels different. It's heavier, for one thing. It sits on your shoulders differently, makes it harder to move. It's something you don't notice until maybe your second or third one. This time, it was pills. Last year, it was a jump from a building. We buried Tyler in his old leather jacket, covered in patches from all of our favorite bands that we would cross state lines to see in a shitty Ford Taurus. There was the Fall Out Boy patch, largest on the back of the jacket. We got it at the show in '04, where Pete threw his bass guitar into Andy's drum set and then put his foot through a speaker but couldn't pull his sneaker out of it, so he just left it in there and walked off stage with one bare foot. Tyler was almost a foot taller than me, and at that show, he grabbed some suburban scene trash by the collar after the kid tried to make some crack about me being the only Black kid at the show. And look, I know that memories don't actually bring a person you love back to life. Real life, I mean. It doesn't make them touchable in the way we most need them to be.

In 2005, Pete downed a bottle of pills in a Best Buy parking lot while listening to Jeff Buckley, who drowned in the Wolf River Harbor at age 30 and who was the son of Tim Buckley, who overdosed on heroin at age 28. And so what I'm saying is that our heroes spill from their heroes and their heroes before them, and at some point, everyone wants out. Pete lived because his mother came and dragged him out of his car and sat next to him in a hospital room, talking him awake. And on the night Tyler died, I was driving through the darkness to make it to Chicago by morning so that I could surprise a girl who I wouldn't remember in a year. And there was only a missed call on my cell phone when I looked down at it around 5:30 in the morning, when the sun was just beginning to bend itself around Chicago's sprawl. So I'm not saying that I would have been able to talk him away from that which was beckoning him. I'm not saying that I would have been able to hold his face to mine on the concrete and tell some story that would have kept him alive until the ambulance lights flooded our little corner of Ohio.

I think I am trying to say that I like to imagine Tyler was calling to say goodbye, and couldn't bring himself to do it to a machine. But what I am mostly trying to say is that the air at a funeral feels different when someone finds their own way to the grave, but we scene kids all decided to still wear black leather to bury Tyler today, even with summer bearing down on our backs. Sometimes, it is truly about the aesthetics. It helps, in the moment of the casket's lowering, to think about suicide not as a desire for death, but a need to escape whatever suffering life has dealt.

Once I hit a certain age, I never imagined a life where I didn't lose friends. I dated someone during this year who told me she'd never been to a funeral. She was 22 years old. I couldn't decide if I thought something was wrong with her, or if something was wrong to me—the way I learned to cling to my relationship with death as if loving it hard enough would make it into a full person. A person who looked, at least a little, like everyone I had loved and lost.

Infinity on High dropped three months before the funeral and we listened to it in Tyler's van, where he said it was the album that Fall Out Boy finally sold out on so I didn't tell him that I thought it was brilliant. Jay Z was on the intro for the album's first song and they called the song "Thriller" because I guess Pete decided that if you're going to be famous anyway you might as well fucking go for it. In the second verse, Pete wrote "the only thing I haven't done yet is die / and it's me and my plus-one at the afterlife" and me and Tyler played that line back at least ten times.

Columbus, Ohio, 2005

In some *Rolling Stone* interview, Pete says *there are the songs you actually love, and then there are the songs you pretend to love when people are watching.* It has been one of those endless summers again, and "Sugar, We're Goin Down" is always on the radio, coming out of the rolled down windows of cars in almost every neighborhood. Me and my pals tell all these new fans that we were there from the *beginning* of it all, presenting it as currency in a world where you start to feel something you love slipping away from you. When Tyler's parents got divorced and he was crashing on my couch, we'd play *From Under The Cork Tree* all night long behind a closed door, but then tell the dudes at the record store that we only liked Fall Out Boy's old stuff, talking about their B-sides as a way to regain some of the credibility we felt we'd lost during our nighttime listening parties.

The album is about the aftermath of Pete's relationship falling apart, and my post-college girlfriend moved to California in April and stopped calling in May. I scrawled lyrics in pencil on the wall of my apartment that I pushed my bed up against so that no one knew they were there. It was the summer of all our scene pals getting hooked on some drug or the other and sleeping on top of each other all day while me and Tyler played video games on their couches and spun the first Fall Out Boy split 7" until we got back to his van, where we'd play the chorus of "Sugar, We're Goin Down" and sing all of the words.

It's easy to convince people that you are really okay if they don't have to actually hear what rattles you in the private silence of your own making. I sometimes imagine that this is what Pete was trying to say the whole time. Public performance as a way to hold yourself together until you could fall into what actually kept you alive in your secluded moments. By the time this summer was finally done with us, it all felt plastic. Like we were all playing the roles of someone else.

Austin, Texas, 2010
During the hiatus, it's like the band never existed. No one talks about them like they were real, and the band members themselves were briefly ghosts. My ex-girlfriend Marissa tells me that Pete never leaves his house in L.A. and that his marriage to Ashlee Simpson is falling apart. It all seems so impossible. There was a collapse, and then everyone became something new and distant. My crew from the scene doesn't really talk anymore since Tyler's funeral. I saw a couple of them outside the Newport after a show a few months back, and we made small talk about all the new trash hardcore bands our other old pals were diving in and out of, but none of us talked about how we were feeling. It was like once we lost the band we decided was the mouthpiece for all of our most confessional moments, we decided we didn't need those moments anymore and we didn't need each other either.

I wear a patch on my jacket now. I found it underneath a pile of records in Tyler's apartment when his mom came to try and clean everything out but instead cried with me in a circle of his old t-shirts. It's a patch that says "DESTROY WHAT DESTROYS YOU" in bold and sharp white letters. He got it for free at some NOFX show that we hated in 2003 because we took the girl working the merch table to score weed a few hours before the show and I imagine it was the least she could do.

I'm wearing the patch on a jacket in Austin, Texas, at South By Southwest, where I am because some startup music mag sent me here to cover the festival for the first time, even though I have no idea what I'm doing. In a bar called Dirty Dog Bar, a restless crowd of emo and punk kids are waiting in the dark. A surprise solo performance from Patrick Stump has been rumored all day, which seems both unlikely and exciting. No one had seen or heard much from Stump since the hiatus began, other than reports that he and Pete weren't speaking, frustrated with each other, I imagine, about how much each of their legacies managed to be tied to the other.

When the drumming starts, It's still pitch black in the room. The crowd murmurs, some crane their necks. People begin taking flash photos with their cell phones to try and get a glimpse of this might be Patrick. Then the drums begin looping, and a keyboard starts. The keyboard begins looping, some '80s pop riff. And then, leaning out of the shadows to pick up a massive white guitar, is the face of Patrick Stump, several pounds lighter than when he was last seen in October of last year. Dressed in a dark blazer and with his blond hair neatly shocked across his head, not obscured by a hat, as it had been for the past several years, it is almost impossible for people to process the fact that they are looking at Patrick. Until he gazes, briefly, up at the growing and silent audience, gives an uneasy laugh, and retreats back into his comfortable shadow. An audience member breaks the silence by yelling, "We love you, Patrick!" and, lit briefly by a camera phone, you can see a smile starting at the edges of his mouth.

Patrick once said, "I sang because Pete saw, in me, a singer," and I think what he meant is that Pete saw, in him, a vehicle. This was the band's great fascinating pull. That they were a bit of a mutation: a shy and otherwise silent frontman with a voice like a soul singer, belting out the confessional emo lyrics of a neurotic narcissist. Pete, who wanted the attention, but not enough to sing the words himself. I'm thinking about this again in a bar in Austin, Texas. Wearing a patch taken from my dead friend's old bedroom, and considering the things we saw in each other that kept us whole for our brief window of time together. Tyler fought kids who fucked with us at punk shows because I saw, in him, a fighter. Until he stopped getting out of bed some mornings and I told myself that I saw, in him, a burden. Until the dirt was shoveled over the black casket and I saw, in him, nothing beyond a collection of memories.

Patrick is running around the stage, frantic. He has played a total of six instruments, looping all of them himself. The songs he's playing are rooted in funk, jazz, and '80s soul-pop. The audience, expecting to see Patrick maybe play solo versions of old Fall Out Boy songs, has thinned out. Those who remain cast strange looks at the stage, while Patrick barely makes eye contact or speaks between songs. It is a bit forced and obviously strategic, him trying to unwrap himself from the mythology of emo, which he had grown to be visibly uncomfortable with. He's showing that he can be a Real Life Musician, outside of the machinery of Wentz. Destroy What Destroys You. Halfway through the showcase, it becomes clear that this exercise isn't connecting with the audience, because it isn't an exercise *for* the audience.

By the time the end comes, he sits down at a piano, out of breath. He gasps, "This song isn't going to be on my record, because I didn't write it. Bobby Womack wrote it."

By the time he gets into the chorus of "If You Think You're Lonely Now," Patrick has arched his back with his eyes closed, leaning away from the microphone, yelling the same lyrics over and over: "If you think you're lonely now / if you think you're lonely now / if you think you're lonely now / just wait"

This part. This is the part that's for the audience.

LaGrange, Illinois, 2002

The heckling starts slow, first in the back, and then making its way to the front. The band on stage is, decidedly, not hardcore enough. And this is, after all, a hardcore show. Some of the faces are familiar enough from the Chicago hardcore scene: there is Pete Wentz, Chicago scene celebrity, who most recently screamed in Arma Angelus and thrashed around in Racetraitor. And Joe Trohman, the scrawny guitarist from Arma Angelus. The drummer is Mike Pareskuwicz, from Subsist. The problem, the crowd has decided, is the kid fronting the band, with his clean vocals and craving for melody. "This is a fucking hardcore show," someone yells in a silent moment. "I didn't come here to listen to this wannabe Marvin Gaye."

I'm here because a few months earlier, I came alone to Illinois to see The Killing Tree, former Arma Angelus frontman Tim McIlrath's newest band. In what seemed like a solid, he let his old bandmate Pete Wentz open the show with his new project, a band that had been soliciting advice on a name from their friends, according to a group of people smoking outside. When Wentz finally took the stage that night, he mumbled into the microphone, uncertainly.

"Hi... we're uhhh... well, our name is, uhhh... we're..." Someone from the side of the stage cut him off.

"Fuck it, you're Fall Out Boy."

And then, someone else.

"Fuck yeah, dude. Fall Out Boy Forever!"

The small crowd laughed at the nervous new band.

That night, during The Killing Tree's set, I got knocked down in the pit, which happened often due to being short, less aggressive, and sometimes invisible, as the only Black kid there. It is hard to describe what this is like, to be on the ground with no room to get up, waiting for the feet to grow less restless and violent, so that you can get a small escape. Right when I began to cover my head, assuming I'd be kicked, a massive shadow pushed through the pit and pulled me up nearly effortlessly. I yelled thanks, and the tall kid nodded before bouncing off, throwing elbows behind him as he went.

At the end of that show, the kid who saved me from the pit found me leaning on my car. Checking out my license plate, he leaned in. "Ohio? Can you drop me near Columbus?" Most of the Midwest scene kids all found their way to Chicago for these shows, often without a means to return to wherever they came from. It wasn't uncommon for us to pile in whatever car was headed back to the state that we came from. Skeptical but indebted, I told him sure. "But you can't smoke that in my car," I told him, gesturing to the cigarette he was preparing to light. "You fuckin' straight edge punks," he laughed, lighting the cigarette and jumping in the passenger seat. "I'm Tyler, by the way."

When Tyler heard that Fall Out Boy was playing a show in LaGrange tonight, he called me, insisting on a road trip. I was on the fence, arguing that they weren't that good the first time we saw them, but Tyler persisted, claiming that they had to have gotten better. He liked the singer, and I thought the lyrics had promise.

So, in an indoor skate park in LaGrange, Illinois, the band known as Fall Out Boy is getting heckled while standing at the bottom of a skate ramp and playing through fast, sloppy songs. Everyone in the room is standing mostly still in a traditional unmoved hardcore pose: arms crossed, nodding slowly but unimpressed. Someone from the front of the stage yells, "What the fuck? Play something to get the pit going!"

Pete looks at Patrick, smirks at the audience, and confidently says, "All right. This is a new song. It's called 'Dead On Arrival.'"

Thirty seconds into the song, arms begin unfolding. Someone starts pogoing toward the front and bodies begin a collision, first gentle, and then rougher. When the pit reaches its peak, Pete moves to the front of the skate ramp made stage, visibly considering a leap into the crowd. At the last moment, he pulls back. An issue of trust, I suppose. Don't throw yourself to those who would heckle you until you bow to them.

When the show is over, outside of the venue, someone drunk and barely standing yells, "FALL OUT BOY SUCKS" before throwing up into a sewer.

Knights Of Columbus, Chicago, Halloween 2003
(We got kicked out cuz everyone was packed to the ceiling and I mean the ACTUAL ceiling and Joe had his face painted like a skeleton and Patrick was sweating everywhere and I do mean EVERYWHERE at the end of "Saturday" Pete jumped into the crowd with the mic and he nearly got buried by everyone trying to grab his head and sing into the mic because it was the only song of theirs we knew all of the words to and he was climbing over everyone trying to make it out of all the arms grabbing at him and he put the mic in Tyler's face for a moment and Tyler sang the part about never really living and then the whole entire stage collapsed and I mean REALLY collapsed so the band had to stop playing altogether and it's probably for the best because the room was over capacity by at least 25 people and when the door guy saw the river of us pushing our way out into the streets he said *goddamn, you kids are gonna get the city burned down*)

Subterranean, Chicago, 2013

Pete is in the crowd already, mere seconds into the band's reunion show. He's jumped from the stage into the front row, and the brief moment he was in the air felt like an eternity. There is a part of me that thought they wouldn't show up, even as the opening notes of "Thriller" poured out of the loudspeakers. But then there they were, for the first time in four years, together. On a stage that could barely fit the four of them, like the old days. But they're adults now, Pete's hair trimmed to a shorter and more reasonable length. Patrick in a slick leather jacket, with glasses. Joe, more restrained than his usual whirlwind of activity. Before they started playing, they huddled briefly, slapping each other's hands. It felt, more than anything, an acknowledging of no hard feelings. Or, an acknowledgment of that which we all spend a lifetime searching for: the permission to come home again, after forgetting that there are still people who will show up to love you, no matter how long you've been away. No matter how obsessed you've been with your own vanishing, there will always be someone who still wants you whole. Pete, for all of his songs about racing toward an abyss, returned to us with two kids. Patrick and Joe returned married. No one wanted out anymore, at least not that night.

Cleanliness is next to Godliness, sure, but you can be both God-like and unclean. Pete Wentz is no longer afraid to dive from a stage because he knows he will be caught, no matter what sins or regrets make the trip with him. That is the true ending of Fall Out Boy's story, no matter what comes after tonight. The Boy With The Thorn In His Side, finally made good. And all it took was dragging an entire band through the fire of his own making, and managing to come out clean.

There's a thing Pete and Patrick have always done on stage during every show since the beginning, even during their bad nights.

The full line in the second verse of "Saturday" that echoes into the ending goes "Read about the afterlife / but I've never really lived / more than an hour / more than an hour."

When the second rotation of "more than an hour" hits, Patrick and Pete turn toward each other, no matter where they are on stage, and they sing the line at each other, sometimes giving each other a slight bow before returning to their microphones. They do it tonight, and touch hands on their way back to their corners of the stage. I think it's a way to remind each other that they've made it, for one more day. There is something about setting eyes on the people who hold you up instead of simply imagining them.

Tyler's patch had fallen off my jacket a year or so ago, after the adhesive wore off when the jacket sat in the closet for too long. I hadn't worn it since I got back from Austin, Texas, in 2010. I carried the patch with me to the show tonight. At the end, when the band is playing the final notes of "Saturday," I toss it into the pit, and let it fall into the forest of writhing bodies.

No one decides when the people we love are actually gone. May we all be buried on our own terms.

You can put a murderer in a suit, and he's still a murderer.

Allen Iverson

IV.

By the time Marvin gets to "...bombs bursting in air..." you can see his hands finally stop shaking. A rhythmic clap begins to grow from the audience.

I watch fireworks in July 2013. Two weeks later, George Zimmerman walks free, and Trayvon Martin is still dead.

(Marvin Gaye sings *If you wanna love, you got to save the babies,* and a Black mother pulls her son close.)

I watch fireworks in July 2014. Later that month, the world turns to the internet and sees Eric Garner choked to death by police officer Daniel Pantaleo.

(Marvin Gaye sings *Trigger happy policing / Panic is spreading / God knows where we're heading,* and thousands of people march from New York to Washington.)

I will watch the fireworks in 2015 and Black churches are burning in the South. I will watch the fireworks in 2015 and no one marched for Renisha McBride.

I will watch the fireworks in 2015 and people I love can be legally married on Saturday, and then legally fired from their jobs on Monday.

(Marvin Gaye sings *In the morning, I'll be alright, my friend,* and a group of Black children watch the sky light up, seeing darkness turned inside out for the first time.)

Ric Flair, Best Rapper Alive

ONCE YOU REALIZE THAT IT'S ALL PERFORMANCE, the medicine goes down easier. The boy on the playground who doesn't really want to fight dances around and talks his shit at a volume that shakes the birds from the trees. There was a point where most feared rappers are the ones who could best convince you that they have killed someone before, even if they hadn't. Perhaps if they had only held a gun and dreamed of the history it could unwrite. Before the internet, it was even more possible to believe in anything a performer presented. It took more work to track their histories, their more unprepared moments. I feared N.W.A most when they wore all black and looked like they might not run from any manner of violence that arrived at their doorsteps.

Look, all I know is that Ali started this shit, bouncing around his opponents and daring them to lay some small violence on him. What a gift, to be both invisible and as bright as the sun itself. All I'm saying is that no one knows where Richard Morgan Fliehr came from and that ain't even his birth name but no one knows that either, not even him. The Tennessee Children's Home Society spent the '40s and '50s illegally removing children from their birth mothers and stripped them of their histories before putting them up for questionable adoptions with desperate parents, and that's how Richard Fliehr ended up in the world, so it's hard to trace exactly when and how the fire started.

(But it did start in Memphis, where Three 6 Mafia once played at a nightclub on Lt. George W. Lee Ave. after they won an Academy Award for a song about the difficulties associated with being a pimp, and Juicy J had the academy award on stage and the light hit it just right and reflected back into the crowd and Juicy J said, "This right here is for Memphis, Tennessee," and everyone was blinded by its immense presence, and then he threw a handful of dollar bills in the crowd that arched and then collapsed in the middle of the club floor and this was in 2006 in the South when everyone was just trying to survive and so a fight broke out right there in the middle of the club while Three 6 Mafia played their song "Stay Fly" which samples the Willie Hutch song "Tell Me Why Has Our Love Turned Cold" which is one of those samples that you can't unravel from your memory once you hear it nested deep in the song and so while watching a man straddling another man on the ground preparing to throw a punch, all I could hear was Willie Hutch singing "tell me / tell me / tell me" so what I'm mostly saying is that Memphis is a wild place to fight your way into and then fight your way out of.)

And speaking of staying fly, Richard Morgan Flieht was going by Ric Flair in 1975, when the twin-engine Cessna 310 he was in ran out of gas in North Carolina and fell from the sky, hitting the ground at 100 miles per hour. In the picture of the plane after the crash, the entire front window is gone, the plane's front smashed. The pilot, Joseph Farkas, eventually died from the crash. The crash also paralyzed wrestler Johnny Valentine, one of the biggest wrestlers of the era. When the plane went down all of the seats were jarred loose, pushing the weight of all the wrestlers onto Valentine at impact. Before the flight began, Ric Flair switched seats with Valentine, after being nervous about sitting up front near the pilot. Ric Flair walked away from the flight with a broken back, and returned to the ring in six months. Doctors told him that his bones were healed but there was no telling how they'd hold up under the stress of the ring. Valentine never walked again. Ric Flair never talks about this.

But he sure could talk, sometimes about flying, sometimes in jets while wearing $8,000 sequined robes in the 1980s. There is almost dying and then there is truly almost dying. The thing about that is you get a grasp of all that which you cannot take with you and then you sometimes wear it on your body at all times. Ali had the mouth, but was always too humble for the gold. Ric Flair walked from the wreckage and became The Nature Boy. All of the best showmen hid behind their names and their gold. The people didn't scream for Antonio Hardy like they did for Big Daddy Kane. The women weren't always running for James Todd Smith, but for LL Cool J, sure. It is more than just the name. At the start of rap, it was about stepping into a phone booth and coming out as something greater than you were. It was easier to sell a personality than it is now, with every nuance of a person's life splayed in front of us. Rappers can go by their real names now, with no persona attached, and still be legends. Ric Flair, already an invention, walked from a plane crash reinvented.

I imagine the rivalry between Ric Flair and Dusty Rhodes was only a little bit about wrestling and a lot about the fantasy of hard work seeing a triumph over flash. Dusty Rhodes wasn't built like a bodybuilder. He was built like a man who you might live next to, and see mowing the lawn on a Sunday morning. He sold himself as a plumber's son, a part of the working-class America who kept his adornments modest by comparison to his peers. Dusty Rhodes was more of an idea than a wrestler. The American Dream that could still be touched by anyone who just worked hard enough. Nestled up next to Flair, sold as the golden boy, born with a silver spoon and reaping the benefits of a hardened, steroid-enhanced body, the battles became that of someone fighting for the people against someone fighting for his own, gold-drenched legacy. In promos, Dusty Rhodes would scream at Flair about how he was going to defeat him in the name of blue-collar Americans everywhere, and Flair, on a split screen, would laugh, flip his blond hair, and let it fall perfectly back into place.

The fundamental difference between Rhodes and Flair that sat in the middle of their feud is a difference that also sat between LL Cool J and Kool Moe Dee during their near-decade battle with each other: a different understanding of what the people need. Moe Dee, like Rhodes, was interested in selling the people a living dream, while Flair and LL were more interested in selling the possibility of dreaming larger. The idea of making yourself anything, as large as you want to be, so that someone might think twice before coming for you. Moe Dee thought that he could pick LL apart by mocking his muscles, his appearance, the consistent licking of his lips. This scored some direct hits, sure. But LL just covered his chest in bigger chains, came back with bigger muscles, became loved by more of the masses. This idea was simple: there is no victory like fame. Popularity so heavy that no one can take it from you, even if they tried. It didn't matter if Ric Flair lost to Dusty Rhodes in the ring if he made people believe that he would never lose to him in life.

I grew up too poor to admire the fantasy of the slow-rise of the working class. I admire the things I could see when I closed my eyes, always a bit out of reach. When I started making my own money, I bought all of the sneakers I saw rappers wearing in their videos because it seemed like a way to separate myself from the times I opened an empty refrigerator. Ric Flair wasn't born with a silver spoon in his mouth, but none of the best MCs were. The only way to build yourself into something unstoppable is to become intimate with all of that which would otherwise attempt to stop you where you stand. Hunger is not glamorous, but under the bright lights, far removed from its grasp, it is a currency. A thing you know well enough to not desire a return to.

The greatest Ric Flair promo is called "His Kingdom." In it, he directly addresses Lex Luger, who was challenging him for his heavyweight title. The promo is vintage Flair, starting out tense, but calm, and then slowly losing his cool as the promo goes on, eventually stripping out of his expensive jacket, loosening his expensive tie, and tearing off his expensive sunglasses. The promo hits a climax with about one minute left, when Flair decides to rip off a bandage that was covering a wound on his head. As his eyes bulge and the veins pop out of his forehead, blood lightly begins to descend from the wound, making a slow journey down the front of his face. It was the height of his performance as Ric Flair, who walked away from a plane crash and ran into the ring still broken. Who never talks about facing death, who maybe before would be ashamed to show his own blood, who maybe would be ashamed to show the damage done to his stunning and flawless image. And as he hit fever pitch, his eyebrows raised and holding back the small river of blood from falling into his eye, he yells, staring into the camera, "No one is going to determine my destiny in this sport but me. So, pal, either bury me, or do nothing at all."

And he spun and walked away, carried through a crowd once again, on the back of the realest shit he ever wrote.

It Rained In Ohio On The Night Allen Iverson Hit Michael Jordan With A Crossover

AT LEAST THIS IS HOW I REMEMBER IT AND SO, then, this is what I need you to believe with me. Memory is a funny thing, though. Memory is a funny thing. Here is one way that memory is funny, though you may not laugh: I don't remember Michael Jordan inspiring any of the kids on my block to be a basketball player. Some of this was surely age—many of us getting to experience him most clearly after he returned from his first retirement, where he was still spectacular, but existed in a different way than he did before. His swagger was much more cerebral, as opposed to the explicit gold-chain, dunk from the free-throw line brand. Upon his first return, from the mid-'90s until the late '90s, it could be argued that he was at his best. Deadly from mid-range, and with an improved feel for the game, he was both unstoppable and fiercely clutch, playing with a chip on his shoulder larger than the one he had when he left. This was, perhaps, the most fascinating part. He had already won the championships that eluded him. He had already had a two-act career that, for most, would have been good enough. But in his third act, he was most ferocious. Seemingly most dedicated to staring down the clock and pushing back against age.

This is how we found Michael Jordan at the top of the key in 1996, guarding Allen Iverson, then a rookie from Georgetown University. Iverson hadn't yet grown out his soon-to-be signature cornrows, and was several tattoos short of where he would end his career. He hadn't yet harnessed all of his abilities yet, but throughout his rookie season, he showed the exciting, franchise-saving ability that made him a #1 overall pick the previous summer in an overwhelmingly stacked NBA draft, one of the best of the modern era. And at the top of the key, on what I remember to be a rainy night in Columbus, he faced his idol. Who he stood next to on the court before tip-off that night and stared at, like he was watching the sun from a closer distance than anyone had ever seen it before.

The thing about a crossover is that, perhaps more than any other signature dribble move, it relies on trust: a defender willing to trust you, and what they understand about you, and your willingness to deceive them. It is a basic dribble move, one that existed in several forms before Allen Iverson entered the national conversation. Dwayne Washington, while playing at Syracuse in the 1980s, perfected the original crossover: a small switching of direction, the body moving with the ball, just long enough to send a defender briefly off-balance. In the '90s, Tim Hardaway introduced the Killer Crossover, a more exaggerated version of the original, relying on a wide step in the opposite direction and a head-fake, before jerking back in the direction away from the defender. Allen Iverson was the master of the final iteration of the move, the one that is most well-known now: the double crossover.

The double crossover is the final act. A culmination of the crossover's lineage, at least for now. It is the move, in all of its iterations, sped up and performed almost with a violence. It is exactly what it sounds like: the player performs a killer crossover to throw the defender off balance, and then quickly drags the ball back in the other direction. What made Allen Iverson so efficient and unstoppable in his early career was this move. Defenders, used to only having to shift direction a single time, were thrown off by the small, added movement. It seems like nothing, really. But, depending on pace, the things that can throw us off balance are often the small things.

The main strength of a crossover is that it works best when you are being closely guarded. When someone is hovering over you, the crossover allows for a shuffling of feet, a quick backtrack. This is why defenders who are on the business end of a mean crossover sometimes fall to the ground—the quick lateral shuffling of feet when trying to close space means that their legs sometimes get tangled. It creates a thrilling scene. When I was in high school in 2001, a few years after Iverson's most iconic moment, but still firmly in the middle of his career, our basketball team's starting point guard hit a teacher with a crossover during a lunch game, and the teacher fell, sliding across the gym floor in his tan pants and sweat-soaked shirt. The gym erupted with students screaming and running in all directions. The teacher, for the remainder of the day, had to walk around with a dark streak on his light pants, like a scar, showing the results of his humiliation. That, too, is part of the ritual: a crossover, more than about getting space, is about who can be briefly humiliated inside of the space you make.

The thing about Allen Iverson is that it felt like he should've never made it because in 1993, it was said that he threw a chair during a fight in a bowling alley, which broke out because him and his boys were too loud and it was a big brawl in Hampton, Virginia, and when the police came, only the Black people were arrested and so maybe it wasn't just that him and his boys were too loud. Allen, then a high school senior, bound for sports glory, said, "What kind of man would I be to hit a woman in the head with a damn chair?" but a judge still gave him 15 years with 10 suspended, and so Allen went off to the Newport News Correctional Farm for four months until the Virginia Court of Appeals overturned the conviction due to a lack of evidence.

During those four months, Iverson had to finish his high school career at Richard Milburn High School, a school for at-risk students, instead of Bethel High, where he was an all-state football and basketball player. Because of this, his scholarship offers dried up, despite his overwhelming talent in both sports. Only one coach, Georgetown's John Thompson, came to visit him. And this is how Allen Iverson began to make it, despite.

The narrative about Allen Iverson is that he's difficult. Difficult to coach, difficult with the media, difficult to the people he loves most. He often clashed with authority figures even if he loved them. Hugging John Thompson one minute, and storming away from him the next. The logic, at least as it always appeared to someone watching from afar, was that Allen Iverson loved the game, loved his people, in a way that couldn't be understood, even by those people he loved so much. It is the kind of love that would, perhaps, force a high school sports star to put his career on the line if his boys were in danger.

During Allen Iverson's now-infamous "Practice" rant, which came after his 76ers were eliminated in the first round of the 2002 playoffs, after making the finals the year before, everyone always hones in on the fireworks: Iverson, repeatedly, bemoaning the fact that he is in a press conference talking about practice. He was worn down, and it showed. The season had weighed on him, littered with reports of him taking plays off and missing mandatory practices leading the rumors of him being traded away from his beloved Philadelphia in the offseason. And it is entertaining, if nothing else. Iverson, fed up, had gotten one too many questions about his practice habits. It is humorous to watch him, in full demonstrative fashion, yelling, "Practice? Practice? We're talking about practice? Not a game. Not a game. But practice?" repeatedly, but there's a reality to it: he simply can't fathom why anything but the game is important. Basketball is a game that literally saved his life, and so it seemed, to him, like being asked to give his all to it in a game was the ultimate sacrifice. Practice was extra—something that didn't move him.

And he did give his all, for years, throwing his body all over the place for the city of Philadelphia, and dragging lackluster teams to the playoffs, and then to the finals. He was a 6-foot wrecking ball, who wouldn't practice hurt, but who would play hurt for what felt like half of the season. The era of witnessing Allen Iverson was the era of learning a language for your limits and how to push beyond them.

But the true work of the press conference lies outside of that brief section. It is a man, at the end of his rope, trying to convince a room that he loves the city he plays for, that he's hurt and afraid, that he is concerned about his family and the game he loves. That he thinks his body may be starting to betray him, and he still wants to give the game all he has. Toward the end of the rant, an exhausted Iverson leaned forward on the table to share the most jarring and human moment of the afternoon, which also gets lost. During the season, Iverson's best friend Rahsaan Langford was murdered. He hadn't been very open about the loss until this moment, dropped into a hostile press conference about a game he loved, but was uncertain about his future in.

I'm upset because of one reason... we are in here. I lost my best friend, I lost this year [in the playoffs], I feel that everything is going downhill for me as far as my life.

I don't want to deal with this, man, I don't want to go through this shit, man.

At the top of the key in 1996, Michael Jordan is stretched out in his typical defensive stance. He was, by this point, one of the NBAs elite defenders, a skill he entered the league with but perfected in the early '90s, while trying to get past the Detroit Pistons during his first title run. His defensive stance on the night is perfect: arms stretched wide like the wings of a hunting bird, knees bent, and leaning forward on the tops of his feet. There are no statues of him in this stance, though there should be. It is the part of his game that most looked like he had to work at it. By this point in Jordan's career, he could make everything on the offensive end look easy. His knowledge of the game, and the way he'd shifted his style of play to preserve his body, led to an understanding of offensive movements that seemed to make the game slow down for him. But on the defensive end, he was still tenacious, like he was fighting to earn his way off of the bench.

Michael Jordan never threw a chair during a brawl, as far as we know. He had his share of indecencies, many of them rooted in gambling and infidelity, things that came fully to light after he was out of the game for good. But Jordan, in some ways, was the anti-Iverson. No one would ever call Michael Jordan a thug, a label Iverson was saddled with from the first stages of his career, and probably for much of his life before he entered the NBA.

Michael Jordan spoke clearly to reporters and flashed a wide smile with perfect teeth. Michael Jordan endorsed good things like healthy cereal and sports drinks. People died over Michael Jordan's shoes, but let's not talk about that part. Michael Jordan was the kind of Black person people wouldn't mind living next to. Michael Jordan was just as competitive as Allen Iverson but he wore it better. Michael Jordan probably didn't love his teammates as much though. Punched one of them in the face during a practice. But at least he showed up to practice. You can't terrorize your teammates at practice if you don't show up. There were two NBAs, it seemed. The one of Black players who fit into the Jordan personality archetype. And, by the time Allen Iverson came along, Black players who decidedly did not.

My parents were from New York and so they loved the Knicks and so I kind of loved the Knicks and my brother loved John Starks and my mother thought Charles Smith seemed like a "nice guy" and Michael Jordan maybe could have gone easier on the Knicks in the early '90s is all I'm saying really I'm saying I grew up in a home of people who maybe believed Michael Jordan had a bad thing coming

If you listen closely, especially in replays, you can hear Bulls coach Phil Jackson yelling for Michael Jordan to approach Iverson at the top of the key once Iverson gets the ball. "Get up on him," he yells out. The double crossover, when sped up, doesn't seem like much. But Iverson is a technician. First, he gave Jordan a small cross, just to see if he'd bite on it. Jordan did, lightly, shifting his body to his right, and giving a slight reach for the ball.

This is the moment where, looking back, you know Michael Jordan is done for. It isn't the second crossover, the one that actually finishes him. It's when he bites on the first, smaller one. When he admits a willingness to be fooled. It's all a negotiation of what someone will open up their body to. A negotiation of disbelief, really: what can be sold and who is willing to buy it. By the time Jordan re-sets his feet, Iverson goes in for the larger cross, the one that sends Jordan back to his right, this time more aggressively, opening up the left side of his body for Iverson to slide past.

Had Iverson not made the jump shot after the move, the archival of the moment would not exist. Or if it did, it would be an afterthought—something briefly brilliant, but unfinished. People pull off grand moves every day before missing a shot, or throwing a pass out of bounds, or dribbling the ball off of an opponent's foot. Allen Iverson, with Jordan lunging to get a hand in his face, made a shot from the free throw line before falling, and jogging to get back down the court, staring briefly at Jordan, not entirely with arrogance, but with disbelief.

If a guard did change in this moment, it was within the way the game was played, and who it was played facing. The street-ballers, those who valued style over substance, the short people who couldn't dunk but could definitely dribble, now had a lighthouse.

Eventually, in 2005, when Allen Iverson grew out cornrows and wore tall and baggy shirts, flat-brimmed hats, and covered himself in gold chains at press conferences, David Stern's NBA instituted a dress code. Michael Jordan always dressed well, after all. Players were to wear suits now, to look presentable in front of the media. It was the Iverson rule. Something to stifle what some were calling "hip-hop fashion" before it bled into the NBA's locker rooms. Allen Iverson pushed back against the code, racking up fines so that he could still wear his jewels, his baggy clothes. So he could never let anyone forget where he was from. So that he could never let anyone forget what he gave up to get here. So that he would always remember that he was different from what the past was: that he blew through it one night in 1997 and never looked back.

If you believe that it rained in Ohio on the night Allen Iverson hit Michael Jordan with a mean crossover, you will also believe that I know this by the sound that lingered in the air after my small cheering, the way rain can sometimes sound like an echo of applause if it hits a roof hard enough. You will also believe that I know this by the way an unexpected puddle can slow down a basketball's dribble on blacktop, especially if the basketball is losing some of its traction, some of the grip that it had in its younger days. You will also believe that in my neighborhood, even in basketball's golden days, none of the players would take to the courts on the day after rain, because it was too risky: the court at Scottwood Elementary, known for legendary full court games filled with Eastside Columbus basketball royalty, was already uneven, and the slickness of even a little rain made the court treacherous, something that many players, also stars for their high school teams, couldn't risk. You will believe that I once wore baggy jeans that dragged the ground until the bottoms of them split into small white flags of surrender and you will also believe that I dreamed of having enough money to buy my way into the kind of infamy that came with surviving any kind of proximity to poverty. You will believe, then, that I remember all of this by the way the ball felt in my hands as I stood on the court alone the next day, pulling the wet ball from one hand to the next and feeling the water spin off of it. You will believe that I only imagined the defender I was breezing past, and pushing my way to the foul line. And even as I missed shot after shot after shot, I still cheered. Alone in the wet aftermath of a night where I first saw the player I imagined myself becoming. A shot, finally finding the bottom of the net, and my hand, still extended, to an audience of no one.

There Is The Picture Of Michael Jackson Kissing Whitney Houston On The Cheek

& IN THE PICTURE WHITNEY IS ALL TEETH THE way she was at the end of the '80s the way she was in a white dress as wide as heaven's door at the grammys where she couldn't dance in those heels but still sang a song about dancing & in the picture Michael is about six years removed from having his daddy's nose & what better way to sever ourselves from the sins of the father than to rebuild the temple & the kiss in the picture

is gentle the way it might be for an old friend or a lover or two
kin leaning for a moment out of the damned American engine
of pop music again at their backs & howling for them to shake
their skin to the ground & sing the hits

& in the picture Whitney and Michael are under a tree & on
a bridge somewhere South & it is easy to imagine a song in the
leaves & it is easy to imagine a song in the water beneath them
which once perhaps ran through a preacher's hands or over a
baby's head & history repeating itself wouldn't be so bad if not
for the chorus of violences accumulating along the landscapes
where small miracles sometimes took place & in the picture both
of their eyes are closed & I wish for a home in that darkness a
small & black eternity

it is likely true that we only get one livable youth & I wasted mine
thinking myself beautiful & throwing rent money into jukes &
scrawling my phone number on skin in summer & watching it
sweat off outside at goodale park where we just had to dance
to the song we all knew & performing self-worship as a survival
& giving myself, unkillable, over to a parade of death instruments & racking up just enough sins to make praying worth the
time & leaving socks tangled in bedsheets & sneaking out of a
room before sunlight ruptured its silence & locking arms with
a motley crew of hooligans in the drunken hours & shoving
five bodies into the backseats of cabs & opening the doors &
sprinting down Livingston when it came time to pay the driver
while he cursed the names of our families a small penance for
keeping the cash we'd spend on the pills that we'd never be bold
enough to take & in the mirror, I would try to smile as wide as
my mother who, in the early '90s, would sing pop music while
steam hung over her afro in the kitchen & who would crane her
neck backwards to laugh like the jokes were spilling from god's
own pockets & I am telling you all of this to let you know that

I, too, want to *feel the heat* with somebody or, at worst, I want to be a child of the heat's eager production, the smoke that rises & dances thick in the air, a ghost over those who labor in our names & then become the ghosts themselves & it's a shame our wings don't arrive until after we've already raced off the cliff & met whatever waits below & it's a shame to still have living hands & barely anything left worthy of touch.

the joke hiding in *Thriller* is that if you play anything for long enough, it's like the dead never left. Revived, swaying in leather down another boulevard, I tell my boys that Michael was most Black when he died without being able to save his land and no one gets that joke either.

it seems the nightmares about drowning have again mounted my dreaming hours & have left me gasping into the stillness before morning & yet I still have not learned to swim. In the bath, I sit with the water just below my chin, a height that would not cushion my hunger for sleep. The world is undoing itself & I must tend to my vast & growing field of fears. In this new country, a nightmare is nothing but a brief rental home for the mind to ransack & leave the sleeping body unharmed.

around the porch after the cookout, the big homie says *in the '80s police were locking niggas up for putting anything to their lips & lighting a match so wasn't really shit to be smiling about* & then he closes the photo album on the picture of him as a boy in a single white glove.

science says that two dead stars collided once & that's how earth got all of its gold & it is not vanity to cover yourself in what your people created underneath a summer's worth of Southern branches & it is not vanity to grow weary of telling the world you cannot be fucked with & it is not vanity to cloak your casket in excess & it is not vanity to have the people who love you bear the weight of your excess for one last time & I imagine it as a question of comfort. Heaven as the only chart worth topping.

& it turns out that I want all pictures of me loving my people to be in color. I want the sunlight whistling its way across our faces to be always amber & never an absent hue that might mistake our lineage for something safe. I am talking of artifacts again & not of how I cup my hands to the chins of those I love & kiss them on their faces & this type of love will surely be the death of us all. this type of love will shake the angels loose & send them running to their horns.

Black Life
On Film

Doughboy: I ain't been up this early in a long time. I turned on the TV this morning, they had this shit on about... about living in a violent world. Showed all these foreign places. ... I started thinking, man, either they don't know, don't show, or don't care about what's going on in the hood.

IN THE SPRING OF 1991, I WAS SEVEN YEARS OLD, and my family moved from one neighborhood on the east side of Columbus, Ohio, to another, slightly less dangerous neighborhood—one that, at the time, would still be considered "the hood" by those on its outskirts. Compared to where we lived before the move, there were more poor and working families, but still gunshots at night, still police sirens during the day's long and slow hours, still worried parents at their windows, praying for their children. I was too young to understand violence as a thing that lived outside our doors, that would claim the lives and years of friends in a future that was near but still too distant to be visible. Instead, I reveled in having a backyard for the first time. I ran through the sidewalks with my older siblings, on the hunt for new friends.

On the television news, there was a grainy video of Rodney King, his body thrashing from the force of a police officer's kicks, a baton cracking down on his ribs. I learned a new type of fear this way, through the confusion and anger of my parents and siblings, watching a man none of us knew being beaten viciously, broadcast for the world to see. It was something that some would say I shouldn't have been watching—a plain type of evil, the type that cannot be disputed or softened. Still, I watched, in a room with my stunned family, in search of an explanation. Around that time, televised trailers were airing for a film called *Boyz n the Hood*. All I ever saw of it was a black screen with a slowly emerging white statistic: "One out of every twenty-one Black American males will be murdered in their lifetime." Then came gunshots. I remember my mother turning off the television.

Years later, in the bygone era of older brothers with VHS stashes and the forever-era of little brothers raiding anything that their older siblings want to keep from them, I blew into the mouth of an old VCR and pushed the *Boyz n the Hood* tape inside. By now I was 12, maybe 13. I had already watched Los Angeles burn, already seen boys playing basketball at the court one day, vanished the next. Once you understand violence, once its presence is constant enough, it can become something you survive until survival becomes normalcy, and fear becomes something you lie about when your friends are listening. Watching the previously forbidden film as a preteen in a basement during summer with friends didn't allow for much critical analysis beyond the adrenaline that comes with getting away with something. But looking back on *Boyz n the Hood* now, having watched it at least a half-dozen times in the 25 years since its release, I think that it's less a movie about death, or about visualizing the ghetto as a living, breathing entity, as it is a movie about loyalty that spans generations. Much like the very hood I knew myself, it shows mothers and fathers doing their best to protect their children, their boys and girls rapidly becoming men and women. It shows loyalty among crews, and the lengths any of us would go to in order to keep ourselves close to our chosen family, despite their most glaring flaws. *Boyz n the Hood* never demanded the watcher to choose a narrative of the "good" Black life against the "bad" Black life, despite Cuba Gooding, Jr.'s book- and street-smart college-dreaming Tre and Morris Chestnut's football megastar

Ricky having vastly different chosen paths and dreams than Ice Cube's gang-affiliated Doughboy. Wanting to get out of the hood can be just as honorable as wanting to stay behind, or wanting to keep your hood with you when anyone tries to strip you of your roots, when a city tries to strip the land of its homes. With that in mind, I found Doughboy, though not painted as the most honorable figure, to be somewhat sympathetic. He was someone I knew, resigned to the machinery of what he understood at all costs.

Upon watching *Boyz n the Hood* for the first time and seeing Ricky murdered, I remember not being surprised. Even as a boy, I had lived long enough to understand that the person we think shouldn't die is the one who, of course, sometimes dies. The sports star, the kind and warm convenience-store clerk, the loving single parent down the street. It was an end that I could almost see coming, even before I blew the dust from the VCR. I saw this end in the way my neighborhood basketball star, four houses down the street, was held close and watched over by his mother. I saw this end in the way the gang members who burned out on sports protected the high-school football stars, knowing that envy sometimes comes with a gun at its waist. Ricky's death was easy to process and understand, even with the jarring scene of Doughboy carrying his bloody body into the house of his weeping mother, a scene that still rattles me to the core.

I always wanted more for Doughboy himself. Revenge, yes—of course the revenge for his brother's death had to be a part of his destiny. Unquestioned, as if called down from the heavens. And, truly, fortunate is the death dealer who does not get a taste of their own medicine. But when the movie's epilogue rolled out, detailing the fates of the characters, it pained me to see the words at the bottom of the screen telling us that Doughboy, too, had been murdered. I wanted Doughboy to live in the hood for 50 more years. I wanted him to protect himself, protect the hood. Perhaps help keep it alive, despite all the dying around it.

Growing up as a hip-hop fan in a landlocked state that had delusions of East Coast grandeur, liking Ice Cube was acceptable, unlike enjoying most of his West Coast peers. In the early 1990s, the music coming out of the West Coast was great for a cookout or a house party, but it was largely inaccessible listening to people in Ohio. If you were truly committed, you might have put some gold Daytons on a drop top Chevy and pulled it out on a summer morning, before the rain inevitably came in the afternoon. But the things happening in mainstream West Coast rap didn't resonate with a bunch of kids who had never seen the ocean or felt sand between their toes.

Ice Cube, N.W.A's most skilled MC, embraced a more East Coast-influenced sound in the early '90s, first working with Public Enemy's Bomb Squad, then using their heavy, frantic, urgent sound as a blueprint for four albums between 1990 and 1993. Those albums played loud in the parks and spilled heavy out of cars, and I grew up endeared to Ice Cube the MC. I still count him as one of the five best rappers of all time. Versatile, political, sometimes nuanced, and a stunning writer, Cube was South Central to his core, but he felt like one of the New York rappers I admired so deeply. Even in the late '90s, when he dove back into a West Coast sonic aesthetic, he stretched the imagination of regional rap. For an entire decade, Ice Cube matured me as a rap listener. Without his '90s run, I wouldn't have the ear that I do, or the willingness to take listening risks. He built a map, and I followed.

The criticism of Cube's performance in *Boyz n the Hood*, at least on my streets, was that it wasn't real acting, it was just Cube playing the dude he plays behind a microphone—the same sneering and careless troublemaker from N.W.A, or the antagonizing street-smart hood from *AmeriKKKa's Most Wanted*. Cube was, in some ways, playing the role of America's worst nightmare, a role he was deeply familiar with living. But, of course, he was so much more.

If you play the movie *Friday* in a room full of Black people, one of us will quote a line as the character says it onscreen. Then another of us will do the same, and perhaps another. Maybe, by the time you're an hour in, you'll forget that there are characters on the screen at all. Every character is there with you in the room, on the couch, on the floor, laughing and slapping the wall. I find it important to always remind people that Ice Cube wrote *Friday*—making it a script by someone who truly knew and understood his people, the full scope of our neighborhoods and the characters within. Yes, I have known a Deebo. Yes, I have known a Felisha. Yes, I have wasted a slow and hot day on someone's porch because there was nothing else to do. *Friday*, at its core, is a buddy comedy with a simple premise. But to me, it's much more. It's a masterpiece, one of the great Black films of a generation.

Ice Cube grew up and got old and made the kinds of movies that some of us roll our eyes at, with some gems in between. It's funny, isn't it? The meme of young N.W.A-era Ice Cube situated next to Ice Cube in a family comedy like 2005's *Are We There Yet?* makes for a striking image, but it doesn't quite represent what I find to be a fascinating trajectory. Ice Cube can no longer be who he was in the '90s, but give him his due for what he has done, more than once: Ice Cube has, for years, spoken to various levels of Black sanctuary with anger, humor, and emotion. I see my hood in every *Barbershop* film—the joy of the space, and the fear that it may no longer exist. Ice Cube's most intense political music still echoes down an entire generation, years after it was made.

Like many of the Black men who helped raise me, Ice Cube is complicated, sometimes problematic, and still often endearing. I fight internally with this, the same way I fight internally with the Black spaces we all glorify: the misogyny of the barbershop, the respectability politics of the cookout. I come back to Ice Cube because he embodies this, too. The full scope of every Black man I know and have grown with, including myself, is incomplete without our emotional and social failures. I cringe at the occasional Ice Cube interview, I cringe at the occasional remark from my barber, and I value both of these men for what they have given to a world that I am lucky enough to share with them, despite our failings.

And I suppose that this, too, is loyalty. That's the lesson I first learned from *Boyz n the Hood*, and the one I carry with me even now. I learned at the feet of Ice Cube once, and I love him forever now. The hood is not glamorous or romantic, but it is mine. It is ours, those of us who still sleep with its whispers hanging over us. And I am loyal to this. I return to where I am from and give a hug to my man who has done dirt and will do more, because we were kids once, riding our bikes through these same streets, and I love him for that. I have sat in a chair and looked through glass at a person in an orange suit and seen them as I remember them best, shooting jump shots with me on a bent rim in a dirt field—and I do this because I love them. I buy a DVD from the DVD hustler outside the corner store because his daughter held my hand the day of my mother's funeral and I love her, and so I love him, and so I love what feeds him, and so I love his hustle.

It is summer and there is a video again. A Black person is dead on camera again. And I think now, after so many of these incidents, about the urgency that comes with discussing the whole and complete life. I think about the necessity of going beyond the snapshot of death and the wedging in of binary narratives. A person is a whole person when they are good sometimes but not always, and loved by someone regardless. I love the people where I'm from because they would fight to humanize me if I died violently on film. We would do this for each other, despite anything in our pasts, because no one else would do it for us. We know that we are more than only good and only bad, despite what happens to the names of the dead after they are no longer around to speak them.

There's a scene in *Boyz n the Hood*, toward the end, the morning after Doughboy gets revenge on his brother's killers. He sits down with Tre in the morning sun, a 40 oz. in his hand. In a rare moment of emotional humanity, he tells Tre that he feels alone, in the wake of his brother's death and his mother blaming him for it. "I ain't got no brother," he says. "No mother either." As Doughboy begins to walk away, Tre yells after him: "You've got one more brother left."

Doughboy turns back, nods, walks away, and vanishes into the sun. Alone, but briefly loved.

Tell 'Em All To Come And Get Me

"We speak of heaven as if we've been there. As if heaven was a mile away."
—MarShawn McCarrel

THERE ARE FEW THINGS I LOVE MORE THAN watching Black people joyfully greet each other. There is much to be made of the act, in almost any setting, even though the tone of it may vary. The familiarity of a too-forceful slap on the back during a hug, or the more gentle How your mama doin'? pitched across a parking lot while someone throws down their bags and makes their way over for a hug. The more subtle nuances of a joyful greeting, sometimes rooted in relief or exhaustion: I walk through a sea of white faces in Salt Lake City, or Portland, or anywhere in America where I am made especially aware of the space I am occupying and how I am occupying it. From the sea emerges another lone Black face, perhaps two. We lock eyes, raise an eyebrow, smile, and give a nod. One that says: I see you, and you see me. Even if no one else does, we know we're still here.

It is an art, really. One that, like all institutions of Black joy, gets dissected, parroted, and parodied—but only the language that comes from the body, and rarely the language that is spoken. On the other end of the jovial How you been doin'? that bursts from the mouth of someone who you haven't seen in awhile is often a response of "all right," or "fine," or, a favorite among people I know, "I'm working on it."

I sometimes consider this, how marginalized people quantify their own lives when compared to others who occupy the same world as we do. I say that I'm "all right" even when I've had good days. My father, a caring and deeply thoughtful person, has been "all right" for all of the years I've known him. The Black woman who works in the market next to my apartment sighs, pats my hand, and tells me she's "all right" as she hands me back a receipt for another purchase.

If there is a cost to this, the reality of fear, the fights that grow and seem insurmountable, the obsession with your grief in America as a beautiful and moving thing, it is a lowering of the emotional bar. Waiting for the other shoe to drop instead becomes dodging the avalanche of shoes, occasionally looking back to see the avalanche claiming another person you know, love, or have been on this journey of survival with for so long, you could be family. I celebrate expressions of unbridled Black joy because I know what it takes to unlock this, to have the joy of the body drown out the anxiety of the mind, if only for a little bit. I know that Blackness, when turned away from the mirror of itself and back into America at large, is most appealing when there is a type of suffering attached to it—sadness, anger, struggle, dressed up and packaged to the masses. A quarterback dances to celebrate an accomplishment in a violent game, and words like "class" appear, hanging in the air for months. The daughter of a Black man murdered on camera by police records an ad for a presidential candidate and the white people who support the candidate are so moved by her retelling of a life without her father. And I do imagine that it must be something, to be able to decide at what volume, tone, and tenor you will allow Black people to enter your life, for praise or for scolding. I think about this when I go to the gym and hand my gym card over to the same front desk person, always a white man. I ask how he's doing. Most days, he says "Good. Really good."

The link between Black music and Black survival shows up most urgently when the stakes are at their highest. When I say that music is how Black people have gotten free, I mean Harriet Tubman echoed songs along the Underground Railroad as a language. I mean the map to Black freedom in America was built from music before it was built from anything else. Black music is the shepherd still pointing us toward any needed liberation, giving us a place to set our emotions, a room of our own.

More than any other song on Kendrick Lamar's *To Pimp a Butterfly*, "Alright" signaled the arrival of a new song to nestle itself into this new historical movement, led by young Black people from all backgrounds: Black women, Black college students, Black queer and trans communities. The Black song that sits in the movement has often been a reflection of Black people in America, hope rooted in a reliance on faith, but still so often looking over its shoulder, checking for an exit. There are trains or chariots coming to take us away to a better place, a place just for us ("People Get Ready," "The Gospel Train," "Swing Low, Sweet Chariot"). There is the imagery of water, that which carried Black people to this place, and that which will save them from it ("A Change Is Gonna Come," "Wade in the Water").

I've always viewed "Alright" as part of the evolution of these songs. It's a song that clings to the idea of a hope that rests primarily on spirituality, but also a song that meets the people where they are and doesn't try to take them away. The dynamics of "freedom" have changed, the idea of freedom and escape becoming less physical. When Kendrick Lamar, before the first chorus hits, tells us "I'm fucked up / Homie, you fucked up," it feels like permission to revel in whatever we must in order to feel alive. The song is a gradual unpacking of the author's failings, his rage and vices, all held close in the idea of surviving. Where so many songs from the past promised a new and improved paradise on the horizon, "Alright" promises nothing except the fact that there is pain, and there will be more to come. We can push our backs against that door and hold out the darkness until morning, but the night has been so long it feels like it might never end. "Alright" tells us to, instead, revel in the living, despite it all. When a smiling, joyful Black person says they're "doing all right," I imagine it's because they know "good" may be too close to the sun. I imagine it's because they've seen things burn.

The heaven that Kendrick tells us is touchable might not be real, or I maybe saw heaven this fall, when Yale students marched across their campus in a demonstration against racial insensitivity. It was a seasonably chilly November day, and the well-attended and vocal march was visibly draining some of its participants. To fight for a country to see you as human is an exhausting thing, that exhaustion compounded by the physical exertion of marching, chanting, making your space your own. After the march wound down, someone found a loudspeaker, pressed play on "Alright," and this imagined cloud of despair pulled itself back. People danced, hugged, rapped along with what parts they knew. I realized then that the magic of "Alright" is the same magic that exists in the body language of the joyful Black greeting. It fits so well into these movements because it pulls so many people on the front lines of them to a place of healing. It works as both a rallying cry and a salve. It meets you at eye level and gives you what you need—an escape from the fight, or a push to get back into the fight. It is the warm nod and knowing smile from a Black face emerging in a sea of white.

There is something to be said about an artist who can face their people while rolling out the welcome mat for whoever might choose to sneak in the back door while not being ultimately concerned with their sneaking. Kendrick Lamar says "God got Us" and the Us crawls out of the speaker and wraps its arms around the Black people in the room. The way a good preacher might say "We" in a Black church and the congregation hums. The way I say "My people" and My People know who they are even if we've never met, or even if we've never spoken, or even if all we have is the shared lineage of coming from a people who came from a people who came from a people who didn't intend to come here but built the here once they arrived.

There is something most comforting in this part of the song: Kendrick's promise that God has Us. All of Us, sure, but Kendrick is talking about the Us who most need to remember that there is a God out there to be named, even if it isn't the one we pray to, or even if we are not of a praying people. There is a God to be pointed at, and pulled close. There is a hope in Black gospel that I find alluring, even though I wasn't raised in a church, which echoes here. An urgency, even. Always a cliff to run toward, with the certainty that something will catch you.

In February of 2016, an activist and poet from my home town, MarShawn McCarrel, took his own life on the steps of the Ohio Statehouse. I found this out when my wife called up to me in the office of our apartment, miles away from Columbus, where I knew MarShawn. Where we spent countless hours joking around at poetry open mics or bullshitting at local action events. I am used to the feeling of knowing the dead, having a touchable relationship with someone who is no longer present. Yet the immediate moments after the news arrives never get any easier to manage. MarShawn ran toward the cliff and there was nothing there to catch him this time. I went to MarShawn's Facebook page and saw his final message of "My demons won today. I'm sorry." Right below was a picture of him and his mother, smiling at the NAACP awards. Right below that, a screenshot of a threat that was emailed to him from someone telling him that they wouldn't rest until he "shut his nigger mouth."

The truth is, once you understand that there are people who do not want you to exist, that is a difficult card to remove from the table. There is no liberation, no undoing that knowledge. It is the unyielding door, the one that you simply cannot push back against any longer. For many, there are reminders of this every day, every hour. It makes "Alright," the emotional bar and the song itself, the best there is. It makes existence itself a celebration.

I hadn't spoken to MarShawn in months, a thing that we feel most guilty about after a person is gone, especially if we are miles away from home, or on a plane to somewhere even farther from home, on the day of a funeral. The last time I saw MarShawn was at a protest. We hadn't physically seen each other in a while, and we embraced. I slapped his back, perhaps a little too hard, and asked how he was. He told me "I'm all right, you know. I'm still here."

Maybe all of these heavens are the same—Kendrick Lamar's heaven, the heaven that all of the trains and chariots took our ancestors to, the heaven on the other side of Harriet Tubman's river. Maybe all they ask is that we help hold back the darkness for as long as we can, and when we can't anymore, they'll save us a room. They'll make sure "Alright" is playing, and we'll feel the way it felt hearing it for the first time, in the face of all this wreckage. Full of so much promise, as if all of our pain were a bad dream we just woke up from.

Burning That Which Will Not Save You: Wipe Me Down And The Ballad Of Baton Rouge

I. Shoulders

WHEN PEOPLE TALK ABOUT HURRICANE KATRINA, particularly in the national conversation, they focus almost exclusively on New Orleans. That city, of course, bore the wrath of the storm's center—uncovering a failing of local and national government and infrastructure before, during, and well after the hurricane, with effects from it still lingering to this day. But with the lens pulled back, the full story of Hurricane Katrina is not only about water and the dead. It's also a story of the living, of place and displacement.

Think of Baton Rouge, which Katrina's weather impacted in less direct ways. In the days leading up to and especially after the hurricane, when New Orleans became uninhabitable, the population of Baton Rouge swelled, almost overnight. Tens of thousands of New Orleans residents made the short journey up Interstate 10 to seek shelter in Louisiana's capital city, causing it to burst at the edges. The school system took in nearly 6,000 new students, causing immediate overcrowding. Traffic swelled, making navigation of the city nearly impossible. No matter how good a city's infrastructure is, there is no preparing for an unexpected population increase that rapid.

There was also a swelling of violence. In the years after Katrina, while many of the evacuees settled into their new city and gave up on returning to their old one, the murder rate across Baton Rouge briefly soared, well beyond that of other cities its size. In 2004, homicides per capita in East Baton Rouge parish were at 14.5 per 100,000 people. By 2007, that number had jumped to 21 per 100,000. Residents and law enforcement insisted that this wasn't simply due to the influx of new bodies in the city, but rather to the lingering state of crisis and uncertainty, where crime can thrive.

So the story underneath the story is about the weight one city can carry on its own. The edges of New Orleans broke open, and there was a flood, and those fortunate enough to escape the flood became a flood themselves, and pushed the edges of another city to its breaking point. Homelessness in Baton Rouge rose, briefly and dramatically, in the years following the hurricane. People were making homes wherever there was land not touched by the ruin of the hurricane and its memory.

In 2007, less than two years after the face of Baton Rouge shifted, the remix to Foxx's "Wipe Me Down," featuring fellow Baton Rouge MCs Lil Boosie and Webbie, was released as a single. The original version, released a few months earlier, was a Baton Rouge street classic, but got little traction elsewhere. Comparing the original version's music video with the video for the remix, released months after the single began creeping up the charts, is an almost comedic endeavor. The original video is blurry and shot at odd angles, while various tags and ads tremble across the screen. In the remix, there is gloss, jewelry, all of the trappings of the mid-to-late-2000s rap video aesthetic. It is like watching the difference between a city that's trying, and a city confident in a light at the end of the tunnel.

Baton Rouge hip-hop has a small history, but it also has the misfortune of being positioned less than 100 miles from the storied music culture of New Orleans. This is particularly hard for rappers from the area, given the massive influence that New Orleans had on Southern rap beginning in the mid-'90s, when Master P relocated No Limit Records from the Bay Area back to his hometown of New Orleans and began working with local rappers, garnering immense commercial success. In 1998, Cash Money Records, which had been toiling away in New Orleans with little success since 1991, got a big break, signing a $30 million deal with Universal Records, in part due to the proven commodity of New Orleans rap.

"Wipe Me Down" was a song made by three born and raised Baton Rouge rappers who were all under 25 years of age at the time of its release, which means they were, in some ways, children of the rise of Louisiana rap music. Young enough to have watched the rapid ascent in the '90s, and old enough, by the mid-2000s, to want a small piece of that for their own city.

The song is absurd enough to anchor an inspiring sing-along, perfect for both club and car, and with enough nostalgic staying power to still be a point of discussion 10 years after its release. Though not overwhelmingly skilled, the rappers, Boosie, Foxx, and Webbie, find a home on the beat (produced by Baton Rouge legend Mouse on Tha Track) and work it for all it's worth. It matters that this was a Baton Rouge song, made by a Baton Rouge producer and three Baton Rouge rappers who were icons within their city, in a time when Baton Rouge was in the business of recovering its own identity, waiting for someone to carry it to the light.

II. Chest

To tell someone say it with your chest is about a negotiation of confidence. If I do not believe in what you're telling me, I won't believe in you. It is not exactly a measure of volume—rather, a question of defined intent, articulated in a way that people can get behind.

The first line in "Wipe Me Down" is one of the greatest opening lines in all of rap music. Foxx says, "I pull up at the club VIP / Gas tank on E / But all drinks on me," and he says it with his chest. It is the entire thesis of the song, distilled to a fine point: I don't have much, but what I have is yours. For this, I think of what it is to grow up poor in one of your city's worst neighborhoods and dream of money. To grow up with an eye toward gold while young Black men who look like you and come from a neighborhood like the one you come from in a city just a highway away are covered in gold from rapping. To get close enough to afford some things, but still sacrifice others.

The thing I think people get wrong about the act of the stunt is that it isn't entirely narcissistic. Or, at least, it isn't always an act of self-worship. There is generosity in one who goes out of their way to look fly and raise the bar of the room they're in. There is generosity in having some cash in your pocket and an empty gas tank, and a room full of friends who are harboring a thirst, with maybe less cash in their pockets than you have in yours. To grow up poor, especially with any proximity to wealth, real or imagined, is to think sometimes that money can save you. To think that money can pull you and the people you love out of the feeling of any grief, or sadness.

To then get money, especially rapidly, is to find out that isn't true. It's all a myth, especially if you are of any marginalized group in America. The only answer is to dispose of that which will not save you. What Foxx was really saying, I think, is that it doesn't matter how one gets home in a room full of people they love. You make your home wherever you and your people stop.

As someone who grew up with no money, I know what it is to want to show someone, anyone who will look, what little you have earned. Whether it's drinks, or jewelry, or some combination of both. Whether it's donating to a school or throwing a fistful of dollar bills to the sky. I believe all of these to be noble acts. This might seem like hyperbole, but I mean this. I say it with my chest, as I might on a night when I know my money is good in a city I love. The act of stunting, when it gets you free, is also charity.

At the end of his verse, Webbie, the youngest of the three rappers, boasts, "This chain hit me for a couple grand / Oh, no, I ain't complaining / Just watch how you wipe my chest." It strikes me now, that the best way to show off is to hide that which you are showing off in something else: a joke, a memory, a warning. I once knew someone who wore a thick gold rope and kept it tucked into their shirt, so that the weight of it rested against their bare chest, but the unmistakable thickness of it could be seen around their neck nonetheless, like an opulent snake. It occurred to me that this, perhaps, was truly the way to show off: keep most of what you have at a whisper, but keep just enough of it so loud that it won't be forgotten.

III. Pants

Many years ago, I found myself in New Orleans in the early fall, not long after Katrina blew through the city, and the water, in some places, was still high. It was settled, done with its wildest moments, but still dark and mostly unmoving. I remember making the trip to New Orleans because it felt like the vague Right Thing To Do. I was young, and didn't consider what I might do there, if I would be a burden to a suffering city with my aimless wandering. Many of my college friends planned trips to go south and "help," which, I realized when I arrived, mostly looked like an exercise in witnessing: to see the damage up close, to stare, take it in, and to leave without actually doing much beyond sighing for several hours at a time, wondering what could be done. An older and wiser version of myself would have, I hope, chosen another action. But in September 2005, I stood on a curb in New Orleans while water pushed itself over my feet and onto the bottoms of my jeans, which were baggy and heavy, hanging thick over my sneakers, immersed in the dark brown water.

Everything in the music video for the "Wipe Me Down" remix is large and colorful. Eras of rap fashion tend to move so fast and become so comical to look back on immediately after they're done that the video, released in the spring of 2007, already feels like it is from an era that can barely be remembered. From 2005 until about 2008, the entire aesthetic was about how much of your body could be folded into something two, or even three times, too large. I wore extremely tall tees despite not being tall by any stretch of the imagination. My pants, too, were almost clownlike in how much of me they consumed.

In the "Wipe Me Down" video, there are airbrushed shirts swinging to the knees of the people wearing them! There are women dancing in outfits that aren't coordinated at all, and some are wearing what looks like heavily modified pantsuits! Boosie is wearing brightly colored polo shirts that are also too big, but at least he dressed up for the occasion! They are all wearing gold like they just discovered what gold was! Webbie's pants are so low, the waist is visible even with his tall tee dangling far and long!

The thing our parents would always say to discourage us from wearing our pants baggy and low was that we'd never be able to run away from anyone. I most love the "Wipe Me Down" era of rap fashion because it didn't consider the need for escape as a barrier to being the flyest person in the room. Of course it is absurd to look back on now, but in the moment, it felt like the most extreme reaction to young Black people being told, for years, to wear clothes that fit as a means of acceptance. Young rich Black people in 4XL t-shirts and jerseys, belted pants still being held up by a hand, and no one feeling the need to run from anyone or anything.

Somewhere along the way, when established rappers began to take fashion more seriously, clothing started fitting around bodies better. Pants didn't sag as much, shirts didn't hang as low. And immediately, the era of hiding yourself in what adorned your legs and torso seemed foolish. We became our parents almost overnight, laughing at pictures of ourselves from less than a year earlier. And why wouldn't we want to wear clothes that would allow us the freedom of escape? And why wouldn't we want pants high and well-fitting enough to not become victim to a small and merciless drowning?

IV. Shoes

In *The Bluest Eye*, Toni Morrison writes, in part, about the human investment in objects and material things as a way of tipping the scale of the righteous vs. the wrong, of poverty vs. wealth, of what gets you through the day versus what doesn't. In the second chapter of the book, the narrator focuses on the history and makeup of the home that the Breedloves live in. A focal point of this section is the description of the sofa. The Breedloves purchased the sofa new, but the fabric split down the back before it arrived, making the sofa look tacky and worn down. The store didn't take responsibility, meaning the Breedloves had to continue making payments on the damaged sofa. This is most striking because of the relationship we are to understand them desiring with the sofa: something large and new, signifying status and a financial freedom that the Breedloves did not possess, but desired nonetheless.

I own more sneakers today than any one person should. Some would suggest that a person only needs three or four pairs of shoes to make it through a year: a couple good pairs of dress shoes, one good pair of sneakers, and perhaps a pair of casual shoes that fall somewhere in the middle of the dress-shoe/sneaker spectrum. I have considerably more than that. I used to say this with a lot more pride than I do now. I've become more conflicted about it as I age and think more about the ethics of how things are produced, or the ethics of growing up poor and now living in close proximity to people who are growing up poor, or the ethics of spending large amounts of money on that which doesn't secure a future for yourself and whatever imagined offspring might exist for you.

I consider all of these things, and yet, I still have several sneakers. I still love the seeking out and purchasing of sneakers. I still feel the same satisfaction that I did as a young child, purchasing my first pair of Jordans with money I earned on my own. In my particular part of the Midwest, weather was unpre-dictable, even more so than it is in most places. In Central Ohio, especially if you were a child in school all day, sneaker choice was important. You could wake up to sun, and walk outside to a muddy rainstorm. For this, I always purchased black sneakers for myself. If I could only afford one good pair of shoes per year, I'd want the pair that I could keep clean the easiest, even in the most unpredictable moments of weather.

White shoes, for me, were the signifier. White shoes were my un-torn sofa, new and sitting wide in a living room. To own a pair of white sneakers meant that you had enough money to have options. That you could, if you wanted to, keep a pair of sneakers in your closet for a special occasion and wear the other pair when it rained, or snowed, or wasn't perfect.

My senior year of high school, I got my first pair of white sneakers—all-white Nike Air Force 1's. I kept them in the box for weeks, taking them out only to try them on in the safety of my own home, away from the elements. When I wore them, I felt like a different person.

I am also from an era where people were killed for sneakers. Yes, it does still happen now, of course. But in the '90s and early 2000s, there was such fear around big sneaker releases that there were tricks to the process: wear an old pair of sneakers on release day and keep the new ones in your book bag. Dress down, so no one will suspect that you're hiding expensive shoes anywhere. In our twisted and sneaker-obsessed youth, I think we found some small corner of that thrilling. To own something that another person would kill for.

The first day I wore my all-white Air Force 1's outside, it did not rain. I checked the forecast tirelessly the night before to make sure of this. When I got to school and stepped out of my car, I accidentally brushed my foot against my tire, scuffing a long and permanent black mark along the side of the shoe. And that was it. The torn fabric down the back of my sofa. My one signifier, tainted. Now simply a dirty sneaker.

It is fitting that the chant that runs through the "Wipe Me Down" hook is anchored by "shoes." The whole point of someone wiping another down, it seems, is in the performance: if I know I'm fresh, I don't need to tell anyone out loud, but lend me a hand and make sure people know I'm on point. The thing I love most about sneakers, perhaps the thing that keeps carrying me back to them, is that there is no confidence I have found like that which comes with something on your feet that you can believe in. Lord, let me walk into every room as confident as the shoes on my feet make me feel.

"Wipe Me Down," on its face, is an exercise in boasting from three young rappers who just got money, but surely not as much money as they would have you believe. But that's the trick of it: they could have you believe anything. The song is about doing whatever it takes to fake your way into the rooms that people might otherwise kick you out of. And beyond that, it was just a hell of a lot of fun.

The ride was short-lived. Foxx still trudges away on the underground scene; he's released more than a dozen mixtapes since 2009, though none to any notable commercial success. Webbie found some mainstream success with his *Savage Life* album series, the second one, 2008's *Savage Life 2*, offering up another Boosie-assisted hit in "Independent."

Boosie, arguably the most naturally gifted of the three, lost what could have been his most promising years to prison behind 2008 drug charges. He spent five years in the Louisiana State Penitentiary, from 2009 to 2014. He released one album, *Incarcerated*, from behind bars in 2010. During this time, also in 2010, he was indicted on federal first-degree murder charges for the murder of Terry Boyd. If convicted, he would have been staring down a maximum sentence of the death penalty, but a life sentence seemed likely, in part because of the fact that prosecutors leaned heavily on the sometimes violent content of Boosie's lyrics and the fact that he, at the time of indictment, was involved in several other cases. In 2012, he was acquitted of the murder charge due to a lack of evidence. Upon his release, he dropped the album *Touch Down 2 Cause Hell* in 2015, after changing his name to Boosie Badazz. The album was both critically and commercially successful. Boosie now raps with a clarity that comes with both adulthood and, I imagine, incarceration. Still draped in gold, he is now more introspective, considering things like heaven, family, faith, and the future.

Baton Rouge has also, in many ways, recovered. Homicide rates have dropped in recent years, as have the rates of homelessness. When visiting it last year, I talked to longtime residents who praised the city's ability to balance itself out after a hard decade. People were in love with their homes again. People finally stopped looking backward.

For all three of the rappers at the center of "Wipe Me Down," but especially for Boosie, the song feels like a brief and bright moment, with comical fashion, which burned out as quickly as it arrived. But there is something special in that, too—in three young Black rappers, trying, in a moment of peril, to put their city on the map. To build themselves bigger than they were. From the sneakers up.

Rumours And The Currency Of Heartbreak

WHEN I WAS FRESH INTO MY 20S, A PAL OF MINE moved into a small one-bedroom apartment with his girlfriend. Our group of friends thought she was wonderful, but still had our concerns, not all of them tied to the fact that he was splitting from our established post-college but pre-adult house and leaving his portion of the rent uncovered. The concept was entirely foreign to me: I hadn't yet loved anyone enough to want to share a space with them that wasn't temporary and then potentially quickly forgotten. The shared machinery of love and trust has many parts and therefore many flaws, and therefore many opportunities for disaster. At the time, it all existed on too thin of a ledge for me to imagine walking. When my pal and his girlfriend broke up three months into the lease, they stayed in the apartment together. Breaking the lease was too expensive, but so was one of them taking on the rent alone. There is also something about remaining inside of the wreckage that is more seductive than pushing your way out of it alone. It seemed, at the time, like stubbornness gone off the rails, but it is a judgement call. If I have the destruction of something that I once loved to carry with me at all times, isn't it like I still have a companion?

The summer of the breakup, my friend would stay at our house late, making sure he could get home after his now ex-girlfriend fell asleep. They would avoid each other in the mornings, one sleeping on a tiny couch in the living room. Though it seemed like an absolute nightmare to me then, I remember both of them on the day we helped move them out of the apartment, as sad as I'd seen them in any of the months before. There are endings, and then there are endings.

In this way, heartbreak is akin to a brief and jarring madness. Keeping up the fight—any fight—to not have to reckon with your own sorrow isn't ideal, but it might help to keep a familiar voice in your ears a bit longer than letting go would. Heartbreak is one of the many emotions that sits inside the long arms of sadness, a mother with many children. I suppose it isn't all bad, either. For example, I am heartbroken at the state of the world, so I take to the streets again. But the real work of the emotion and all of its most irrational callings happens beneath the surface. When the room you once shared with someone goes quiet, there are few good ideas. I have gutted a record collection because too many of the songs reminded me of someone I didn't want to be reminded of. My friends have fled jobs, bands, states. I don't enjoy being heartbroken, but I'm saying I enjoy the point of heartbreak where we convince ourselves that literally everything is on the table, and run into whatever will dull the sharp echoing for a night, or a week, until a week becomes a year. It is the madness that both seduces and offers you your own window out once it's done with you.

At some point, a person figured out that the performance of sadness was a currency, and art has bowed at its altar ever since. Sometimes it's a game we play: if I can convince you that I am falling apart, in need of love, perhaps I can draw you close enough to tell you what I really need. Other times, it is not entirely performance. In 1976, Fleetwood Mac was in desperate need of a massive album to cement their shift from blues-rock obscurity to more radio-friendly pop. Mick Fleetwood had higher aspirations than kicking around small clubs, and could sense the band's time running out. Their previous album, 1975's self-titled effort, was the first with California duo Lindsey Buckingham and Stevie Nicks. Containing songs like "Rhiannon" and "Landslide," now seen as Nicks' signature tune, the album saw success, paving the way for a monster follow-up. But in the two years that followed, everything began to come apart. Here, the part everyone knows: first bassist John McVie and keyboardist/vocalist Christine McVie divorced at the end of a tour after six years of marriage. Then Buckingham and Nicks, embroiled in a volatile on-again/off-again relationship since joining the band, finally permanently turned it off, which didn't reduce any of the volatility. Mick Fleetwood, the only one not in an intragroup romance, found out that his wife, Jenny, was having an affair with his best friend. The press, catching wind of what was believed to be the band's collapse, circulated inaccurate stories. In one story, Christine McVie was near-death in the hospital. In another, Buckingham and Nicks were labeled as the parents of Fleetwood's child. The band was breaking apart, but not broken up, reveling in the false stories before falling into piles of cocaine to forget them. When the spring of 1976 came, they retreated to a recording studio in California. No longer at the edge of chaos, but fully immersed in it.

The lyric that opens up *Rumours*, the band's most iconic album, is Lindsey Buckingham's: "I know / there's nothing to say / someone / has taken my place" opens the song "Secondhand News," and just like that, the tone is set. There are few lyrics that set an album's tone like this one, and few songs. Nicks' vocals weaving in to clash with Buckingham's in the verses, littered with bitter proclamations. What sells *Rumours* as more than just high drama, spun out on record, is the clean brilliance of its pop leanings. While their last album felt like what it was, an old blues band trying on some new clothes, *Rumours* was the sound of the band fully committed to their new role as a pop band playing the game, aiming for the charts. The collaborative spirit of Buckingham and Nicks, even fractured, played into this more than anything else. Taking on the bulk of the album's writing and vocal duties, there was an ability to fashion a dual tone: Nicks, both remorseful and hopeful on "Dreams," Buckingham angry and spiteful all the way through the album, most impressively on "Go Your Own Way." Even beyond this, the album's most interesting character, in some ways, is John McVie. He was the band's most private and reserved member, and didn't provide lead vocals on any song. This meant that the narrative of his failing message could only play out on record through Christine, the most brilliant and stunning example being "You Make Loving Fun," an ode to an affair she'd had. She told John, at the time, that the song was about a new dog. It's hard to ignore that the women made *Rumours* exciting. Christine McVie wasn't as flashy as Nicks, but her familiarity and comfort within the band, paired with her and Buckingham's musical rapport, allowed space for her to emote with ease and nuance in a way that often made Buckingham sound like he was having a frantic, exceptionally skilled temper tantrum.

These are the politics of splitting apart: we run to our friends and tell them the version of the story that will ignite in them a desire to support our latest bit of grief. It becomes a bit tastier, of course, if your friends are millions of pop fans. If, in the telling of your heartbreak, you have to share a microphone with the person who broke your heart. If, perhaps, the drugs wore off just in time for you to remember watching your ex-partner going home with someone else the night before. This is what made the album, particularly the collaborations between Buckingham and Nicks, so interesting, and slightly troubling: a real-time plea to see which of them could come out of the breakup more adored than they were inside of the relationship. Buckingham lost, of course, and didn't stand much of a chance. Nicks, gifted, charming, and singular, was the greatest and most fully developed character in the album's soap opera, despite only taking lead vocals on two songs. But beyond winners and losers, the formula had already been figured out. For the voyeur who prefers public collapse, there is no better combination than someone who is both sad and willing to lie to themselves about it.

Without a healthy investment in the art of denial, the album doesn't work. That, truly, is the album's greatest performer. Only denial of an emotional desire for escape could lead a band to complete an album when, at their worst moments, they were unable to talk to each other without screaming. In the Sausalito studio where the album was recorded, there were no windows. Mick Fleetwood, after a few weeks of recording, removed all of the clocks from the walls. When there is no image of time to make stand still, everything can become a type of stillness. The album represents the sound of '70s excess at every turn, asking the band how much of the process and all of its demons they could take into themselves. It all spoke to the band's interest in self-torture for the sake of Mick Fleetwood's mission, his desire to make The Great American Pop Album at all costs, even if Fleetwood Mac had to be held together by cocaine and scotch tape.

"The Chain," the album's most acclaimed song, is haunting, angry, teeming with regret and disgust. It is the whole of the album, condensed into just over four minutes. It was crafted largely in separate rooms, pieced together with past parts of old songs. It churns along painfully, driven by a McVie bass riff that sounds like a caged animal finally coming to terms with its surroundings. On the song, Buckingham and Nicks engage in a tug-of-war on the chorus, "If you don't love me now / you will never love me again" and it is like they are shouting at each other from across the studio. Buckingham, toward the end before he takes on his howling guitar solo, feels like he is almost shouting. It is the one song on the album that makes me feel like something could be broken at any moment. It is the song you play for someone when they ask you what the fuss about *Rumours* is. It is the entire emotional cycle of dissolution, peaking at the end of the song with the band singing "Chain, keep us together" in unison, more as a plea than anything else.

It helps to think about *Rumours* as not just an album, but a living document. Once you push past the theatrics of it, the massive album sales and the thrilling gossip, it is a deeply sad project. One that reflects the human conflict of leaving and not leaving and trying to find some small mercy in the face of what has left you briefly torn apart. The songs are perfect, of course, drenched so richly in the late-'70s California aesthetic that, for a moment, you may forget what the songs were born out of. For anyone who has ever loved someone and then stopped loving them, or for anyone who has stopped being loved by someone, it's a reminder that the immediate exit can be the hardest part. Admitting the end is one thing, but making the decision to walk into it is another, particularly when an option to remain tethered can mean cheaper rent, or a hit album, or at the very least, a small and tense place that you can go to turn your sadness into something more than sadness. It's all so immovable, our endless need for someone to desire us enough to keep us around. To simply call *Rumours* a breakup album doesn't do it justice. Most breakup albums have an end point. Some triumph, a reward or promise about how some supposed emotional resilience might pay off. *Rumours* is an album of continual, slow breaking.

My favorite photo of the band from the *Rumours* era was taken by Annie Leibovitz for the March 1977 *Rolling Stone* cover, the same month the album was released. The band is sprawled on a queen mattress that is resting on the floor. Mick Fleetwood, the glue, in the middle, his long limbs stretching from the top of the mattress to the bottom, a single sheet covering everyone. Buckingham has Christine McVie in his arms, a hand in her hair. Christine's hand is outstretched, reaching over to touch

Fleetwood's foot. Nicks is resting on Fleetwood's bare chest, her legs draped over John McVie's stomach. John McVie is unbothered, reading a magazine. The joke is that they were always too connected to let each other go so easily. I like to think of this as the great lesson hiding in *Rumours*: there are people we need so much that we can't imagine turning away from them. People we've built entire homes inside of ourselves for, that cannot stand empty. People we still find a way to make magic with, even when the lights flicker, and the love runs entirely out.

I see hell everywhere.

Future

V.

The clapping grows. By the last lines of the song, the entire crowd has joined in, clapping on beat with Marvin, breaking decorum to honor such brilliance. No one I know remembers who won the game.

For some of us, denying what this country is, and what it is doing to our bodies, is impossible. We are perhaps at the cross-roads that Marvin Gaye was at in 1970, with the answers as clear as they've ever been, yet still pushing to ask questions. Trying to push our shoulder against one of the millions of doors America built to keep us out. And we are all here, we unlikely patriots. All of us pushed to the margins, trying to fight for ourselves and one another, all at once. Celebrating while still fighting, which is perhaps what represents the ethos of this country more than anything else. To bear witness to so much death that could easily be your own is to push toward redefining what it is to be a patriot in this country. It is even to push toward redefining "country," until it becomes a place where there is both pride AND safety.

And so a transgender woman steps into the hallowed ground of the White House and fights to be heard in the name of undocumented transgender immigrants.

And so a woman scales a flagpole and tears down a symbol of oppression with her bare hands, taking time on the way down to deliver a word from the same God that spoke Marvin into revolution.

And so a community buries more of its own, but does not forget to celebrate, and does not forget to sing.

These are the people who I will remember most when I look up to the sky this year, watch it explode in light, and hear a child laughing.

February 26, 2012

THE DRIVE FROM COLUMBUS, OHIO, TO THE MIDdle of Minnesota isn't particularly a simple undertaking. It is the worst kind of Midwest drive: the one that spans nearly 12 hours over the course of mostly wide-open farming land. For a brief moment, there is the excitement of Chicago, or the rolling greens of Madison, Wisconsin. It's a tedious trip, but one that feels shorter with a person you like, and maybe want to impress. So in the still-dark of morning, I jumped into a car next to a girl I liked and wanted to impress. Atmosphere was playing in Minnesota that night, and I wanted to go a little and she wanted to go a lot and so I, then, wanted to go a lot. It was a Sunday at the end of winter. It was raining.

Atmosphere is a rap duo (made up of Slug, the rapper, and Ant, the producer) from Minneapolis. They are, in many ways, the darlings of the Midwest underground rap scene, the crown jewel of Minneapolis indie hip-hop label Rhymesayers. Their career, by 2012, spanned nine albums over 15 years, all of them filled with Slug's singular ability to either pick apart his own flawed life, or enter the life of someone else and give their stories depth, a softness that might not otherwise be afforded to them by the outside world. His natural eye toward empathy is why, even with fans stretching all over the country, the passion for Atmosphere in the Midwest is at its most eager. Slug is an MC that comes across like the guy you might bump into telling a story at the supermarket or the diner. A pal of your parents who comes by to talk about the days that were both good, and old. Couple this with the fact that they are seemingly always working, piling on hundreds of shows in most years while also dropping a consistent stream of EPs, and their status with kids in working-class Midwest towns is cemented.

The fifth Atmosphere studio album, *When Life Gives You Lemons, You Paint That Shit Gold*, is, by all accounts, a concept album. Slug spends most of the songs looking into the lives of people who are struggling: single parents, minimum wage-earners, just trying to hang on to what they've got before someone comes to take it away. In 2008, I was struggling my way through my early 20s; leaving a good job with the state to sell music at a local bookstore because of some flawed punk concepts about principles. Every hour I worked stocking records and CDs or bantering with some customer about the importance of grunge felt like I was slouching my way closer to some type of freedom, even though there were months I could barely afford to keep my phone on, or times I had to wait until direct deposit hit at midnight on a Friday before I could eat. There are the politics of chosen struggle. What it is to not go home, when going home might be a more comfortable option. *When Life Gives You Lemons, You Paint That Shit Gold* was filled with anthems for me and my friends. Kids who were getting by, leaning on each other when they could. Kids that would pool their money and get a pizza on a Saturday night after working for ten hours. It was this album that played at house parties in whichever apartment had the most space to spare. This album that I would have in my headphones while I walked home from work in the rain, with my dark hood pulled up over my head.

On February 26, 2012, Atmosphere had a show in St. Cloud, Minnesota, which is about 45 minutes outside of Minneapolis. They were playing in the Atwood Ballroom, a banquet hall type venue on St. Cloud State University's campus. Not exactly the ideal setting for an underground rap show, but it was still not enough to turn us off from the journey. By 2012, my struggle was at least more glamorous. A few places would pay me to write words here and there, which would keep my lights on and keep a frozen pizza hanging out in my freezer. The 12-hour journey on that day seemed logical. My Sundays were mine and mine alone. I had just crawled out of the wreckage of a horrible relationship, and the potential to spend that much time in a car with someone who I liked felt thrilling. Someone who maybe liked me back, or at least didn't think too poorly of spending 12 hours in a box with me, traversing the vast landscape of soybeans. We stopped for a few minutes in northern Ohio while the sun rose. We watched the planes take off and wished ourselves, for a moment, winged machines.

On the trip north through Illinois, the playlist was Atmosphere-heavy. This is a thing that I did, often. Listening to the act on the way to see the act, trying to figure out what songs they might play. I was missing the NBA All-Star game for this, something that I had strongly wanted to watch, but was told not to worry about by my smarter friends. One of them rolled her eyes, exasperated. "You like this girl, right?" she said. "Then why would you sit and watch a game that happens every year where it doesn't even matter who fucking wins?"

There was sound logic there, but the NBA All-Star game was, in my life, less about who won and who lost. There was something freeing about it, the tone and pace of it. Seeing all of these players, mostly Black, who spent the entire season restricted by the NBA's structure, sometimes slowed down by coaches. Watching them call back to some of their playground days, ones that perhaps mirrored my own in freedom, if not in talent. Seeing players attempt alley-oop passes to themselves, or dribble moves that would get them pulled from most games. Most of the people I know who hate the NBA All-Star game are white. They complain, mostly, about the showboating, or the lack of fundamentals. They don't understand why anyone would want to watch a game like that. When I think about Black freedom, I think about the small moments of it, in concert with a larger-scale version of liberation. The NBA All-Star game brings me joy as it brought me joy to run on the blacktop and throw a no look pass, or watch someone dribble a ball through someone else's legs and get a chorus of "ooohhhhhs" from spectators. There is something about performing toward our roots in this manner, without an eye toward the white people who may be watching us, following our every movements with fear, or disgust.

My favorite parts of a road trip with another person are the moments where silence allows everyone in the car their own thoughts, and the space to assume what the other person is thinking. The song "Dreamer" from *When Life Gives You Lemons* is about a teenage mother who is raising kids on her own. She fantasizes of a better life until she realizes that her family is the better life. This song filled the car as we crossed through the middle of Wisconsin, and it made me think of the value in someone who is willing to see the world and write about it in the way that Slug does. The consideration of empathy in mainstream spaces does a lot, but what it might do better than anything is convince someone to fight for your life after your life is taken. Or, at worst, it might convince someone that you don't deserve to be murdered because you wore gold teeth or typed a curse word into a box on the internet. For most of the drive I considered this. Slug, championed as the MC who could tell stories accesible enough for everyone in the world to enter. I envied this then, from the passenger seat of a car being driven by someone I desperately wanted to talk to in that moment, but instead pushed my lips to a small bottle of sweet tea to keep our silence ours.

There is a real excitement in seeing an artist play a show in, or around, the city they're from. I've made trips across the country to see punk bands and rappers play tiny dives in the towns that made them. There's a natural comfort that takes the stage. It comes with, I imagine, the comfort of knowing you could fall into your own bed after you're done. I haven't seen Atmosphere since February 26, 2012, mostly because I haven't been able to catch them in Minnesota again. That night, what I remember more than anything is feeling, for a moment, like the floor might collapse under the weight of our collective thrill. I don't mean the usual anxieties about the collection of bodies in a packed space. I mean, during the show, when Slug leaned over the stage and told the audience to jump, everyone jumped, and when I landed, I felt the floor bend itself underneath us all, like it was gritting its teeth just to contain our endless celebration of this hip-hop homecoming. And I did, for a moment, look down and feel like if this were to be it, I would be all right. If the floor gave out and the walls caved in, and we were all trapped under the ruins of the Atwood Ballroom in St. Cloud, Minnesota, I would at least have gone in a room where people were getting free on their own terms.

It remains one of the best rap shows I have ever seen, not just because I was there with someone who made me feel like there was a window for my heartbreak to crawl out of, and not just because I got to watch her smile and sway wide when the first notes of "Dreamer" bled through the speakers. It felt, on that night, like there was a true contract between audience and performer. What Slug does on records so well, the communication of concern, translates even better to Atmosphere's live shows, where there is space to engage in plain conversation with the listening masses. That night, he put a sneaker on the edge of a monitor near the front of the stage, out of breath after playing through what felt like 30 songs in a row. "Listen," he said, waiting a beat for the crowd to quiet. "Whatever else is happening out there in the world tonight, I need y'all to know that we're gonna be all right. We're going to make it."

The feeling I love most is walking into night air after spending hours cloaked in sweat, dancing in a small room with strangers. If the night air is cool, the way it sits on your skin is a type of forgiveness. A balm for all of the heat you've leaned into. Sometimes, I think I still only go to shows for the way it feels to leave them, everyone pouring out of a bar or an arena, a collective gasp rising after everyone feels the same breeze at once. On the night of February 26, 2012, most phones didn't work in the venue. I watched everyone staring, frustrated, at their phone screens, as they were denied the opportunity to post a photo or send a tweet. I eventually turned mine off until I got my fill of the cool night baptism. I turned it back on at just past midnight. Trayvon Martin had already been dead for five hours.

It was Twitter first, that night. Bits of a story: a shooting in Sanford, Florida. A teenage Black boy. Iced tea and Skittles. Neighborhood watch. Emmett Till, Emmett Till, again. Even in the younger stages of Twitter—I had only been on for about a year and a half—the details of the story were being best reported on the scrolling timeline, even though the information was disjointed, coming too fast. I hadn't adjusted myself to the routine like I have now. This was the first time I was reading about the murder of an unarmed Black person in near-real time. The first time I was seeing reactions to it from people online in the same moment it was happening. The boy didn't even have a name yet, he was just a parade of descriptions: Black. Hoodie Boy. Walking, and then not.

On February 26, 2012, people weren't yet insisting heavily that Trayvon Martin deserved to die. People weren't yet arguing over the hooded sweatshirt as a respectable piece of clothing to wear in the rain. The protests hadn't swarmed thick into the streets. His murderer hadn't even been charged. I sat on a bench outside of the Atwood Ballroom, scrolling through my phone, glued to it as I would learn to become in these moments each year after. Over my right shoulder, my date to the show read along with me, first Twitter and then small news hits. Every now and then, she would gasp, something quick and silent. I remember looking up and into the still-lingering crowd and seeing another person scrolling their phone, stopped in their tracks. And then another, and one or two more. I imagined they were all taking in what I was taking in, even if they weren't. I wanted, for a moment, to share in this small horror. What a country's fear of Blackness can do while you are inside a room, soaking in joy, being promised that you would make it through.

On Kindness

I AM MADE MORE UNEASY BY A RAGE THAT RESTS itself beneath silence than I am with something loud, stomping along a house and making glass rattle. Growing up, my father was a mostly calm man, even in anger. Instead of spankings, he preferred long, drawn out lectures, often peppered with stories, to get his point across. My mother's voice, naturally loud, did most of its work when joy was afoot. Her laugh was the type to echo through walls. She was a woman with a loud personality, loud smile, loud walk, the type of presence you could feel coming from miles away. In a largely Black neighborhood, I grew up around parents who were not all like my own: my friend Josh, for example, had two parents that were both loud and stern, laying down strict rules and enforcing them at all costs. Other friends had relaxed, playful parents. These were my favorite. The ones who appeared to let all things slide. Video games played until all hours, basketball dents in a garage. One such set of parents, always gentle and thrilled to see me and my brother, split when we were just teenagers. The mother stayed, the father drifted miles away. We never saw him again. The mother, wrecked by grief, grew more and more silent as the years wore on. She stopped laughing, barely smiled when she recognized me on a bike going past her house. A few years ago, I'd heard that after her youngest son went to college, she stopped leaving the house altogether.

In temperament, I am more of my father's son than my mother's. When I was 16, I was in a car being driven by two of my white friends when we were pulled over on I-270 in Columbus. We were speeding, tearing down the highway at least 15 miles over the speed limit. When the police officer arrived at the passenger window, where I was sitting, I was laughing loud, as my mother would, at a joke a friend in the backseat told to loosen the mood. None of us had ever been in a car that was pulled over before, and joking seemed like the right thing to calm us. The officer snapped at me. Asked, of course, if I thought anything was funny. Demanded to know what I was so excited about. This, before even addressing the white driver for his infraction. High school was the first time in my life that I had white friends I considered close to me. All of my Black friends growing up were loud, sometimes quick to emotion. Among ourselves, among our neighborhoods, it all felt like it was the same volume. A low, and safe hum. Kept within, away from those who may wish to dull it.

Through high school and my playing time in college, my scouting reports for soccer all read the same. The highlights: speed, agility, instincts. The lowlights: balance, focus, work ethic. Toward the end, all of them that I recall had reads on my personality that felt odd. Words like "passionate" and "fired up" and "emotive" would hang in the closing sentences as compliments, I imagine, but uneven ones, given my play. I played sports as I imagine my father would have: all business, the occasional burst of outward emotion, but nothing startling. My freshman year of college, I played for my university as the first American-born player of color. I stepped onto the field for a preseason match, in a sea of white jerseys, white faces, white coaches, white fans. I got a yellow card for clapping in slight frustration, in the direction of the sky, after I allowed a ball to roll out of bounds.

What I am told most often now is that I am kind. I am told this more by white people than anyone else, but I am told it often by everyone. That my kindness is a blessing. People who don't know me particularly well talk about how they can see a kindness in my eyes, or feel a kindness that I have deep within. I generally laugh, shrug uncomfortably, and give a small thanks. I know, particularly when it is by people who aren't familiar with me, that what they are actually complimenting is an absence of that which they perceived, perhaps expected.

I often joke about how I don't wear anger well. To a very real extent, this is true. I didn't see anger translated well growing up, so it isn't an emotion that I have worked through enough times to push outside of myself. Another element of that is rooted in the distance between my anger and the trouble it might cause me if taken in by the wrong audience. I read about a Black man in the Columbus suburbs not far from where I went to college. His neighbor called the police on him because he heard the Black man raising his voice to a level that the neighbor wasn't used to hearing. He feared that something dangerous was happening in the house.

When the police arrived, it turned out the man was just singing. Practicing for his church choir. The stakes are high and the capacity for mercy is not. When I yell, I feel an immediate sense of guilt afterwards. Shame, sometimes fear. People aren't used to my voice pushing above a joyful monotone. In the rare times I am confronted with anger spilling out, I wish to collect it quickly, before it grows all over everyone in the room. Before I become just angry and nothing else.

What I'm saying is that I've been thinking a lot about Black anger lately, and what we do and don't do with it. The relief that people have when a protest centering on Black lives aligns with their ideas of peace. The relief that I have when there are no pictures of police pushing protesters to the ground. I am interested in what we afford each other, in terms of the emotions that can sit on our skin, depending on what that skin might look like. This makes me ask the question of who benefits from this, our eternal façade of kindness? Is the true work of kindness owed to ourselves, and our sanity?

This is not saying that I, personally, am waiting in a rage at all times. I'd like to think that people are largely correct: on any given day, I imagine myself a kind person. Or, at least, a person who is trying. One who reaches for the well of empathy before all others, even if I come up empty at the end. What possibilities would Black people be allowed if their anger, and all of the ways it manifested itself, could be seen as a part of the human spectrum. The way we cut a wide lane for riots after sports games, for punk rock and metal bands fronted by white anarchists who wish to overthrow all unjust modes of government. Our fights aren't going to be equal in the world, but if we are pushing our backs against the same barriers of injustice, I would like my anger to live in the world as your anger does. Reasonably, with expectations that it doesn't make me who I am. It is a task, some days. To think about your consistent kindness as, instead, a product of restraint.

Black women, sitting at the intersection of race and gender, experience this more than I do, more than their male counterparts. Tabbed as angry, and only angry. I think, then, of my mother. How she always made sure to laugh louder than anyone in the room. How in every picture, she smiled with all of her teeth. How in the markets by our house, she would call everyone by their first names. Warmly touch them on their shoulders and ask about their families. How, even then, on a day where she was exhausted, I remember walking into the store with her. She was not smiling, but kind to the white man behind the register, offering short but polite responses to his questions. When handing her back change, he looked at my mother and said, "Everything okay? You just seem so mad today."

And I can't be sure, but I think I remember a smile, forcing its way along the edges of her mouth.

In The Summer Of 1997, Everyone Took To The Streets In Shiny Suits

THIS IS THE ONE WHERE THE MOTHER DIES.

I feel drawn to apology, though I imagine you must have known it was coming. Here, perhaps I should tell you that she died in summer. If I say that I was at least outside rather than cocooned by cold, pressing my grief-slick face to a window, perhaps the image is more bearable. The thing about dying unexpectedly is that it certainly saves you the heartbreak of watching your loved ones fuss over you. I kissed my mother on a June night in 1997, and when I woke up, she was gone. That was it. I think sometimes it was better that way, to have our last moment be a routine farewell. Her throat simply closed in the middle of the night, a reaction to medication she was taking to fight against her bipolar disorder. Sometimes it isn't what we're battling that takes us, but simply the battle itself. Days before she died, she got to watch my brother, her oldest son, graduate from college. It seemed fitting, to go out on the heels of a celebration.

A few months before we buried my mother, a casket was carried through Brooklyn, the Notorious B.I.G.'s body inside, and here is a myth I like to imagine about that day: a line of rappers watching his funeral with their hands out, trading in their street-honed rhymes and still-cocked guns for a shiny jumpsuit, perhaps a pile of chains. A stack of money with the promise of more to come. And no rapper was ever killed again, and every hood danced in the streets for two whole decades, every song dipped in a sweet sample that our mothers learned from their mothers. It's a lie, of course. But 1997 was, for me, a year of far-off myths that I wanted to come to life. I dreamed myself into an emotional survival that I wasn't afforded the opportunity to live in my waking hours.

To have lost a beloved rapper first was a sad but gentle blessing. I was 13 years old and familiar enough with death to have felt its impact, but the loss of Biggie felt different, even more than the loss of Tupac just a few months earlier. If you happened to be alive in the Midwest in the mid-'90s, equidistant from each coast, you got to enjoy mainstream rap at its sharpest and most complete rise, without the biases that engulfed the coasts at the time. After the Notorious B.I.G. was murdered in March of 1997, it felt like the ride was over. It briefly felt like perhaps the peak had been reached, and then came the blood and the funerals, and now the whole genre was on timeout, tearing itself apart at the seams. I remember a brief moment where my brothers and I had to become secretive about our rap intake, our parents growing concerned about the violence of it all. It felt a little heavier to rap along to songs about guns and death. My mother began to eavesdrop on the music I was taking in, cutting eyes at anything with a black-and-white striped "PARENTAL ADVISORY" sticker on it. I was her youngest child and it was still the spring. She did not yet know that she would be gone.

"Mo' Money, Mo' Problems," the Diana Ross-sampled hit from the Notorious B.I.G.'s posthumous album *Life After Death,* was released as a single two days after my mother's funeral. It was my first time hearing it on the radio. Not just a single radio, but every radio. It spilled out of cars, onto basketball courts, people danced to it in parking lots after the sun set. The song sampled "I'm Coming Out," an anthemic 1980s disco soul hit that arrived before I was born but existed in familiar homes in the years after, playing in the hood, or at the cookout, or anywhere you could find space for Black people to dance. "Mo' Money, Mo' Problems" was the first time I considered the true work of the sample: to call us all back to something familiar, in hopes that we might ignore all that is falling apart outside. The music video for the song came out shortly after the single. I watched it premiere on BET one day on a break from summer revelry. The visuals are a celebration. Ma$e and Puff Daddy dancing, cloaked in shiny suits, and even with the ghost of Biggie hovering thick over the song, they laughed, swayed arm in arm, levitated underneath the face of their dead friend.

With that, a new gate opened. The so called "shiny suit era." The commercialization of hip-hop, taken to an extreme. The party that never stopped. Puff Daddy on every single, blinding jewelry in every video, songs drowning and shameless soul and pop samples covering the top of the charts, gold albums for any MC who stepped in the booth. It began with Puff Daddy and Bad Boy Records, of course, but like all successful trends, it spread. It would be a lie to say that all of the music that was produced during this period was good. The results weren't always ideal; MCs like Mic Geronimo and Nas, who weren't organically in the shiny suit lane, attempted to venture in and found themselves clumsy and out of place. Still, rap was at its most commercially accessible after a brief and dark holding period, and I remember being thankful. Drinking in every bit of excess from a small TV screen in Ohio, feeling like both rap and my life hadn't managed to change much at all, despite the hole left in the genre, despite the hole left in my childhood home.

At its inception, what made punk rock great in the face of incredible odds was the general idea that anyone could do it. It wasn't about making great music, it was about getting free. This isn't just something that Puff Daddy understood. Big Pun understood it while dancing in the "Still Not A Player" video. Missy Elliott understood it while spending the late '90s giving us new ways to see, hear, and feel. Big Tymers understood it when they realized that they had no business rapping, but did it anyway. Nelly understood it while becoming a Midwest success story, an MC who still sounds exactly like where he's from and doesn't apologize for it. Cam'ron understood it in 2003 while freestyling on Rap City, counting hundreds of dollars.

This, too, is a response to grief. Covering yourself in the spoils of your survival and making music that sent people dancing in the streets again. What I took away from 1997 wasn't how much I'd lost, though that burden was mighty. I remembered the songs my mother loved once, repurposed for my own pleasures, and this made it feel like she had never left. The shiny suit era, for all of its detractors, was a gift in that summer and beyond. A small light out of the loneliness that had found its way to me.

In New Orleans, the people dance on caskets. They cut the body loose while the funeral rolls slow down a street. Onlookers join in and celebrate the life of the deceased, whether they know them or not. The band plays loud and long into the hot night, and the line of dancing people grows and grows. I watched this once when I was young, in 2002, a few years after my mother's passing, when I'd learned to move on. People, covered in sweat, both crying and yelling out in joy. Strangers hugging each other, and singing along to whatever tune the band saw fit to carry us home with. It made me reconsider the true purpose of a funeral. To see it, instead, as something that makes death memorable for those still living, something less tearful to sit in. A way to show the dead that we'll be all right, that we can go on without them just fine.

After Katrina, when I came back to the city for the first time in a couple of years, there were bodies floating on the water. People were searching for their loved ones. After a couple more days, caskets, unearthed by the flood's ferocity, began floating through the streets. It was haunting, the unburied floating next to the once-buried, both home and far from home, all at once. On my last day there, a man on some higher ground took out his horn and began to play while a few caskets, some turned sideways and empty, floated below us. A few people, weary and sad, started to clap slowly along, on beat. We make our own music to celebrate our dead where we must.

I'm saying that I wish I knew what joys could be unlocked by tragedy before my mother died, but I'm thankful to have learned it shortly after she was gone. No brass band played for her as she was taken into the cemetery, no dance spilled out in her name. But in the summer of 1997, I learned what it is to feel someone everywhere. On the radio, every time I heard "Mo' Money, Mo' Problems," I would think of how it might just have been the one rap song that my mother would have given allowance to. How she might have smiled and swayed at the familiarity of Diana Ross for long enough to ignore the lyrics. The gloss and shine of the era wasn't just for the suits and the sound. It was all a distraction. A small and delightful manipulation. The only way that rap could have survived after being declared dead under a hail of bullets. It was all a trick to pull our eyes away, and it did, for me. And, look, I am not saying that the mass commercialization of rap music saved the genre or saved lives. It had vast drawbacks, some of them still being felt today. Shifts in production and marketing that started to water down the genre then haven't really stopped, leading to a current-day market where there are, quite literally, too many rappers. But I wouldn't take it back. It was what I needed in the moment, and still what I need now. The thing about grief is that it never truly leaves. From the moment it enters you, it becomes something you are always getting over. I will take healing in whatever form I can, and I heard my mother's voice singing underneath that music. I heard her slowly making her way back home.

The thing that I can't promise is that heaven exists. I like to hope that it does, despite growing less and less connected to an idea of a higher power with each year. My mother died without knowing that death was coming for her, and I like to imagine her somewhere comfortable, a place where she can make peace with that. Selfishly, and more than anything else, I'd like to see her again, whatever seeing in the afterlife might look like. I'd love to sit across from her and hear her laugh at something, anything. I'd like to tell her about the summer of 1997 while someone sits behind us and plays a horn, slow and beautiful. I'd like to tell her about how I went outside for the first time two days after we covered her casket in dirt and heard the notes to a song she could sing along to. I'd like to tell her that I played basketball late into the night that summer, with the words to that song fresh on my tongue. That the radio played rap again, even in the suburbs that I hated. I'd like to tell her that I did not cry at the funeral, but I didn't dance either. Not until weeks later, when I finally let go and flailed my limbs to the radio behind a closed bedroom door, crying and singing, feeling myself get closer and closer to freedom with every unhinged movement. You should've seen me, I'd tell her in our new and clean heaven. You should've seen me.

I did, she'd say. I always did.

Nina Simone Was Very Black

IN THE SONG "PIRATE JENNY," ORIGINALLY FROM 1928's *The Threepenny Opera*, a maid named Jenny, who works at a cheap hotel in London, plays out a fantasy in which she gets revenge on the townspeople who have treated her so poorly. A pirate ship—with 50 cannons, eight black sails, and a skull on its masthead—rolls into the harbor and fires on the city, destroying every building except the hotel. The pirates walk ashore, into the ruins of the city, and put all of the townspeople in chains. Upon presenting all of the chained townspeople to Jenny, she orders the pirates to kill them, before sailing away with the pirates to new land.

I first heard "Pirate Jenny" sung by Nina Simone when I was 12 years old. The record, from 1964's *Nina Simone in Concert,* spun in the living room of my childhood home while I played on the floor. In Nina's version, Jenny works at a flophouse in South Carolina. She watches the pirate ship grow closer, larger, out of her window. For years, this was the only version I knew. In the world Nina Simone builds around the song, the already harrowing tale takes on a new, more terrifying life. In hearing it for the first time, with the active imagination that comes with childhood, I could see the black ship through the walls. I could hear the chains locked around the arms and legs of the towns-people. I could hear their cries for mercy before death. I could see Jenny, standing tall on the black ship as it drifted away, sails raised high.

I can only imagine that I still find Simone's version of the song to be so jarring because Nina Simone knew well that Black people have a different relationship with boats, with chains, with the South, with freedom and the haunting that comes with not having it. "Pirate Jenny" was my introduction to Nina Simone, and it has informed how I have chased after her work ever since. Nina Simone opens her mouth and an entire history is built before us, where there is nowhere for anyone to hide from the truth as she has lived it. I view her now much like I did as a child, when I picked up the record cover to see the woman behind the voice. Nina Simone, of dark skin and a nose much like my own, never afraid.

I have been thinking a lot lately about how Black people have to hold on to our stories, or tell them for ourselves. I have been thinking about how I learned to write, to tell the stories I have, largely at the feet of Black women who then became ghosts—ghosts by death, or ghosts by erasure of their living contributions, and sometimes both. I think of Nina Simone's legacy, and I see the legacy of so many Black women I know, who have had their work reduced by all of the hands that are not their own. Today, movements are stolen and repackaged with faces America finds more palatable. Hashtags and viral memes are created by Black girls and women who do not profit from their enduring popularity: Peaches Monroee, the originator of "on fleek," and April Reign, who created #OscarsSoWhite, have had to fight for the minimal credit they've received. Meanwhile, the "Damn Daniel" kid ends up on Ellen after a week. I have always held the legacy of Nina Simone close, because I know how easily it could be taken from me and served back to America as something more pleasing.

It is easy to be Black and non-confrontational if nothing is on fire, and so it has never been easy to be Black and non-confrontational. The silence may reward you briefly, but it always comes at the risk of something greater: your safety, your family, how the world sets its eyes upon you and everyone you love. When you look like Nina Simone looked in the 1960s— dark, with an Afro piled high on your head—the confrontation will find you. It will inform your existence and the way you move through the world. Nina Simone sang songs of protest even when she wasn't singing songs of protest. Every song was a plea to be seen through that which was burning around her. I say "burning," and mean that Nina Simone wrote songs while churches were being blown from their foundations. I mean that I listened to her sing her version of "Baltimore" in a summer when the internet argued about the value of property and the value of a man's spine, the song arriving just in time for a new, burning generation. "Ain't it hard just to live. Just to live."

Zoe Saldana is, in my opinion, a fine actress. The kind of actress who I will not rush out to see, but if I am at a movie and she is in it, I don't feel as though her performance is distracting. When I saw the trailer for *Nina*, the Nina Simone biopic that was released in 2016 before, I shared a feeling of disappointment with many others. It was more jarring for some, myself included, because it seemed, for a time, that this idea had been scrapped. The initial announcement of the film's concept, in 2012, was not well received, and Nina Simone's family did not give the film their blessing. To have the trailer arrive at all seemed to be a small injustice, one that visibly upset the Simone estate. The trailer portrays Simone, of course, as a mess, during a period when her life was at its most out of control, needing to be pulled back from the brink of destruction by a man. This is how it goes for women on screens in America: a loss of control driven by anger, or "complication," followed by a man to help them regain the control that they have lost. In the trailer, we see Saldana in very obvious makeup used to darken her skin. She has a nose that looks very different from her own, and a kinky Afro wig.

This is the Nina Simone that is being presented to America now: clichéd and predictably polished.

I came of age during a time when I was constantly reminded of the darkness of my skin, the width of my nose, the size of my lips. I am similar to Nina Simone in this way. When I chose to take up jazz at 13, driven in part by Nina's influence, my white jazz teacher told me that my lips were "too big to play trumpet." This led to my father marching into his office with record after record of large-lipped Black trumpet players, spreading them all out on his desk while I sat in a corner and watched. Louis Armstrong, Freddie Hubbard, Mercer Ellington; my father, born in the era of Nina Simone's most confrontational living, standing over the desk of a white man who tried to tell his son that he didn't belong.

America, so frequently, is excited about the stories of Black people but not the Black people themselves. Everything is a Martin Luther King, Jr. quote, or a march where no one was beaten or killed. This is why the telling of our own stories has always been important. The idea of Black folklore as community is still how we connect to our past, locking in on our heroes and making them larger than life. This is, in many ways, how we make our own films. I tell the story of my father walking into my jazz teacher's office in a place other than here, perhaps on a hot porch at the end of a long summer. In that version, my father storms into the room and pulls out a Miles Davis record. He puts it on, pulls a trumpet from the sky, and plays along with every note. When the record dies down, he places the trumpet on the teacher's desk, and walks out of the room with me on his shoulders. In any version of the story I tell, he is driven to do loud things, to be the type of Black that has to be loud in order to not vanish.

When I see people talk about diversity in film rooms and writing rooms, I often see numbers and percentages, but not often very plain talk about what the repercussions are when no

Black people are present. Of the core team that created and brought Nina to life, there is only one Black person: the film's co-star, David Oyelowo, is one of the executive producers. Nina Simone's Blackness—not just her politics rooted in it, but her aesthetic Blackness—is not a footnote. The fact that no one in the room was able to point this out serves as this film's undoing before it is even released.

Because Nina Simone unlocked a part of my imagination that I have always returned to, I hoped the story of Nina Simone to be one that was larger than life, because that is what she has always been for me. I wanted to hear folklore, a story of a great Black woman surviving violence through more violence, driven by her incredible gifts. Here is the story I hope we tell: Nina Simone's Blackness didn't wash off at the end of a day. Nina Simone sang "Sinnerman" for ten minutes in 1965, and the whole earth trembled. Nina Simone played the piano like she was cocking a gun. Nina Simone was dark, and beautiful, and her hair piled high to heaven. Nina Simone survived what she could of the civil rights era, and then got the fuck out. Nina Simone rode away on the troubled ocean, standing on the deck of a black ship, looking back while a whole country burned, swallowing itself.

Blood Summer, In Three Parts.

I. A Black Jesus On Stained Glass:
16th Street And The Necessity Of The Black Church

"It is only when we are within the walls of our churches that we are wholly ourselves, that we keep alive a sense of our personalities in relation to the total world in which we live."
—Richard Wright

THE BLACK CHURCHES WHERE I COME FROM ARE still standing. Most of them around my old neighborhood are toying with the idea of collapse, worn down by the type of hard use that only a Black church can endure. The foundations lean from years of the stomp, the clap, the holler. Paint is peeling back from the walls where a picture of Black Jesus hangs, often crooked, but still smiling.

I say this to point out that I don't know what a church on fire looks like. I've never had to walk past what used to be a Black church and see a pile of smoldering bricks, or smell the wood still burning from whatever is left of the old piano. I get to write about the Black church without knowing a neighborhood afraid to go to one.

Like most people, when I think of the 16th Street Baptist Church bombing, I think of Addie Mae Collins, Cynthia Wesley, Carole Robertson, and Denise McNair. I think of the 22 injured, some who never fully recovered from their injuries. I think of Reverend John Cross Jr., who in 2001 recalled how the girls' bodies were found, stacked on top of each other, clinging to each other for dear life.

Though the church holds ceremonies for our dead, no one goes to church to die. I know that which makes the Black church a sacred thing also makes it a thing that is feared. The African Methodist Episcopal Church (A.M.E.) was founded by Rev. Richard Allen in 1816 Philadelphia, formed from Black Methodist congregations along the Atlantic, eager for independence from white Methodists. Still, during America's decades of slavery, nothing shook white slave owners more than Black religious meetings. Prayer meetings and religious movements of slaves were closely watched by slave owners; some slaves were whipped if they prayed to Jesus. After emancipation, Black Americans in the South built sanctuaries of their own as a way to find refuge in a country that still didn't feel like the Promised Land. The greatest mission of the Black church, historically, has been to care for the spiritual needs of Black people, with the understanding that since the inception of the American church, the spiritual needs of Black people have been assigned a different tone, a different urgency. It is the difference in looking out on a land that you believe is yours, and a land that you were taken to, forced to build.

During the civil rights era, Black churches served as holy ground. A place where Black organizers could meet, strategize, pray, and give thanks. The organization of Black resistance has always sparked white fear, never greater than when violent bigots see a building where Black people are praying to the same God that they do, and doing it with so much fire, so little worry. When a place like this also becomes a base of power for social and political movement, it becomes a target. Taylor Branch, a historian of the Civil Rights Movement, once estimated that from 1954 to 1968, there was a church bombed almost every week. During the freedom summer of 1964, it is estimated that a bombing happened every other day.

The thing that we do on a day like this, where history arrives and reminds us of who it has buried, is that we look back and think about turning points. How a monumental day of violence changed everything that came after it. What hurts me the most is that we don't get to do that here. We do get to mourn Addie Mae, Cynthia, Carole, and Denise in the best way that we can. We do get to reflect on what it means to live in a world where little girls can get dressed up to go to church and not make it out alive. But there isn't the satisfaction of knowing that we live in a world where this could never happen again.

In the mid-'90s, 59 Black churches burned, mostly in the South, leading then-president Bill Clinton to sign the Church Arson Prevention Act. But churches still burned. The Black church was still a target. In the summer of 2015, Dylann Roof walked into the Emanuel African Methodist Episcopal Church in Charleston and unloaded a handgun. In the days following, six Black churches were damaged or destroyed. I imagine this to feel like the whip being taken to the back of any Black community that dares pray to the same Jesus as its white counterparts. When the fear of death is omnipresent, when it has followed you into houses of worship for as long as you've known how to say a prayer, praying becomes an act of immense urgency. To be Black and know how sacred this is, to see a whole history of your sanctuaries burned to the ground, or covered in the blood of your brothers and sisters, it demands you to give yourself over to a loud and eager prayer. One that echoes through an entire week, until you are called back again. The Black church, where we can do this without apology, without the politeness of anxiety. Yes, be loud, and free, and rattle the walls with song.

Yes, clap, and stomp, and sweat on whomever you must. Yes, leave baptized and clean. Yes, survive another week and pray for another.

When the 16th Street Baptist Church was rebuilt and reopened in 1964, it did so with a new stained glass window. The Wales Window depicts a Black Christ with his arms outstretched, his right arm pushing away injustice, his left arm extended in an offering of forgiveness. There is a replica of this window in a church near my old neighborhood in Columbus, Ohio. It is said to be inspired by a verse from the gospel of Matthew: "Truly, I say to you, as you did it to one of the least of these my brothers, you did it to me." I think about the image often, though not of the Black Christ. I think about that expectation, to hold off injustice with one arm while still consistently offering forgiveness with the other. I think about how often that is what Blackness in America amounts to. Even when grandmothers are burying their children, and their children's children. What forgiveness looks like when there are still churches being blown apart, still Black bodies who arrived to pray, and ended up murdered.

When the right arm is reaching into a fire to push away decades of injustice that still presents itself, how long before the whole body is engulfed in flames?

I don't know what a community does when it has no more forgiveness left, or when it knows what forgiveness in this age truly means. I don't know how a country can forgive itself for the deaths of those four sweet girls in 1963, just as I don't know how it can forgive itself for the consistent assault on Black sanctuaries ever since. Still, as thankful as I am to come from hands that still reach out for forgiveness, I am even more thankful to come from a people who know the necessity of rebuilding. Who know what a church does, know how to drink all they can from it, and refuse to let it be torn from them.

II. Another Rope, A Newer City:
The Legacy Of Ida B. Wells And
The Death Of Sandra Bland

"Our country's national crime is lynching. It is not the creature of an hour, the sudden outburst of uncontrolled fury, or the unspeakable brutality of an insane mob."
—Ida B. Wells

What makes the dead body worthwhile is that it was once living. It is true that in every instance of Black death, we adorn the dead body with its accomplishments. We name the people who loved the person who was once alive. We look for the pictures where they once smiled into the sun, their camera turned on their own face. And we do this, consistently and loudly, because we have to. Because we have seen enough death to know what untruths feed on a body at rest. I say this to illustrate the point that I do not want to talk about Sandra Bland getting her dream job, or the joy that seemed to fill her life before she lost it. I want to speak plainly about the hanging of Black bodies from anything in this country strong enough to hold them. It took three men to remove Ida B. Wells from a train car in 1884, and for his trouble, one of them got her teeth marks in his arm. She should have never been asked to move from her seat to the smoking car of the train and she knew this. She measured the fight and took it on.

This is my favorite story about Ida B. Wells' life. It's the one that will show up first when you click on a Google doodle, and I tell it to someone every year on the day of her birth. It makes sense to tell the story every July 16th. I like to think that Ida B. Wells always knew what we see so clearly now. When Black men die, they live on, almost forever. When Black women vanish, they often simply vanish. When enough outlets tell you that your life is an exercise in rehearsing invisibility, when you become invisible, it just seems like you're performing the grand closing act. I admire the work of Ida B. Wells, of course. But more than that, I admire her consistent refusal of silence. It is present in all of us, I believe. But I become most inspired when I see it in Black women. I come from a long line of Black women who spoke, who moved with authority—direct descendants of The School of Wells.

It took two men to arrest Sandra Bland on the side of a road last week. One was holding her firm to the ground while she cried out in pain and, perhaps, fear. We are to believe that she assaulted one of the men, though we do not see it. We so rarely do. We are to believe that Sandra Bland was hanged three days later, though we are not clear on how her body was fixed to a metal bar, or what was used to hang it. But we are to believe that it hanged, nonetheless. We are to believe that this was due to a traffic stop. We are to believe that she was planning a bright future. We are to know that it will not exist.

It is impossible to even mention America's history of lynching without mentioning the woman who fought most fervently to dismantle it at a time when men were being dragged from their homes and hanged for not paying debts or being too drunk in public places. Or, in other cases, for displeasing law enforcement. There is sacrifice in that. In being a Black woman who fights and is alive at any time in this country's history is a sacrifice. It can still get you a death sentence, though the knife is fashioned differently. When Ida B. Wells couldn't go home to Philadelphia, she fought in Chicago. When the mobs came for her in Chicago, she went to England. And like so many Black women, she fought and lived and loved a family and built a home and wrote and pushed to the front when the front did not want her there. And she did not want to stop the fight until more Black women had room of their own, until Black men stopped being hanged from trees.

But Ida B. Wells died an unceremonious death in 1931 and we are to believe that Sandra Bland hanged from a jail cell on a summer day in 2015. It was the failure of kidneys that took Wells at age 68, not any of the violent mobs, their whetted teeth shining against the moon. I write about Wells today, how much she hated the rope, the Black bodies left hanging in the South. And I write about Sandra Bland today, the all-too-familiar death, the dead body that this country has come to know, the one that we write about even when we are not writing about it. And my hands can't help but shake. I don't know anything more about Sandra Bland than anyone else, other than the fact that I want her life to be one that is not forgotten. I want us to honor the living Black women who fight and I want us to fight for the Black women who no longer have the honor of living. I want us to respect the legacies that were remarkable by virtue of boundary-pushing and I want us to respect the legacies that were remarkable by virtue of being alive and loved. I want these statements to not be "brave," or "unique." I want them to be expected.

III. On Black Grandmothers And The Art Of Dying On Your Own Terms

During the time in my life when my grandmother was still living and wholly present, I rarely recall her smelling of anything other than smoke. She smoked More cigarettes, a brand that currently can only be purchased online (and, I'm told, at a few corner stores in the Florida Panhandle). More cigarettes were mostly notable because they used brown paper to wrap the tobacco instead of the traditional white paper that most cigarettes use. My grandmother seemed to always have her thin brown fingers wrapped around a stick of thin brown paper, so often that on some days it seemed like the smoke was rising from her hands all on its own. If she needed to get into her purse for any reason, she often had to sift through a graveyard of emptied red and green packs of cigarettes, cursing under her breath the whole time. The smell of them, though, was distinct. I had no language for it as a child, sitting outside of her room and breathing it in while watching her watch *Supermarket Sweep* in the evening, or watching her watch some soap opera during the summer days when school was out. I found myself not even having language for it as it lingered on my clothing after a good hug. It wasn't until years later, while taking a road trip through the South in my early 20s, that I could name it. In South Carolina, after a hard rain, I walked through an old plantation. And it was the smell descending from the trees after they made room for the storm. A humble attempt at forgiveness.

Almost every Black grandmother I know smokes. I once hugged a friend's grandmother while she was holding a cigarette, and it burned a mark onto my t-shirt. After which she took a long drag, looked me up and down and said, "You gotta watch that, honey." I have known some who put out their cigarettes, look down at them with disgust, and say, "I swear, I'm gonna quit one of these days," which we understand to mean, "I swear, I'm gonna die one of these days." My particular Black generation is the one who, if they are lucky, have two (or more, in some cases) generations of living women that survived despite being pressed up against all manner of relentless tragedy. It's why we laugh at the stories of the grandmother who takes no shit, but we know not to laugh too long. It is the unspoken fear, the unspoken knowledge of what many of these women gave. We know that if the officer's gun didn't kill them, and poverty's hunger didn't kill them, and the violence of marginalized and silenced Black men didn't kill them, there is no measure of swallowed smoke that will shake them free of the earth quickly and easily.

There is pretty much no violence in this country that can be divorced from this country's history. It is an uneasy conversation to approach, especially now, as we are asked to "behave" in the midst of another set of Black bodies left hollow. The Southern Black church has always been a battleground in this history of violence. Most notably, of course, during the Freedom Summer of 1964, but even beyond. The church, if we are to believe that it still exists for this purpose, is a space of ultimate humbling and vulnerability. In the South, the Black church is also a place of fear. To attack the innocent where they feel most secure is cowardly, of course, but it is also a reminder. There is no safety from this. There will be no reprieve from the sickness that spreads and calls people to take up this level of violence. There will be no calm before the storm. There will only be the storm, and then another, louder storm. It will follow you to your homes, press itself between your sleeping children, hang over your shoulders at work, and yes, it will walk into your church, pray to the same God as you do, and then stand up and open fire. There is no way to talk about this without talking about the history of instilling fear in Black people in this country. Without closing our eyes and feeling the warmth from a flaming cross. Or smelling a wet body, limp and descending from a Southern plantation tree.

The weight of this tragedy hung over me on the day after the Charleston shooting. I slept two restless hours in an Ohio hotel, spending most of my time rolling over to scroll through news feeds and news stories. I mostly thought of grandmothers. I thought of the grandmother who told her 5-year-old grand-daughter to play dead so that the killer would pass her over. So that she might live long enough to see her name grow fresh in the mouth of someone she loves. It is impossible for me to imagine that this is the world we live in. One where Black girls must learn to play dead before they learn to play the dozens. But it is not impossible for me to imagine what her grandmother has lived through. What she knew that we did not. Survival is truly a language in which the Black matriarch is fluent. Much like this country's violence, there is no survival in this country that can be divorced from this country's history. A grandmother who has maybe stared down death more than once, passing that burden on to the child of her child. I don't know if there is a name for what it is when you are moved to praise something as impossibly sad as this. I don't know if it can be found in a church, even as a little girl is not among the dead inside of it. I imagine that I am writing this because I don't know these answers. I think of this child growing up and knowing what it is to escape death. Wrapping herself in the trauma of that. Knowing at such a young age that to be a Black woman in America is, in a way, to feel like you will survive until you decide to stop surviving.

But, the Black people who pray still must pray. In a good Black church, all manner of sweat, holler, and joy lives in the walls. I'm not sure what it is to set foot in a place of worship where you saw members of your community fighting against an inevitable death. I imagine that to be impossible. I prayed last night in a hotel bathroom. Like many of us, nothing draws me to prayer quicker than desperation. Not knowing what to do with my hands, my heart, or my mind. Sometimes, I don't even know what I'm praying for. Last night, I think I prayed for a Southern Black church that didn't also smell of smoke, of cooked flesh. Where the memories weren't of burial. Where Black children could fall asleep in the front row, their small bodies still, but breathing.

My grandmother began to smoke more as she got older. When she moved to her own apartment, down the street from my childhood house, I'd visit and see empty packs of More cigarettes littering the table. Occasionally, when she'd tell me that she was thinking of quitting, I never knew if she meant the cigarettes. I'm not sure that she ever stopped, though I don't imagine she did. She died in the South, in Alabama. I don't know what smell rises off of the trees there after a storm, but I like to imagine that it's the same smell that is rising in South Carolina today. The way I'd like to imagine it, our grandmothers are with us, even when they're not with us. Teaching us how to pray. Teaching us how to survive.

August 9, 2014

IT IS EARLY, AND ~~INSIDE OF AN AIRPLANE SITTING outside of the San Francisco Airport,~~ a mother is asking ~~a person two seats ahead of me to switch seats, so that she can~~ have a window seat for her son, ~~and he looks at the world outside of this metal container that is dragging us~~ back to somewhere in the ~~waiting~~ Midwest. I have this fear of ~~heights, but I do find the appeal in looking out of windows during flights. In Oakland, where I spent the past five days reading poems in hotel rooms with friends that I only get to see a couple times a year. Two nights ago, one of them ran up to the roof of the hotel at night and looked over, everything below was~~ an impossible darkness. ~~It's that kind of height I find myself uncomfortable with.~~ Some would tell me not ~~a fear of heights so much as a fear of falling. Planes work if you can manage~~ to not think of the machinery. The way I walk into a store and buy what my body is demanding without thinking of the labor that carried the product to that moment. ~~But,~~ this mother wants her son ~~to understand the world from this height and the person in the window seat she wants isn't moving. So~~ she is loud now, shouting in the name of her child, who ~~also~~ isn't moving, ~~and who seems preoccupied with the small screen in front of him, where two cartoon characters are wrestling each other over some treasure.~~ I am thinking of what it must be like ~~to not have a desire~~ to get close to heaven at a time like this. A time when ~~there is just a hint of morning coloring the sky as the waning darkness fights against it, making it so that~~ everything ~~above~~ is the color of blood pushing its way across

a dark surface. ~~This is the part of the flight I live for.~~ being pulled into the impossible ~~beauty above and feeling like I
could touch it if I wanted to. I'm not particularly excited about
going back home today, though I do miss it.~~ The dying summer and covering the Midwest in a kind of heat ~~that doesn't
afford anyone the mercy of Oakland's proximity to water. It is
one thing to love where you're from and miss it, and another to
fall in love somewhere else and then have to pull away. When
the mother gives up on the person two seats ahead of me, she
makes eye contact with me and my precious window seat.~~ I pretend to not notice, ~~nodding my head along to imagined music
coming out of my detached headphones. But I'm a poor actor, and have no luck convincing her of my being~~ oblivious to
her suffering. ~~Standing over me, she pleads, explaining that her
son has never~~ even ~~been on a plane before,~~ though ~~has loved
watching them from below. And she wants him to have a window seat so that he'll be maybe less afraid. And~~ I know that I
have been afraid and found comfort in seeing. ~~In the turning
of my head to that which I fear.~~ And so I ~~surrender my seat and
I~~ watch the eager mother carry her son in her arms, to that
which she thinks will make him whole. ~~I push myself into an
aisle seat and prepare for the long flight home, considering that~~
perhaps life is too short for fear. There is always going to
be something outside, waiting to kill us all.

Fear In Two Winters

WHEN PEOPLE SQUINT AT MY NAME ON SOME-
thing in front of them and then ask where I'm from, I tell them
"Columbus, Ohio." When they look again and then, perhaps
more urgently, ask where my parents are from, I tell them "New
York," smiling more slightly. Occasionally, I'll get a person who
asks where THEIR parents were from, and I humor that as well.
No one has ever gone beyond two generations before me, but I
look forward to the day where it all plays out: me in line at the
bank, or at a deli, someone attempting to trace my lineage to
a place they feel makes sense. Me, eventually saying, "Well, I'd
imagine Africa came into play at some point, but now I'm here,
so who can say really?"

What people are asking in this exercise is never about where
I'm from. The question they're asking is "why doesn't your name
fit comfortably in my mouth?" and we both understand what
this is asking, and my toying with the asker usually doesn't win
me any points. The answer they are digging for is less exciting:
my parents converted to Islam in the 1970s, when many young
Black American-born New Yorkers found their way to the religion. A desire for reconnecting their roots to something that
felt more like home than Christianity. My father, before Islam,
was Catholic, though I'm not sure of my mother's religion. They
took new names. The name "Abdurraqib" means "servant of
the observer" in Arabic. It is hard, even now, for people to imagine that any Muslim people are not people who came here from
another country. In the mosque I went to as a child, I felt most
comfortable because I didn't have to repeat my name to anyone

I spoke it to, but I did have to apologize for my flimsy Arabic, or my distance from tradition. In this way, I was often too Muslim for one world, but too steeped in American culture for another. But the person who has to prepare themselves to yell out my coffee shop order as a line grows, snaking behind me, is asking where my parents are from. So they are asking how I got a name like this. So, today, I simply say, "It's Arabic."

The distance between curiosity and fear is tragically short. They are, like sleep and death, within the same family, a quick nudge pushing one directly into the other. Because it has been so long, what people maybe don't remember about Muslims before September 11 is that there was always curiosity that felt like it could take a sharp turn into fear at any minute. My freshman year of high school, I found myself pressured by teachers and administration to come to school without my kufi, the traditional male head covering. I was told it was "a distraction," as it sometimes led to other students snatching it off and running through the halls with it. The school attempted to lean on its "no hats" policy, which caused my father to come into the office, with Islamic texts by his side. This was in the late '90s, when a public school surely should have had to reckon with students of different faiths before, but seemed unequipped to do so. When they were met with resistance, when it was begrudgingly decided that I could still wear my kufi to school, the curiosity shift happened.

The leap from fear to anger can be even shorter, particularly when people feel the need to defend otherwise abhorrent actions. On the morning of September 11, 2001, I woke up in my freshman college dorm and started to walk down the hallway. It was my new friend Brittany's birthday. In the early stage of college, finding and clinging to new friends is vital. Brittany played volleyball and I played soccer, so our teams had to show up to campus early to train. She was from a small town in Ohio, telling me on our second night at school that she had only ever seen a few Black people in her life. This was casual, not something said while sitting, fascinated in my presence. She would talk to me about her town and all of its moral grayness. When you are not surrounded by any Black people, and therefore not directly threatened by their presence, it becomes harder to justify seeing Black people as threatening when you encounter them in real life. Brittany and I got along because we were both escaping, like most people on our small, suburban campus. We bonded in the fact that we weren't escaping things that were especially harmful to us. All of our siblings had gone to college. Our parents supported our dreams. We were two athletes, playing sports in college. Brittany simply wanted to escape the mundane of her small hometown. And I wanted to escape what I, at the time, imagined as a strict Muslim household. One that restricted my pleasures, my ability to fully dance into my rapidly changing personality. With me, freedom was emotional, and mental, not tied to geography. My father's house was a ten-minute drive from our college's campus. And yet, I lived in a dorm. On the top bunk that I jumped off of on September 11 to start down the hall to Brittany's room. I got her a card and a small bag of candy that she liked. As I walked that morning, I noticed all of the doors in the hallway were swung open, and people were sitting at the edges of their beds, unusual for a Tuesday. In one room, a boy on the baseball team was holding his crying girlfriend. In another, someone on the phone with their mother, asking to be told that everything was going to be okay. When I got to Brittany's room, she was sitting on the floor. We watched the second plane hit the building together. We watched the smoke swallow the sky. We watched, as the people jumped, and jumped, and jumped.

By the time I got to college, I had largely stopped practicing Islam. I still participated in Ramadan, the act of fasting for 30 days in an attempt to cleanse the mind, body, and spirit. I relied on that, and the structure it provided. I stopped wearing a kufi, stopped praying daily, unless I was visiting home. I spoke little to no Arabic, which I was always self-conscious about doing anyway. It felt easier this way, fitting in without having to offer explainers. I was making the curious parts of myself invisible in the hopes that curiosity never turned to fear. When I look back now, I find it amazing that I didn't imagine the path that the September 11 attacks would set us down, and how that path would open up the door to global violences against Muslims. The greatest emotional impact on Americans toward American Muslims is that it took curiosity out of the timeline. There was now only fear, turning rapidly to anger. In an age before rapidly updating social media sites, I would read about attacks on Muslims in schoolyards or mosques being set on fire, sometimes days after it happened. I would worry about my father, going to work in a state building every day. And my sister, studying in Madison, Wisconsin. Beyond that, I felt oddly divorced from it all. As if, when I stopped answering the calls to prayer, I inherited a type of safety. By the end of September, when all of the reports and findings about the background of the attackers were being rolled out, news reports would have large banners at the bottom asking things like: "DOES ISLAM HATE US?" and when professors called my Arabic name out in class, it was easy to imagine the fresh and sharp stares I got as something else, something less burning.

The thing about praying five times a day is that it gives you five distinct opportunities to talk to God. To bow and ask for forgiveness, even if you're only returning after an hour. I was bad at sticking to a prayer schedule as a child. When you are young, and everything outside is beckoning, it's hard to not look at that which brings you inside as a task and nothing else. But I appreciated the idea and routine of it, nonetheless. Even when it didn't feel useful, the persistence of bringing myself before some higher power and asking to be made clean, again and again. In the months after September 11, 2001, I found a quiet spot on campus to pray Maghrib prayer in almost every evening. Maghrib, the sun prayer, was the only one my family consistently made together. It worked out, logistically: Maghrib is made at sunset, so during most times of the year, it was made at a time when my entire family was home. There's something mythical and perfect about it, about praying the sun into its resting place every night, waking up and getting to rise with it in the morning. I was the only Muslim on my college's campus. I would pray in a room alone, and then ask forgiveness. I found myself, often, foolishly praying for the country's mercy, as if I could push my back up against a door that was already being broken down from the outside. Brittany went home for winter break, back to her town where there were no Black people and certainly no Muslims. When we came back to school in January, she barely spoke to me. We faded into the background of each other's lives. Some things, it seems, are inescapable.

On the day the new president signs an executive order banning refugees from countries that have primarily Muslim populations, I step out of my car and head to terminal 4 at the John F. Kennedy International Airport. It is still cold, and the sun isn't out. The sun hasn't been out much since the new president was inaugurated eight days ago. It came out briefly on the East Coast the other day, just long enough to see what it had been missing. I began to wonder if someone I love prayed the sun into its resting place and forgot to wish it back. On the way here, I stopped to get tea and someone asked about my name, where it came from, where my family is from. I was patient this time. I explained, thinking of the friends I had accumulated since college: Muslims with families that, unlike mine, were refugees from some of the countries on the list of places that America was now banning refugees from. People with loved ones from these countries, not all of them citizens. People who were afraid, wondering if they should sever their own ties with this newer, even sharper America.

At JFK, a white woman is holding a sign that says "WE ARE ALL MUSLIMS" and I appreciate the messaging, but I don't know that it lands for me when thinking about the future dead that might pile up along some borders while trying to flee some state-manufactured terror. I consider how little I feel Muslim today, even less than I did in college. I haven't stepped into a mosque in five years. My name, the only thing tethering me to people's idea of what Islam is. But I am afraid today, as I was in the winter of 2001. This protest is spontaneous. The executive order was signed last night, and when word began to spread that there were travelers, some citizens, being detained in airports, people took to the streets. Lawyers pushed themselves into airport fast food joints, picking up the WiFi signals so that they could start to do work to get detained people free. It is a comforting and uniting protest, one that isn't rooted in much shared ideology beyond people simply being angry. One man next to me tells me that he didn't vote at all, but he was "pissed off" when he read the news this morning. "You just can't cross a moral line like that," he said, in a thick New York accent. "Fuck that guy. The Statue of Liberty is right over there."

It is eight days in to this new and violent empire that is building upon a legacy of violent empires before it, and I have finally stopped trying to tell myself that everything is going to be all right. There is no retaliation like American retaliation, for it is long, drawn out, and willing to strike relentlessly, regardless of the damage it has done. September 11 is used as a tithe in our church of brutality, even 15 years and endless bombs down the road. The U.S. ignored the Geneva Convention, raping, sodomizing, and torturing prisoners of war at their black site bases around the world. The military bombed wedding parties consisting mostly of women and children in Iraq at Mukaradeeb, and in Afghanistan at Wech Baghtu and Deh Bala. Here, we are saying that we will tear your country apart, we will give birth to the terror within, and then we will leave you to drown in it. This feels, tonight, like a particularly immense type of evil. Real power, I am reminded, doesn't need a new reason to stop pretending to be what it actually is underneath. All of the old reasons are enough to seduce. On my phone, a Muslim friend texts me to ask how my family is. If any of them are in danger. I tell her no, that I am standing, now, in the city where my mother and father were born. There is no border that my living family can be pushed to the edges of, even though a country glares at our name and wishes otherwise.

I still say *Allahu Akbar* often. It simply means "God is Greater" in Arabic. In the rare times that I would be called to lead prayer in my home when I was younger, I would stumble through all of the Arabic without confidence, except for the ending of the prayer, when I would easily and proudly shout *Allahu Akbar,* the only Arabic that fit comfortably over my tongue. Now, it is associated with a call of terrorists before some vicious act is committed in the name of Allah. The perversion of it hasn't pulled me away. I still say it in praise, even when it doesn't fit a specific situation, or when something like *Alhamdulillah* ("Thank God") might be a better fit. I like the translation, mostly. Even though I don't pray, I still like the idea that there is a God and that they are Greater. Than us, than this moment, than this wretched machinery that we're fighting against and sometimes losing. It is the last lifeboat of Islam that I find myself clinging to. As the protest tonight stretches long and hundreds more people stream into the terminal at JFK, until it is overflowing and spilling out of every edge of geography. I think of how foolish I was, to once pray for a country's mercy, and how thankful I am that those prayers were not answered. How, through this resistance, we might find a freedom where no mercy is required. We might find a humanity that is not asking to be seen, but demanding instead. How we all pray for the wrong things sometimes, but somehow, God is greater.

On Paris

PERHAPS IF YOU WERE ONCE YOUNG AND BLACK, or young and brown, but definitely young and Muslim in the heart of a Midwestern city surrounded by corn fields, trees, whole stretches of land where you were feared. Perhaps then you would sneak out of a house, or take the money your father gave you for food or college textbooks, and you would go to see a live show wherever you could find a band playing some songs that you knew enough words to.

You might find some other weirdos like you. The outcasts, the Muslim kids who also knew what it was to have a head covering torn from them in a crowded school hallway, the ones who knew what it was to both run into a fight and run away to survive. You might find a small corner and dance together, sing together, revel in being alive and imagining yourself, for a few hours, un-feared and un-killable.

Having "a place to belong" is something that often works on a sliding scale. The urgency of owning a space with people who look like you and share some of your experience increases the further against the margins you are. Live music, even at its most unhealthy and potentially violent, has historically provided a small mercy for young people who found no mercy elsewhere.

A live show was the first time, as a teenager in Columbus, Ohio, that I found a few other young Muslims who had the same relationship to music that I did. At an early Fall Out Boy show at The Basement, a venue in my hometown of Columbus that is, very literally, a basement, I first noticed them. Muslims who I noticed from school or Friday prayer at the mosque, camped out in the back of the venue. Ones who didn't grow up in a house like mine, where most music was accepted (or, at worst, tolerated).

We connected through mutual passion for feeling most at home during a concert, or our family histories. How we all learned to sneak rap albums past our parents (the trick, back when "Parental Advisory" stickers were actually stickers, involved peeling the sticker off your cassette or CD before you made it back to your house). How our homes varied from understanding to fiercely strict, and how we still found ourselves at live shows with each other. Occasionally, we would travel to a concert in another Midwest city, Chicago or Detroit, and see more of the same. Teenage Muslim music fans who we connected with online at the dawn of social media, who shared our passion and our stories.

These were also the spaces where I understood that my fears were not entirely unique. The ways that I felt about navigating the world were shared by others, the few of us drawn together by both our need to escape into music, and the things that drove us to the escape.

I was a college freshman on a small Ohio campus in September 2001. A time where the word "terrorism" most loudly latched itself to my Arabic name, latched itself on the shoulders of my Muslim friends from Pakistan, Syria, Lebanon. I did not go outside often in that winter. When I did, it was to make the short trip to some cheap show, indie or punk rock, underground hip-hop. Wherever I knew I could see some of the other Muslim kids I knew, and we could sit in between songs, covered in sweat, and speak of our survival.

In Islam, live music and concerts are a tricky thing. In many Muslim households, the act of going to a concert is seen as haram, or sinful. I knew young Muslims who would go to concerts only when they told their parents they would be elsewhere, and had others cover for them. This may never change. In 2015, I read about Muslim teenagers in Turkey and London, rushing to Justin Bieber concerts. Muslims at Coachella and Bonnaroo, basking in that small window of freedom, sinful as it may be.

Hasn't that always been the way of it? We all choose our sins, and their measure. The ones we believe will render us unforgivable, and the ones that we will wash off with a morning prayer. This is something that I find particularly hard to ignore as we again look upon an act of terror that has overshadowed all other acts of terror. Even the ones that have spanned decades, or centuries. As we again discuss selective outrage. Rather, the merit of life, or what we do with how others choose to mourn. Most importantly, as we again ask questions of what Muslims around the world "deserve" and what they "need to do." Then again, have we ever really stopped doing this?

It is a luxury to be able to tear your gaze away from something; to only be made aware of old and consistent blood by a newer shedding of blood. It is a luxury to see some violence as terror and other violence as necessary. It is a luxury to be unafraid and analyze the very real fear of others. I know and understand all of this, and still, as I turned to Paris, even with my knowledge of the world's many horrors, I was particularly struck to read about the shootings that took place in a concert venue. Many concert-goers, mostly young, were gunned down while taking in an Eagles of Death Metal show. I considered the dead, how many among them may have gone out hoping for an escape from whatever particular evil was suffocating them. I considered how many may have been young Muslims. Then, as always, I considered all of the young Muslims still living.

Historically, when people who identify as Muslim kill a large group of people who are assumed to be non-Muslim, the world wishes to see dead Muslim bodies in return. In America, men stand outside of mosques with guns. People urge others to violence against anyone who they believe to be Muslim. Worldwide, in response to this senseless violence, Muslims are assaulted, ostracized, and further misunderstood. I still hear and read stories about Muslims who navigate airports differently, aware of the discomfort that others have around them in that setting since September 11. There are few things like being feared simply due to having a body. There is no way to easily come to terms with this. Those who fear you may wish that you simply make yourself small, if you refuse to disappear. This is how a simple, public space becomes something entirely unpleasant. This is how a place of release and joy becomes something you hold an arm's length away.

It is hard for me to put these things together. Young Muslims around the world, afraid and eager to find a cleansing space. A concert venue, much like the ones where I felt most unafraid, covered in blood. A world, eager for revenge, people to hang their rage on. The idea of feeling most like yourself when watching live music seems small to some, I'm sure. I can only speak for how I found safety and comfort, while also considering how spaces of safety and comfort have become increasingly rare for young Muslims over the past 15 years. Attacks and intimidation at mosques aren't entirely surprising. Much like assaults on Black churches, people will always come first for where you pray. But knowing what music, specifically live music, can do in these times, I worry about Muslims being afraid in those spaces. Or worse, being feared in those spaces.

It is jarring, what we let fear do to each other; how we invent enemies and then make them so small that we are fine with wishing them dead. How we decide what "safety" is, how ours is only ours and must be gained at all costs. How we take that long coat of fear and throw it around the shoulders of anyone who doesn't look like us, or prays to another God. There is something about a dark corner crowded with your people, a song you know, and a night you can bookmark to reminisce on whenever the world is calling for the death of everyone you love.

On the song "Hurt Me Soul" from Lupe Fiasco's classic 2006 debut album *Food and Liquor*, Lupe opens the track by muttering *Astaghfirullah* before the beat drops. Heard frequently in my childhood home, in a literal sense, it means "I seek forgiveness from Allah." But what I always found interesting was how often it was used to express shame. To say *I shouldn't have to do these things, but I don't know how else to survive.*

I imagine Lupe Fiasco, a Muslim making a living performing live music, understands this the way that I do. The shame that exists because of what we have to do in order to remain alive, be seen as human. I consider this while the smoke clears, and we watch young Muslims today do what we always watch young Muslims do in these situations. They plead with the world to be spared. They work tirelessly to show their humanity, show us all the acts of good they have done. They tell the world that they are not like the ones who have killed, as if the world itself, awash with blood, deserves this explanation from the innocent. When I see this now, it breaks my heart. In part, because I recall doing this myself, in the early 2000s, to anyone who would listen. But in part because I know that these are young people in the world, thrashing against what many of us did in our youth, while also coming to terms with their new life as a target. There is shame in this, absolutely. Though I'm not sure that the burden of it belongs on Muslims around the world.

Yet, here, I still write about the living while so many continue to die. I write about music while bodies are prepared for burial. I write about fear from the safety of my apartment, and someone may call it brave. Me, a man who no longer bows to anything five times a day, who had pork just yesterday, who only speaks light Arabic when visiting his family, still writing about how I wish for Muslims, especially young Muslims, to be safe. To have a haven, a place where they can find each other and say I see you. I'm still here.

Then again, as we've come to understand so often, it isn't only music. I know that there are still awkward, anxious Black and brown kids, Muslim kids from all backgrounds, who look for places where they can be themselves, songs that they can hear their experiences in, a world they can dance into and imagine themselves free. Who are still learning that everything can be weaponized, from their bodies to the spaces that they believed to be theirs, and I still hope for them. I think of them today and always. I hope that they can still slide the music they love past their parents and vanish into an album good enough that it makes them forget about everything outside. I hope they always have a place where they are not outcasts for two hours when the house lights go down. I hope they have somewhere to be unafraid and un-feared, like I did.

Through the bombs and the burials, the threats and the anger, I hope they find each other in a room where a song that they know all of the words to crawls up the walls and rattles the lights above their heads. I hope they can still sneak out of their homes. I hope they can still spend their textbook money on live shows that their parents would disapprove of.

This, too, is survival. Astaghfirullah.

My First Police Stop

MY FIRST CAR WAS A 1994 NISSAN MAXIMA THAT I got the summer before my senior year of high school. It was an odd shade of brown, a fading gold stripe encased the body, and it had a loud muffler. Still, it was mine, and growing up without a lot of money makes you cherish what is yours. Shortly after I drove it off the lot, I started to have an issue with the car. The car's alarm would be triggered by me unlocking the driver's side door with the key. An electrical problem that, I was told, would cost almost as much as I paid for the car to fix. This resulted in two solutions: either I unlocked the door and quickly started the car to silence the incessant combination of loud horn and flashing lights, or I would have to unlock the passenger door, which did not trigger the alarm, and climb across it. It was a typical high school car, faulty and deeply loved.

In early September of 2001, after a few weeks of locking myself in my dorm room in between soccer practices and a rigorous new class schedule, my roommate dragged me to my first college party. Admittedly, I wasn't much of a hard-partying person in high school, but I briefly celebrated the idea of reinvention, despite the fact that my college, Capital University, was only a few miles away from my father's home. I would still, largely, be within walls with people who didn't know anything about me. People I'd be spending at least a few years with, and a blank slate to rebuild. The infant stages of college always seemed to be thrilling in this way: after years of observing who you could have been in high school, you can step into it, in front of people who don't know any different.

After a few hours inside, mostly clinging to the safety of a wall, I skipped out of the party, eager to escape a house imprisoned by a thick cloud of body heat and drink in the night air. I rushed to my car and put the key into my driver's side door. Before turning it, I looked around the street where I parked. The towering and expensive homes, the paved sidewalks, the darkness and silence. I opted for what I was sure my father would say was the smarter choice: I unlocked my passenger side door, clumsily climbed across the seats, and started my car. As I put it in drive and began to accelerate, I first saw the police car's lights.

I spend a lot of time trying to pinpoint exactly how fear is learned. Rather, how we decide that fear is a necessary animal that grows out of our relentless expectation to survive at all costs, and how I have been afraid and been feared at the same time. When I reflect, I think the fact that I lived for 17 years without a direct fear of the police makes me lucky. I knew of the warnings from my father: *don't go on a run at night. Don't reach into your pockets too quickly. Be polite in front of them.*

Growing up in the neighborhood I did, police were often present, and yet I never learned to be afraid. Police would drive slow past the basketball courts in summer, scanning the games and the people watching. They would follow my friends and I around corner stores, eyeing our hands and the items in them. I had seen them make life difficult for people in my neighborhood who were not me, and yet I never learned to be afraid. Until the early fall of 2001.

Bexley, Ohio, sits on Columbus's east side. A small and flourishing mostly white suburb that centers on Capital University, it is sandwiched by two significantly poorer, mostly Black neighborhoods, one of them being where I grew up. This has always created an interesting tension within the city, especially as Bexley has expanded on each side in recent years, pushing the poor on its borders further toward the margins. For years, there has been an odd tug-of-war happening between the residents of

Bexley, between their fears and their progressive-leaning stances. For example, the person who punches a Democratic ticket on Election Day might also clutch her purse tighter when walking past a Black person on the street. Because Bexley is a sheltered suburb that is sandwiched between two poor, mostly Black neighborhoods, the residents have a proximity to Blackness that is rooted primarily in a vision of monolithic poverty. This breeds sympathy, for the conditions, but not much interest in actually engaging the people. In 2001, despite Black people pushing against its borders, Bexley remained 90 percent white.

It wasn't always like this. The east side of Columbus was once a place for young Black people to come and flourish. A small-scale Harlem, in some ways: there were nightclubs teeming with jazz players, theaters, block parties, horse races, and a good way for most hard-working folks to make a living. Livingston Avenue and the King-Lincoln Bronzeville district were the city's cultural hubs up until the early 1950s. Columbus, as most cities do, chose construction and convenience over the lives of its Black residents, setting in motion a project to construct the sprawling freeway of Interstate 70, and its sibling, Interstate 670. This demolished much of those communities and pushed the people in them deeper into the southern parts of the city, away from the downtown area, and out of the city's once-thriving center. The clubs and theaters were replaced with bigger houses to lure in more wealthy, white residents who would find themselves working in the new and expanded downtown, or people moving in to have access to the freeway. The Black residents who could stay suffered, losing many of the work opportunities they once had in all of their old haunts, but also too prideful to move homes. This was their neighborhood, after all. That is how Bexley found itself both at the center of two Black neighborhoods, but also built to ignore them.

In 2001, Capital University recruited me to play soccer. They were one of a small handful of schools to do so, as I was a very capable high school soccer player who also didn't have the height to play the position that my skill set most aligned with. Soccer was, admittedly, an interesting choice for me, given my background. Most of the young Black kids in my neighborhood played basketball—a sport I also played, though not nearly as well. I stood out on most soccer fields. I was the only Black player on my select team, even though the team had a Black coach—a detail my father scouted out during the team selection process. I didn't see myself as choosing soccer to be different from my peers, at least not initially. I had a natural skill set that translated well to the sport: a blend of speed and instincts that allowed for a versatility of position, and the coordination and balance to tie every skill together. At 17, with an offer from a college a few miles from my father's house, I didn't consider the idea of existing as Black in a place that historically worked to erase all signs of Blackness from their communities. Bexley was the suburb down the street. A place where the grass was greener. In the late summer of that year, I stepped on the field as the first American-born player of color in the Capital University soccer program's history.

When I hear people talk about "the right things to do" to make sure that police don't kill you, I imagine that I have learned to face police differently than they have. When you are asked to step out of a car that you own, and your body no longer belongs to you, but instead belongs to the lights drowning it, first one and then another, a harsh reality exists. There are two sides of a night that you can end up on: one where you get to see the sunrise again, and one where you do not. You don't exactly consider this in the moment, which I think is important to point out. When demands and questions are being leveled at you, particularly at a high volume, particularly with skepticism in their tone and a light in your eyes, it is easy to fall into an idea of wanting to prove yourself. To reach for anything that might show that you are a whole person and worthy of staying that way. I recall becoming close with fear, with the instinct to stay alive.

That particular night, police officers, first two, and then three more, responded to a call of suspicious behavior. This is where the story becomes unremarkable to many. I was asked to exit my car before I was asked for ID. When I mentioned that this was my own vehicle, I was silenced, held outside of my vehicle by two officers while others huddled around a squad car. When finally asked to produce ID, I reached in my pocket, remembered that it was in my bookbag that I placed in the trunk, and moved to get it. Upon moving, I was grabbed and forcefully held in the grass. People walked from their homes, and I wondered silently which one of them called the police on me. I thought about my pants, now stained by the grass, and how much they cost me. How much the car cost me. How much it cost me to get here, to this college, out of a neighborhood just five miles away that no one on this block would ever venture to. But I mostly thought about how I perhaps owned nothing. Not even my own hands, pressed behind my back.

I was eventually pulled up after what felt like hours, but must have only been five minutes. My car ransacked, my license and college ID eventually located, as the rest of my bookbag's contents spread across the pavement. After the officer stared at my face and stared at my ID repeatedly, he mumbled, "Interesting name. Sorry for the trouble."

After they left, my belongings still scattered in the street, I sat on a curb and watched my hands shake for an hour. No one left their homes to help me or ask if I was okay. No one from the party witnessed the incident. None of the people I wanted to make myself new for witnessed this undoing of pride. It felt, of course, like I didn't belong. Like I was a trespasser, waiting to find my way back to another home.

I have had many interactions with police since 2001, some better, and a few just as bad. In 2008, I was detained in a store for hours, again without a simple ID check, because I "matched the description" of a shoplifter who I looked nothing like. In 2014, I was pulled over in Pennsylvania for not following a law I wasn't aware of. The officer who pulled me over politely explained the law, bantered warmly with me a bit about Ohio, where I was heading, and let me off without a ticket. Like everyone, my interactions with the police exist on a wide spectrum. Unlike everyone, my expectations for interactions with the police only exist on one part of that spectrum: I expect to fear and be feared. But, I have survived every interaction. The difference now is that when I see the news of another unarmed death, a boy who didn't react to orders fast enough, or a man who reacted too quickly, I know how this can happen. I have entered that space and come out through the other side unscathed, but with a new layer of anger, a new layer of fear. The fact that I was afforded survival once used to make this type of death remarkable. Over the years, I find it to be less and less. With each body, I wonder how their stories began. If they began something like mine.

Serena Williams And The Policing Of Imagined Arrogance

BY ALMOST ANY MEASUREMENT, I AM A WHOLLY mediocre basketball player. Good enough to never be picked last, but never good enough to win a game on my own. My greatest on-court skill is not turning the ball over, a skill that I imagine I picked up after playing with two older brothers for over a decade and being afraid to let them down. Mostly, every athletic skill I have is rooted in fear. Which doesn't exactly make me a desirable NBA prospect. None of these facts stopped me last summer in Oakland, after making two jump shots in a pickup game with some fellow writers, from holding my follow through, glaring at my defender, and saying, "I'll be at this all day. You better get a hand up."

I missed every shot I took for the rest of the afternoon, but I say that with the knowledge that it doesn't matter. For those who are well-versed in the language, we know the secret. Trash talking isn't about an individual's ability to be consistently great. If you are from any place in this America where you have seen all breeds of struggle grow until they cloak an entire community, and you are fortunate enough to survive, few things become more urgent and necessary than reminding the world when you're at your best. Because you know how fleeting those moments can be. You've seen how quickly they can vanish.

When I talk about Compton here, I need people to understand it as it once was, and not as the re-imagined area it is slowly becoming as crime rates drop to the lowest they've been in decades, and the wealthy residents who started to flee in the early '90s begin to inch back to the edges of the city. The Compton I need to bring to life here is the one that N.W.A blew the dust off of. An area that we saw in blockbuster movies which often shared a common theme: the Black life who died at the end, usually by the gun, was promising. Or had turned their life around. Or had done "all of the right things" to get out of what we were to understand as an urban killing field.

The Compton that needs to be understood when discussing Serena Williams is the one that America has used so often for entertainment and irony, while simultaneously turning its back on the infrastructural failures that plague so many of the neighborhoods that kids from the suburbs have the luxury to wear on their tongues, and on their bodies, but never in their hearts or minds. The avatar for all things Black and dangerous, both a real place and a vague idea. This is the Compton that briefly held the young Williams sisters, and the Compton that claimed Yetunde Price, Serena's elder half-sister, who was shot and killed after a confrontation in 2003. Though Serena Williams only resided in this Compton for six years, it is perhaps essential in understanding the father who pulled his two daughters from the national junior tennis circuit before they were teenagers, due to white parents talking down to them. It is perhaps essential in understanding the competitive nature of the Williams sisters, though especially Serena. It is ABSOLUTELY essential in understanding how Serena revels in her dominance.

When I talk about crack cocaine in the '80s here, I need people to understand it for what it did to the individual home. Or the individual block of homes. Or the individual Black child. And not so much as the epidemic that is often discussed now in broad-brushed terms, with no eye toward its very real impact. In places like Compton, and places like many I know and have lived, neighborhoods were already swelling with gang violence by the time the '80s hit, even before the introduction of crack cocaine. Once-flourishing industries had long left these areas, leaving whole families without one steady income. Many of the people who were pushing crack were just everyday people, trying to silence a child's cries. Though this didn't stop wars from being fought over territory, over prices, over who got to feed their family and who did not. These things are what our entire American history is littered with. Who will not make it home alive so that someone else can be fed. Still, when it happens in the Black community, it takes on a different idea; a different tone altogether. Everyday people killing everyday people in the hopes of being able to provide for the everyday people who became addicts, not above robbing and killing in order to rest in the comfort of their addiction. It is almost impossible to ignore the governmental root of this cycle, but, while it certainly bears mentioning here, that is a much larger thing to unpack. It is one thing to sit in a movie theater and watch the fragility of Black life play out on a screen in front of you. It is an entirely different thing to sit in a movie theater, watch the fragility of Black life play out on a screen in front of you, and have no escape from it once you leave. It is an entirely different thing to have its presence hang thick over your home, over your young and talented daughters.

I remember the fear I felt when I realized that I had buried enough friends to think of death almost casually. Something that I expect and know will come for people I grew up with and care about. When I see a childhood friend's number flash across my caller ID, I exhale and prepare myself for an all-too-familiar routine. There's a sadness in that, but there's also an urgency. Witnessing the taking of sacred things is how we learn to covet. It is enough to make a father take his children to a place where he is the only one who can fail them.

As someone who observes culture in all of its forms, if the past three years since the death of Trayvon Martin have taught me anything, it's that people have found so many new ways to say "silence." It is what is meant when we look at a peaceful protest and hear people say, "Well, why can't they just do it more peacefully?" It is perhaps what I mean when I look at a text that I am not too keen on returning and text back: "I'll get back to you in the next hour." And it is definitely what is meant when Serena Williams is looked at, careless and immersed in joy, and told, "Be more 'humble'."

There really is no measurement for how America wants its Black athletes to be. Oftentimes, they are asked to both know their greatness and know their place at the same time, a landscape that becomes increasingly difficult to navigate depending on the sport they're in. When Deion Sanders starts high stepping at the 40-yard line, he's still dancing. America has always been fine with its Black athletes doing the dance on the field of their choosing, as long as they do the dance off of it. When Marshawn Lynch doesn't speak to the press, that's when people begin to feel cheated. To be Black and a woman, and a Black woman who is great, and a Black woman who is great at tennis is perhaps the trickiest of all of these landscapes. For many people, the intersection of race and gender is an uncomfortable place, and Serena Williams' greatness sits firmly in the center of it. So much so that any time she wins, there is no way to have a discussion that does not reduce her to her most Black, or her most woman. It isn't always explicit, of course. But one could argue that these things rarely are.

Serena Williams is, almost without argument, one of the greatest athletes of our time. If she was not before, she has cemented herself in that place after her 2015 French Open victory, her 20th major. She did it in a traditional manner, battling back and rallying, using her elite athleticism and strength to overpower and out-hustle her opponent, Lucie Safarova. And she did it with all of the volume and intensity that we've become accustomed to. Serena yelled, both in joy and agony. She pumped her fists, talking confidently to herself when she was most on. Tennis is like few other sports. In most cases, there is only you and a single opponent on an island, sometimes for hours. The mark of greatness in those times is how you sustain, even if you have to celebrate the smallest victories in an attempt to will yourself to the larger one. When we insist that Serena Williams be more reserved, or less "scary," or when we insist that she fit into the mold of decorum that we believe tennis should be, we're really telling her to silence the very things that drive her. We're asking her to not be great so that we can be comfortable. We're telling one of the most dominant athletes many of us will ever see to maybe keep it down a bit, as if any kind of dominance is stumbled upon silently.

When I talk about Serena Williams here, I need people to understand her for where she came from, and not where she is now. Rather, I need people to understand her for what she was born into. I need people to understand both the whole and the sum of her parts. I need people to understand the Compton, the crack cocaine, and the champion. The woman who buried a sister with the same hands she uses to bury opponents. If you do not know what she knows, then you know nothing of the ultimate reward of greatness. The way it feels when every-thing clicks. It is almost unfathomable to tell someone to act like they've been somewhere before when they are intensely aware of the fact that they were never supposed to be there in the first place, isn't it?

And so Serena throws her racket and falls to her knees. And so a little Black girl finds a tennis court on the outskirts of her hood. And so another father finds hope. And so I hit two jump shots in a row in the middle of summer in Oakland. And so I extend my follow through, hold it, and let the breeze blow sweat off of my arm. A reminder of how easily things can be taken from us.

They Will Speak Loudest Of You After You've Gone

WHAT I GOT TO EXPERIENCE IN MOVING TO THE Northeast after living my entire life in the Midwest is the different masks that racism wears. Ohio, in all of its not-quite-South aesthetic, has all of the trappings of bold racism. The obvious type that comes across loud and unapologetic. I was once called a nigger while walking from my high school soccer field. A Black family in a nearby suburb had their house vandalized. Confederate flag stickers were pressed onto bumpers that sometimes revved their engines and yelled at Black kids walking by. There was an understanding that came with the geography, a geography that came with a history of slaves finding their way to freedom along the Ohio River. When you love a place, coming to terms with its lesser qualities and learning to apologize for them is commonplace. My pals who left Ohio for the coasts would come back and talk of how they didn't feel like such a burden, doing more than just surviving and waiting for the next moment of discomfort to rain down from the sky. They had untethered themselves from the comfort of known racism, of knowing who wanted them dead. It was better, they claimed, to live in a place where everyone seemed to welcome your living presence.

The first time I realized I was invisible in my new Connecticut neighborhood, a woman got out of a car with one of those "COEXIST" bumper stickers on them carrying several bags of groceries while talking on her phone. As she approached the bench I was sitting on, she dropped her bags, two of them on my lap. I waited for a moment, but she was unmoved, talking on her phone about Baltimore, a city that, at the time, was in protest, people taking to the streets in the name of Freddie Gray. It was a shame, the woman said to whoever was on the other line of the phone. A shame that police keep getting away with this. I moved her bags from my lap and placed them on the ground in front of me without her even noticing.

Stepping outside my apartment to go to the gym one morning, a man outside of my door, eyeing my apartment building, asked if I knew how much the building was going for. He was interested in moving into the area, looking for a place to live. The building isn't for rent, I told him. People live in the building, I explained, telling him that by "people," I specifically meant "me." He looked me up and down as if seeing me for the first time, taking in my gym shorts, my worn and faded t-shirt, ripe for the trash heap after years of enduring my sweat. "You sure you live here?" he asked. "I thought this space was vacant." When I told him politely that I'd lived there for the past several months, he skeptically started to walk away, glancing back every now and then at me in front of my own door to an apartment that I was paying to live inside of in a city where I barely seemed to exist.

It is summer and white people are sad on the internet about Black people dying again. This time, louder than usual. Everything on social media is in all caps, sometimes with accompanying videos of the deaths in question. In New Haven,

Connecticut, the white woman who cut in front of a young Black girl at the market waves her arms in the air and asks when it all will end, this seemingly endless parade of Black people dying at the hands of the state. At a protest, a white person is all emotion, pulling at his shirt and shouting into a megaphone to a crowd of young people, mostly Black. And everyone is jumping and pointing at the house on fire without considering there are people inside.

I struggle with this, the public grief by white people over Black Death. I have been, and am still, a victim of what my guilt can drive me to. Depending on the day, on the cause, on who I love that might be affected. There is, however, a manner in which this guilt is performed that sets me to wondering what the value of living Blackness is when it rests against white outrage centered on the ending of Black life. It is both essential for us to turn toward our people and ask them to do better, while also realizing that there is a very real currency that comes with being the loudest person to do it in public. It is about going against expectation. I am Black. I am supposed to be sad when the police kill someone who looks like me. I don't gain much by being afraid, because the fear itself has worked its way into me, simply pushing its way to the surface when most appropriate.

I want everyone to be appalled, taken aback by these injustices. A major failing of our ability to process these deaths is that people have, for too long, not allowed themselves to consider the problem as real and systemic. That is the other side of this: my desire for this outrage to exist, even if I think it needs to be reconsidered and perhaps reshaped. What I realize now about my friends who left the shadow of Ohio's sometimes-obvious racism is that they were making themselves comfortable with the silent, liberal racism. The type that sometimes roots itself in faux-concern to present a question of your existence.

It is an odd thing to imagine yourself as someone who may have more value dead, or dying. But surely, if the emotions attached to your vanishing can be currency, isn't your vanishing, itself, something to trade? I don't know what to make of this: the white man who posts on the internet, vigorously, about his disgust with our country's racism. When I approach him about an inappropriate, boundary-crossing behavior, he pretends to not hear me. This is all, it seems, deeper than simply an idea of liberal performance for point scoring. It is the inability to see a body as worthwhile if it doesn't have a value you can trade in on, some sentimental cash out.

I don't want my people to die in order to be loved, or even seen. I understand the type of racism that sits on the coasts now, more than I did before. I'm less afraid of its violence, but more afraid of the toll it takes on the mind and body. How it presents itself unexpected and without awareness, a drunk stumbling home and kicking in your bedroom door before turning on all of the lights. It is troubling to imagine yourself not worth talking about until you are incapable of speaking for yourself, but there is a history of the marginalized being most profitable, or at least easiest to sell, when a hand could be reached into their backs by someone more readily digestible. It was easiest to love Muhammad Ali, for example, as he began to fade. When he was a trembling shell of who he once was. Still proud, but not as loud and boastful as he was in the past. It was easy for some of the racists who perhaps wished him dead in the '60s and '70s to, instead, find him as somewhat warm. In this way, stillness and silence can turn the normally invisible or feared Black person into a sort of mascot.

I suppose it is too much to ask, to be unjustly killed and wish that only the people who truly care about your life speak of the injustice. I think, all the time, about that woman who put her shopping bags on my lap. The man who refused to believe I lived in my neighborhood. The woman cutting in front of the Black girl in line. Surely these are all people who may genuinely feel a type of grief about the loss of Black life, particularly if it's done in a manner that is not just. But it is impossible to not notice the difference in our public mourning. Even the public mourning of a white person who genuinely has a love for Black people who are in or adjacent to their lives. Us, all of us truly in this machine, know that the grief that comes with the killing sits heavy and never leaves. I feel this fear more in my new Northeast home. It is a fear greater than anything I experienced under the cloud of expected Midwestern racism. Here, I can't tell who wishes for me to be gone. Sometimes it's the ones who would mourn for me the loudest.

The state is going to kill Dylann Roof. Dylann Roof walked into a Charleston, South Carolina, church in the early moments of 2015's summer. He killed nine Black churchgoers in hopes of starting a race war. Small Black children had to play dead in order to survive, while their grandmothers were hit with bullets. The night I heard this news, I was traveling by car from New Haven to Illinois. I stopped at a hotel in the northernmost part of Ohio and read the breaking news in my car. Parked next to me was a car with a confederate flag decal in the window, and I wanted to tear it off. In that moment, I wanted Dylann Roof to be dead, in the street. I wanted the police to find him and kill him like they'd killed for less before. I remember this, sitting in my home state, where I was first called a nigger, and scrolling through my phone with unsteady hands, thinking of Black children playing dead and Black people not playing at all. Thinking of fear and prayer and that which will not save us no matter what house we yell God's name into, and I wanted Dylann Roof's death to be immediate then, and buried under the names of everyone's life he cut short.

But that was a long time ago. The state is going to kill Dylann Roof, and my desire for his death has long passed. I don't want him to die unless he can, somehow, carry the insidious spirit of his motivations, which rest deep inside of America's architecture. Everything else feels like the cruel theater of revolving death, which the death penalty often falls into. But I knew what it felt like, for a moment, to wish for a death to cash in on. To want a body as sacrifice, something to help dull the noise, to even a score that could never be evened. I glimpsed, for a small moment, what it must be like to consider someone I didn't know as less valuable living. And the impossible weight of it all.

Johnny Cash Never Shot A Man In Reno. Or, The Migos: Nice Kids From The Suburbs

THERE IS SOMETHING ABOUT CLOSENESS TO THE hood that makes it more appealing. To be Black, and not from the places that some in America imagine All Black People to be from can be interesting, particularly if you live close, or on the border of that space. In the suburb that bordered my decidedly less suburban neighborhood, there was a Black kid or two who would bike the extra blocks into our area, where the houses weren't as big or well-kept. Where the grass was dried and brown, or sometimes there was none at all. The idea was a brief escape, before returning back to the comforts of one's own squalor. I have never imagined this as somehow less Black. Not then, and certainly not now, when I am geographically removed from any hood I held close by miles, and yet still consider myself to be not severed from the cultural roots that I gained there.

I do not know what it is that makes a person real, but I imagine it is in the way they can convince you of the things they have not done. It's a lie we tell ourselves, especially when it comes to our entertainment: we claim we want the real story, told straight, from someone who has actually lived it. That can sell, of course, but only when the living is spectacular. When there is some universal emotion to latch onto. Heartbreak sells, longing sells, desire sells. Violence sells, but mostly when it is a myth. Something invented and then expanded on by the person painting the picture.

In a barbershop tucked into the only Black corner of West Haven, Connecticut, on the week before Migos release *Culture*, their hotly anticipated second studio album, there is a battle raging about authenticity. My barber, always unafraid to run, sword drawn, into a verbal battle about rap music, is yelling. "They're from the suburbs!" he exclaims. "These niggas from the suburbs! They rapping about all this trap shit and they ain't never even been to the trap!"

Migos, a rap group consisting of the rappers Offset, Takeoff, and Quavo, made their name by hustling. Legend has it that in North Atlanta clubs in 2012, they would pay DJs in whatever money they could gather from their parents and have the DJs spin songs from their first mixtape, *Juug Season*. The strategy worked, eventually making them North Atlanta's most prominent party-starters. Their 2013 song "Versace" got a co-sign and remix from Drake, catapulting them directly into rap stardom. Musically, they're more clever and fun than naturally gifted.

They're Future disciples, in some ways, as most Atlanta rappers of their era are, though they run a bit more adjacent to his timeline than some of their younger peers. They are also one of the last rap groups of the past decade to sell records. There is no defined leader of the group, though they all have roles: Quavo is the group's glue, largely due to his ear for melody and ability to pick up the slack on a hook. Offset is the most pure MC, the one who seems to have most studied rappers before him. Takeoff is the group's personality, making up for what he lacks in rapping by providing more thrilling aesthetics. *Culture* is the album that is set to be the group's coronation. The first single, "Bad and Boujee," is the country's number one song. It's being sung in trap houses and in minivans. They have entered into the realm of many rap acts who have had number one songs in recent months: fascination in the suburbs. And in the hood, a gentle resentment.

The thing that most people don't know about Johnny Cash is that he never spent any real time in prison. A few nights here and there, sure. But he never did any hard time the way that his narratives suggest a relationship with not just prisons, but the minds of people inside. It was all tied to country music's outlaw image, something that Cash was a natural fit for in the early stages of his career. In 1951, while serving in West Germany for the Air Force, Johnny Cash saw the movie *Inside the Walls of Folsom Prison*. In the black-and-white movie, prisoners in Folsom Prison attempt to revolt against the cruel and ruthless prison warden. The warden's assistant, in attempts to work toward reforming the prison and making it gentler, is eventually forced out. The movie ends in a riot, where prisoners are beaten, bloodied, and left for dead. The central question of the movie is the one that is still asked today: Is prison simply a place of repeated dehumanization and punishment? Or is it a place where personal change can happen?

Johnny Cash wrote the line "I shot a man in Reno, just to watch him die" in 1954. He recalls coming up with the line after sitting with a pen in his hand and thinking up the worst reason for a person to kill another person. The movie about Folsom still pulled at him, the moral dilemma he felt about punishment pulling him to think up sins so bad they could be deserving of the small hell that prison puts you through. Cash was writing into what he imagined prison life to be, even though, at the time, he was mostly interested in gospel songs. When he first auditioned at Sun Studios, he sang "When The Saints Go Marchin' In," and the story goes that Sam Phillips told him to go home and sin some more until he could come back with a song that could be sold. When looked at through that history, Johnny Cash, a persona from the '50s until he died, makes sense. If the sins don't come to you naturally, you seek them out. You chase them, let them consume you, and the ones you can't touch, you write about like you've lived them.

Cash recorded "Folsom Prison Blues" in 1955, but the song didn't have its signature moment until May of 1968, when Cash released the live album *At Folsom Prison*, to the excitement of his record label, which needed him to get back on track. By 1968, the popularity that Cash had built up in the late '50s and early '60s had started to fade, in large part because of the addiction to drugs Cash acquired. The romantic outlaw image he built during the time was fueled, in part, by a growing addiction to amphetamines and barbiturates, which he first began using to stay awake during tours. It gave birth to a frantic creative output at first, but then burned out, leaving Cash searching for a new direction in the process. When he played at Folsom, he opened his set with "Folsom Prison Blues." The prisoners there were instructed not to cheer at any language in Cash's set that could have been critical of prison life or guards. When he let out the line about shooting a man in Reno, the crowd of inmates was largely silent, afraid to respond. On the record, in post-production, the producer added cheering.

The week that *Culture* drops, I speed out to see Migos play a surprise East Coast show and Offset is making his hands into a machine gun while spitting a rapid-fire shooting sound into the microphone. A banner behind the group reads "NAWF ATLANTA," a small tribute to where they are from. Where they are actually from is Lawrenceville, Georgia, a sleepy suburb just outside of Atlanta's northern outskirts. The kind of place that requires you to name the biggest city it's near when speaking to strangers. *Culture* is everything the hype promised it to be, and more. It is engaging, fun, and full of songs that could be hits, but that also don't sacrifice Migos' roots as a group interested in the club anthem. They have perfected what they've always been able to do fairly well, pulling together a handful of jumbled sounds from various musical elements and condensing them into something catchy in three minutes.

When people bring up the fact that Migos doesn't hail from Atlanta proper, it's signaling some larger criticism about the type of Black people allowed to talk about certain types of things. This is odd, because there is so little to be had in the way of knowledge about their immediate upbringing. They went to a decent high school; Quavo was the school's star quarterback until he dropped out to focus on rapping. Their proximity to Atlanta's street culture afforded them a knowledge of its movements and a language with which to build narratives that sound true, in many ways. They are doing what music has done for years, but what rap's insistence on the idea of realness punishes. They are packaging what sells to people who don't know better, or people who know better but don't mind a gentle lie while the bass floods a room.

In 2015, two months after a fight erupted at a Migos concert leaving six concertgoers stabbed, the group and 12 members of the entourage were arrested at Georgia Southern University for felony possession of narcotics and for carrying a loaded gun on campus. While Quavo and Takeoff were released on bond two days later, Offset remained in custody, with no bond, due to a previous criminal history. The following month, Offset attacked a fellow inmate, causing the inmate severe injury, and inciting a prison riot where prisoners fought each other until guards intervened. The incident was captured on prison security cameras in black and white. It was, some would say, like a scene from a movie.

This is what is *supposed* to make you real, of course. Some blood on the hands you create the music about killing with. The drugs you might have once sold, resting in your pockets. Offset was eventually released on a plea deal in December of 2015, after eight months in custody. The group's songs don't sound any different than they did before he went in. They aren't rougher, or more complex and nuanced. The members of Migos are what they are, and what they've always been. Like Johnny Cash in the middle of the '60s, they spent time getting too close to the fire. It is hard to build a myth so large without eventually becoming part of it.

Rap is the genre of music that least allows for its artists to comfortably revel in fiction, even though all of us know we are watching a performance. So much music is made by someone steeped in persona, building a digestible image. Because of rap's roots, and because so many people who saw it at the start are still alive to turn a critical eye toward it, it comes under fire for turning away from what feels real. Additionally, when Black people singing songs about guns and drugs make it to number one in a country where Black people are arrested and killed for guns or drugs or less than that, it can feel a bit like life as spectacle is more protected than life as a fully lived experience. I understand these things and also say that we've allowed the rappers we grew up with to grow up and still rap about selling drugs with platinum records and sold out tours at their backs, but a suburban zip code is where we draw the line, as if growing up all kinds of Black in all kinds of ways doesn't carry its own unique and varied weight. As if, in the mirror, if you look hard enough, you still don't see yourself as the world sees you.

Culture went to number one on the charts and was released to critical acclaim. It is the album that will do what it was meant to do: make Migos a household name, much to the dismay of my barber, who wishes they didn't feel so fake. But Migos are true to themselves, more than most of their direct peers. Yes, the stories are outlandish and there is the eye-roll that comes with some of the content I come across as I age. But the songs they make are all still with the club in mind. Songs that can be played at the end of a long work week, bass-heavy anthems with catchy choruses that fit into every mouth in the room with ease. I'm less interested in what happens in the hood you're from and I'm more interested in how you can honor that place, especially for people who might not know its history. Migos, more than anything, are still North Atlanta's party starters; now it's the rest of the world that's catching on.

Johnny Cash wore black for entire decades. There was never a performance in his life where he didn't cloak himself in at least some black. He claimed it as a symbol of rebellion; first against a country establishment with singers covered in rhinestones, and then against the hypocrites and in solidarity with the sinners. Johnny Cash, when it was all said and done, finally had enough sins. Real ones, too. Not all sinning ends with blood, which I think he learned too late, after he'd already racked up enough of the big ones to write songs that sold. There's a lesson in that, for those who might want what's real to be tied to what ill one can do to another person. There are few sins greater than the ones we commit against ourselves in the name of others. The things that push us further away from who we are, and closer to the image people demand.

In his final and most iconic music video, for his cover of the Nine Inch Nails song "Hurt," Johnny Cash sits at the head of a table covered in food and riches. It is all very Christ-like. The video was filmed as a race against time, with the 71-year-old Cash declining in health and uncomfortable in the unseasonably cold Nashville weather. The director, Mark Romanek, decided to use the music video as an opportunity to be candid about the state of Cash's health. It is a video filled with humanizing regret and heartbreak. Clips of Cash's earlier career moments juxtaposed with footage of cracked platinum records and an abandoned museum that once bore his name, his longtime wife June, looking at him with both adoration and concern. In a story I read once, Romanek recounts the video's most powerful and unscripted moment. At the end, Cash picks up a glass of wine and spills it all over the feast sitting in front of him at the table before forcefully putting the glass down. Everyone in the room began crying, Romanek said. Cash sat still, looking out of a window, unblinking. Despite wanting to be a man of deeper evil, surviving himself and all of his demons.

June died three months after the video was filmed. Johnny died four months later. He was buried next to her in a black coffin.

Back on stage in New York, Offset yells to the crowd. Something about how good it is to make it out of where they are from alive. The word "from" hangs in the air. The lights fade to black.

The Obama White House, A Brief Home For Rappers

EAZY-E WAS INVITED TO THE WHITE HOUSE BY mistake in March of 1991. It was for a lunch fundraiser being held by then-president George H.W. Bush. Eazy, perhaps in spite of the error, paid $4,000 to attend. This was only a few years after the FBI had set its sights on the members of N.W.A for their album *Straight Outta Compton*, most notably for the song "Fuck The Police." George Bush, a law and order Republican, was holding the dinner for a group called the Republican Senatorial Inner Circle. Eazy-E arrived in a suit jacket, with his signature L.A. Kings hat on his head, curled hair spilling from its edges.

I remember the moment as a news clip only. I watched as a child who only knew that Eazy-E was a part of a rap group that scared people. But there he was, in the White House, with businessmen, senators, and a president who would likely prefer his music to be banned. It was, at the time, a rare access granted to any rapper, but especially one who was seen as too intense for even some of rap's younger, more eager fans. Not everyone was impressed. In the diss track "No Vaseline," Ice Cube opens the final verse, repeating the same line, a thinly veiled shot: "I'd never have dinner with the President / I'd never have dinner with the President / I'd never have dinner with the President."

In the photo that surfaced just a few days before he stepped out of the White House for the final time and left us to our wreckage, Barack Obama is surrounded. At first glance, it is hard to make him out among the mass of familiar faces: Busta Rhymes, Chance The Rapper, J. Cole, Alicia Keys, Common, Wale, DJ Khaled, Pusha T, Rick Ross, and Janelle Monáe, among a few others. What struck me as the best part of the photo were the looks sported by everyone other than Obama himself. A couple of the rappers chose suits, sure. But some, like Ludacris, chose to be dressed down in a sweatshirt and sneakers. Even the ones that chose to be in nicer clothing had their own signature touches: Rick Ross letting his dress pants spill into a pair of black Adidas, Ludacris in a pair of Jordans, Chance in his signature baseball hat. The conversation that was happening in the photo was one of comfort. Coming as you are, not in defiance or spectacle, as Eazy-E did in 1991, to sit and smile in the faces of those who wished Eazy-E to be anywhere but smiling in their faces. There is certainly a power in that, but the door that Barack Obama pushed open for rappers to be seen and comfortable in his White House presented a new type of power dynamic.

The optics of equality, though not doing the same work as actual measures of equality, mean something. Particularly to any people who have been denied access or visibility, or any people who were made to feel like the work they created was not worthy of equal consideration in the eyes of the country it was created in. The history of Black people in the White House is weighted primarily in positions of servitude, or performance. Recently, of course, Black artists and athletes have been invited as distinguished guests, but few like Eazy-E. There is a lot to be said for the river of quality Black art that pushed forward during the Obama administration, particularly during the second half of his time in office, after the shine of the first four years wore off. And though I'm not entirely sure that the right thing to do is tie that art to Obama himself, he made a fascinating companion to the times. What Black people always understood about Obama that often got lost in non-Black analysis of him was the immense difficulty in being the most visible man in the world *and* operating in a way that was often unafraid to nod to Blackness, even clumsily. I am not speaking in political moments here, but in aesthetics presented to a people who craved glimpses of a Black president who, at his most comfortable, was unafraid to briefly talk like our friends or family might talk around a card table. A Black first lady who, in public, would be unafraid to cut a look at someone that would both cause us to laugh and send us a chill, a look that we understood. One passed down from some universal Black ancestor who we all knew.

Even with the aesthetics that nod to a celebration of Blackness that Black people could latch on to, Barack Obama has, also, never been nearly as cool as we've imagined him to be or wanted him to be. Some of that, of course, is due to the constraints of the office. And some of it is, of course, due to the fact that he's a generation or two ahead of us, and one can lead while facing the youth and still look uncool when they turn away from them to face the nation at large. But, even if we imagined it as something greater, Barack Obama's connection to rap music and rap artists always felt logical. Not necessarily because of his race, but because of how he always seemed to carry himself with the charisma and understanding of the stage that an MC has. By this, I don't mean to sell the idea that Barack Obama could be a rapper; more the idea that his understanding of cadence, tone, and crowd control always felt rooted in rap music, which is rooted in a Black oral tradition. People telling stories around porches, and then to instruments, and then to beats. It's why his biggest moments on stage often carried gestures or language with a similar swagger. You could feel it in '08, when he brushed dirt off of his shoulders while a crowd erupted around him. Or when, during the first presidential visit to Jamaica in 32 years, he smiled while waiting for the audience to settle before shouting, "Wha Gwan, Jamaica!" into the microphone, causing the audience to burst into laughter. Or when he dropped the microphone on the floor of the White House during his final correspondent's dinner, two fingers pressed to his lips. It was always there, the promise of the Obama Moment that we could watch and see ourselves in.

For all of the talk about how art can open the human spirit up to empathy, years of Black people rapping about what is happening in their communities hasn't exactly softened much of America's response to those communities or the people in them. This is most disappointing because rap was born out of and directly into a political moment, and the genre, through its decades of growth, hasn't turned away from the core idea of archiving life as a political action. Rap has been a genre of speaking directly to politicians, though rarely to their faces. N.W.A weren't the first rappers to be feared, but they surely incited a widespread panic among the government and government agencies who felt threatened by the group's message. For all of its political motivations, rap's relationship with actual, real politicians has been spotty at best, especially when considering the currency gained by infamy, across almost all musical genres. To provoke someone in power enough that they call for your music to be banned was rap's greatest trick, especially in the late '80s and early to mid-'90s, when the government was easiest to provoke into such responses. It didn't take rappers long to realize that their particular brand of storytelling wasn't the type that could gain sympathy or understanding from white people in power, so why not play into the inevitable fear? When people in power who enforce and back violent policies pretend that the "rawness" of rap makes its creators less human, there is no use in imagining much of a bridge. The question isn't about the obscene, but more what obscenities people are comfortable crawling into bed with.

Obama, as much as we sometimes imagined him otherwise, was a politician. He was an American President, which means that he was tied into all of America's machinery, which means that he was operating with a proximity to some level of violence at all times. But he was more than this, too, a complex and full-storied person. The problem with the way visible and complicated people of color and their histories are approached by the world around them is that they are, all too often, not afforded the mosaic of a full and nuanced history. If, in a song, a rapper has lyrics about enduring or even delivering violence, one might not think them as worthy enough to have any concerns about violence in their communities. It's one of the many fatal flaws of politics: not trusting those who are either living or archiving an experience to know what might be best for that lived experience.

To see Barack Obama throw open the doors to Jay Z and Beyoncé was encouraging, but expected. I was most encouraged to see Barack Obama continually swing the door open or give nods to rappers like Kendrick Lamar and Pusha T, rappers who have lyrics that still cause panic among some of the suits in Washington. To do this, knowing that it would open him up to the most predictable and worst kind of criticism: stale readings of rap lyrics by conservative pundits looking to discredit both the president's commitment to politics and his commitment to their imagined American culture. Conservative pundits who, perhaps, once purchased drugs from drug dealers, now decrying the past drug dealers on television. Obama being a politician meant that a part of this was also performance, of course. But he didn't ever appear to only entertain rappers. He listened to them: Macklemore on addiction, Black youth and criminal justice with Kendrick Lamar and J. Cole. The seat that was given at the table was more than just an idle seat. It was one that put artists in a room where they could be heard.

What strikes me most is that it may never be like this again. When I am asked what I will miss most about Barack Obama, especially when thinking about facing down the coming years, I'm sure I'll manage to think up something greater than the fact that he let rappers into the White House. I'm sure I'll miss watching him in front of a crowd when he was on, and he knew he was on. The way he'd lean slightly away from the microphone and let a smile creep in while being bathed in some hard-earned spectacular applause from an audience full of people who knew that they were watching someone who could get them to commit to nearly anything. I'll miss the way he looked at Michelle. Rather, the way they looked at each other, like no one else was watching them. I'll miss the shots of him playing basketball in sweatpants and a tucked-in shirt, a reminder that he was, indeed, never as cool as I wanted him to be. But I'll remember the door held open for rap and all of its aesthetics somewhere along the line, as the funding for the arts are drained, and the environment speeds toward unchecked disaster, and as we take to the streets again, weary, but willing to fight all of these things and more. I'm sure I'll remember it as rap shifts back into an even more contentious state with politics, and as dinner with the president becomes once again an item of shame and ridicule. I am afraid and do not know what is coming next, but I am almost certain it will not be all good. But above my desk now, a picture of Barack Obama, surrounded. Rappers on every side of him, dressed however they chose to dress. Rappers with their honest songs about the people who live and die in places often used as political talking points, standing proud in front of their proud president. All of those smiling Black people in the Oval Office. Miles away from a past where none of them, I imagine, ever thought they'd get to make it this far.

The White Rapper Joke

IN THE MUSIC VIDEO FOR THE 1991 3RD BASS SIN-
gle "Pop Goes The Weasel," MC Serch and Pete Nice are beating an actor playing Vanilla Ice with baseball bats. The actor,
with large blond hair and Vanilla Ice's signature American Flag
track jacket, collapsed on the ground moments earlier. Serch
and Pete Nice become more aggressive, swinging the bats down
with a type of fervor only reserved for the movies. The song
"Pop Goes The Weasel" is a song aimed at the rapid commercial
shift happening in rap. The first wave of rap's commodification
was starting at the dawn of the '90s, when aspects of it were
becoming less feared and easier for white people to digest, in
part because of pre-packaged megastars like MC Hammer and,
of course, Vanilla Ice. 3rd Bass, a celebrated underground group
from Queens, seemed to be fed up with the rapidly changing
landscape. And so, the actor playing Vanilla Ice is curled on the
ground and we are to believe he is being beaten within an inch of
his life. There is no actor in the video playing MC Hammer. He
is not also on the ground being beaten with bats, though he is as
much a part of this song's narrative as Vanilla Ice is. Both manufactured, with somewhat fabricated histories, created to push
into the mainstream and spread their shadows over everything
they could so that white mothers in the suburbs might think of
them as "fun, wholesome rap music," and feel more justified
wagging their fingers at the other stars of the genre. The fiction-
al attack that 3rd Bass is playing out in the music video, when
looked at through this lens, feels like a type of retaliation.

The joke is that MC Serch and Pete Nice are also white. White rappers taking a bat to a white rapper at a time when the need to separate their whiteness from his was urgent. White rappers fighting to save the world from other white rappers in the name of real hip-hop. The other joke, if you look closely enough, is that the only Black member of 3rd Bass was the DJ. His face wasn't on the cover of the group's debut album. In the second album cover he is there, in the back.

The funny thing about Eminem is that me and my crew fucked with him because he talked that reckless shit like the white boys we'd known from a few blocks over who would scream at their mothers. One of them, Adam, punched his daddy one day, right there on the front lawn of his house. And his daddy didn't even do anything except cover his face and shake his head and tell Adam that he was sorry for not letting him use the car. On the eastside where me and my boys were from, if you raised your hand to your father, you wouldn't be raising it to anything else for at least a few weeks. There is a level of danger that proximity to whiteness makes thrilling, when taken in from afar. Knowing that you could never survive it, or even attempt it in your own life. Eminem was rapping directly into that proximity. For the Black kids in the hood, he gained a type of credibility for the ruthlessness and carelessness with which he regarded human life, particularly his own. We understood nihilism, and a desire for exit. We understood anger, angst, bitterness, and the rage that fueled it. What we didn't understand was a way to express what we understood and walk away unscathed. Eminem's fantasies often involved the blood of people who were living, and it must be funny to be on the other side of a fantasy about death.

Expressive and detailed anger is a luxury. Eminem found a way, despite all of his aggression, to turn most of his rage toward pop stars. Christina Aguilera, NSYNC, Britney Spears,

Mariah Carey. In his videos, he would mock them while wearing plain white t-shirts to complement his blond hair, sometimes patted down with gel. It was another example of trying to swallow what you might not want to be associated with. Eminem looked, some days, like he could be right there in a boy band: white and welcoming, his most rugged edges only existing when he began speaking or rapping. Eminem's biggest and best gimmick was about hiding his relentless desire to be separate from the pop establishment while still playing into the hands of it.

The genre was ready for a white rapper again, after the mid-'90s didn't provide much in the way of white rappers that could be taken seriously in the mainstream. In the underground, absolutely. El-P and Atmosphere were starting exciting careers, but didn't have any intention to break into the mainstream. Rap fans, a growing portion of them white, seemed to be eager for someone in the mainstream who looked like them. The white kids at my public school in the late '90s would complain about *The Source Magazine*, how it had Black rappers on the cover every month. *When can I see someone on a magazine that looks like me?* they would ask. Whenever I tell that part of the story, people can't stop laughing. Eminem came with controversy, cosigns, and actual ability. His face was enough to get him into suburban households, and the window he offered into a danger with no repercussions let him into the hood. He was built for superstardom, and his rejection of mostly white pop stars and violent threats against their harmless masses completed the allure. He was a classroom bully. He was living out a type of white fantasy that the more liberal of us would shout down if it happened to be in a suit, in a boardroom, or in the White House. The fantasy of being able to say whatever you want, with no respect for the masses, with the masses rarely wanting you silenced.

Listening to Eminem was like watching my white friend Adam cuss out his parents in broad daylight. Thrilling at first, but then, as I got older, more troubling. I stopped fucking with Adam when he brought a knife to school and threatened a teacher. He got suspended for two days a week after my boy Kenny from the eastside got expelled for having a small bag of weed in his pocket. I stopped fucking with Eminem when he couldn't stop making rape jokes in his rhymes as he approached 40 years old. There is a time when all of us have to reevaluate the distance we actually have from dangerous moments. Eminem has a distance that never runs out. A distance that only grows wider. And there are those who would call him edgy for not realizing this, while ignoring those who realize that their proximity to danger is a lot slimmer, and yet they've still found a way to stay alive. No one finds this funny.

At the Machine Gun Kelly concert in Cleveland, Ohio, he plays a Bone Thugs-N-Harmony song over the loudspeaker. It is an homage to the city's rap pioneers. Machine Gun Kelly wasn't born here, but he was made here, in Ohio's hopeless northeast corner. He is on the verge of a record deal at the time of this concert, Bad Boy Records winning the bidding war for his services. Tonight is a celebration of sorts. Machine Gun Kelly, on sight, is more punk than anything: tonight, his thin white frame is cloaked in a red leather jacket, open to reveal his shirtless chest, covered in tattoos. The Black people I know in the area haven't entirely found themselves invested in the rise of Machine Gun Kelly, feeling that there are Black rappers in the city who were more skilled, and I think they're right. But the buzz of the skinny white kid from the east side of Cleveland had made it down to Columbus, so I wanted to see him for myself. During his set so far, he's had Black people on stage with him, backing him up, accessorizing his raps about their neighborhood and the interior violence of it. He sounds, at times, like a tour guide, performing for this largely white crowd in a Black neighborhood.

At a show that most of the neighborhood's population couldn't afford tickets to even if they wanted to go.

The Bone Thugs song that he instructs the DJ to play over the loudspeaker is "Thug Luv," the 1997 song featuring Tupac, most notorious for its instrumental that is peppered by the sound of a gun cocking and firing on every seventh and eighth count of the beat. The song opens with Tupac, boastful and proud: "It's time to slay these bitchmade niggas," he shouts. And, on stage, Machine Gun Kelly steps from behind the mic while his mostly white audience shouts out every word. His Black accessories behind him, trying to laugh.

I loved Bubba Sparxxx because he felt genuine. I once watched a rodeo in Bubba's hometown of LaGrange, Georgia. I ate a funnel cake and let the powder from it coat my dark pants, like everyone next to me. During a break in the performance, a group of rodeo clowns came out and lip synced to Bubba Sparxxx's hit song "Ugly" and some people in the crowd square danced. *Deliverance* is one of the few albums by a white rapper that doesn't feel like it's trying to be anything other than what it is. In LaGrange, there are mostly dirt roads. I wore white sneakers that were cloaked in brown within two hours walking around the city. There is the kind of poverty that makes racism easy to bury underneath the performance of shared struggle. In LaGrange, Black people and white people sit on porches, or take to fields with shotguns to hunt for pleasure. In the home of an old Black man, I saw the heads of three deer hanging on a wall. He would have more, but he ran out of room, he told me.

Deliverance gets lost in the discussion of great albums by white rappers because it came a couple of years after "Ugly" and Sparxxx's biggest entry into relevance, but also because it felt so inaccessible to anyone who hadn't touched their feet to the ground in the South. It's an album about survival, success, and facing rural poverty. Bubba Sparxxx is, in many ways, LaGrange, Georgia, personified. Eminem felt like Detroit in some ways, yes. But Detroit wasn't small enough to be singular. LaGrange is the real South, the kind that our grandparents would talk about in the East, in the Midwest. The South where time has frozen, and where stories of making it are currency. Bubba was able to make the South a living, breathing entity that didn't feel manufactured. In a way that someone like, say, Yelawolf, later failed to do. The second song on *Deliverance* is "Jimmy Mathis," where Bubba raps over a banjo and harmonica: "I'm rappin' tonight / but as soon as the light hit / I'm all about the green man / to hell with this white shit." And the joke here is harder to find, but I think it's that money knows no color, but our ability to reach it knows every color, every boundary imaginable.

Deliverance was critically acclaimed, but didn't even get close to going gold. No one, it seemed, was ready for an album by a white rapper with an overwhelmingly thick Southern accent that was drowning in bluegrass instrumentals and stories about mud, shacks, and drinking cheap beer when something better is desired. Bubba disappeared shortly after.

My friends say they wish white rappers would write songs facing their own communities instead of pulling a white lens over our own communities. I ask them what we do if the communities intersect. My friends say that more white rappers should write about the spaces Black people in the hood don't know as intimately as the hood. I play *Deliverance* for them.

No, they say. Not like that.

The thing that should crack me up about Paul Wall is that my homies all thought he was Black for a year until we saw his face in a Mike Jones music video. When we finally did, after a year of only listening to songs from the Houston mixtape circuit, we gazed upon his low fade, his white face, his diamond-encrusted teeth. It never occurred to us that he didn't look the way we looked, and everyone in the room laughed. I didn't laugh. I couldn't figure out if the joke was on me or on him.

Some facts about Asher Roth. Asher Roth never sounded as much like Eminem as people would have you believe when we first heard him. Asher Roth pretended to love college to sell records but never finished college in real life. Asher Roth got his song played at house parties but no one listened to his album. Which is probably fine because it got panned by critics for being frat boy navel-gazing. Asher Roth was never in a fraternity, but he looks like he could be. Asher's first album was the most boring album about partying ever recorded. Sounded like it was written by someone who had never actually spent any time at a party. Maybe that's true. It's hard to talk about wild parties stretching long into the night when you'd rather just get high and fall asleep watching old cartoons. I don't know that from experience. Speaking of getting high, another fact about Asher Roth is that he started rapping like we all knew he could when he grew his hair out and found better weed. In 2009, he was the only white rapper on the cover of *XXL Magazine*'s annual Hip Hop Freshman Class cover, the best class in the cover's history. Critics loved him at first because he was really excited about being white. But not in the way that white supremacists are excited about being white. He just really liked polo shirts and button-ups underneath sweaters. He looked like a guy you could bring home to parents who live in a house with more than two bathrooms. Jay Z could've signed Asher Roth to Def Jam but instead he signed Pittsburgh Slim. Pittsburgh Slim is also white. A true fact is that it is legally impossible for one rap label to sign two white rappers at the same time without a juke joint in a Black neighborhood being replaced by a Seattle's Best coffee shop. Pittsburgh Slim made one shitty album on Def Jam and then got dropped from the label. Just another in the long line of bad decisions made by Jay Z during his tenure as president of Def Jam Records. Asher Roth signed to Universal Motown and they made him wear sweatshirts with the word "COLLEGE" across them in white letters. They made him show up to radio stations with pre-written freestyles. They made him rap about things that they thought might be relatable to young Black people. That's how the bad album about partying happened. The joke is about how Motown used to spend the '60s selling Black artists to white people. Asher Roth was dropped by Universal Motown and didn't make another studio album until 2014. His hair is long and red now. He looks like he should be playing bass in a metal band. *RetroHash* was one of 2014's best albums. It was all about getting high and watching cartoons. No one listened to it. Saw him in 2015 at some festival and a drunk white woman kept yelling at him to play the college song. He never did.

The thing is that I don't think Macklemore feels bad about getting a Grammy. I don't particularly need Macklemore to feel bad about getting a Grammy, but I especially don't need him to convince me that he feels bad about having one. On the day after the 2014 Grammy Awards, Macklemore started his redemption tour, attempting to show the world how sorry he was for winning the best rap album Grammy for *The Heist*. An album that was certainly not the best up for the award, but also certainly not the worst. That he beat out the singular *good kid, m.A.A.d city,* released by Kendrick Lamar, was his biggest burden. Macklemore is the Great White Artist of Burdens. I love him most when he isn't taking himself seriously, but I think he is at his most comfortable when he's taking himself seriously. When he is, at all times, reflecting on the overwhelming feeling of his whiteness and analyzing each corner of guilt that it causes him.

I am sure that there is a place for this, the reveling in guilt for what is afforded to you due to race. It doesn't speak to me, but I know white people who value Macklemore facing them and challenging them. This makes me feel guilty for just wanting him to make songs where he isn't lecturing me on the world that I already understand. It is a hard market for a white rapper who seems deeply invested and interested in anti-racist work. A Black fanbase will undoubtedly show up for the party and leave for the preaching, and a white fanbase will endure the preaching for as long as they can in order to get to the party. What got lost in Macklemore's Grammy hand-wringing is that *The Heist* was, in fact, a good album. It was quirky and odd, but also insightful and honest. It got weighed down a bit by the well-meaning but painfully clumsy marriage equality anthem "Same Love" being its biggest hit, but it offered enough in the way of fun to offset failures in nuance. Macklemore is a more than adequate rapper, his delivery rarely rising above a soothing rasp. He stacks rhymes in a way that would imagine him in the lineage of rappers who truly listened to rap during its '90s heyday. He isn't a great lyricist, but makes up for it with his ability to build a large world in a small amount of time. He's also an engaging live performer, spastic in all of the best ways, unashamed of making a fool out of himself for the greater good of the audience. *The Heist* was the fully realized version of all the music before it, the mixtapes that fell short due to unfocused narratives and a lack of fully formed production. On *The Heist,* the fun served as a complement to the heaviness, which he often times snuck in. "Thrift Shop," as a flawed but enjoyable anti-capitalist ode for affordable clothes shopping. "White Walls" is an anthem for a Pacific Northwest late-night ride-out. During his verse, it's nearly impossible to not laugh when Macklemore, while describing the Cadillac he desires, raps: "I'm from Seattle / there's hella Honda Civics / I couldn't tell you about paint either."

"Same Love" was a blessing for Macklemore's career, but a curse for Macklemore's worldview. It propelled *The Heist* to double-platinum status, a gift for an artist who had done the work of rising through Seattle's underground rap scene. People decided he was important. White people, almost all straight, declared him a beacon of light, an indication of where rap could be going. A "more tolerant and accepting" genre was on the horizon, with Macklemore as its leader. For a few months, the most talked about rapper in the world was white again, and unlike when this had happened in the past, the white rapper met this with conflict. I sometimes think that if Macklemore were either cooler or willing to play cooler, the backlash wouldn't have been as severe. Black people, who were initially open to embracing him, turned on him heaviest when he took what many of us saw as Kendrick Lamar's Grammy award. People in queer communities felt justified frustration at him being the face of their narratives. He was, briefly, a white rapper with only an overwhelmingly white audience in love with him. It seemed unheard of, not seen since Vanilla Ice. On the cover of *The Source* magazine at the end of 2013, he sneered in a brown blazer and a brown suede hat. The cover read: "AMERICAN HUSTLE: 2013's Man Of The Year." In a corner store, I stared at the cover and remembered, vaguely, the white kids in my high school who dreamed of this day. A white rapper, once again gracing the cover of a rap magazine.

All backlash creates an adjustment, and then new backlash. Sometime in between 2014 and 2016, Macklemore decided that since he had the attention of white people, he was going to start telling them about themselves. It was an exhausting undertaking, an exercise that almost certainly would play out better in a living room than on an album. But 2016's *This Unruly Mess I've Made* is jarring in its inability to get out of its own way. The first song, "Light Tunnels," is another seven minute apology for winning a Grammy. "Growing Up" is an awkward open letter to his new child. The album shifts rapidly from confrontational to apologetic, with Macklemore taking aim at his white fans, and then turning to the imagined Black fans to apologize for his whiteness. From the standpoint of someone who already understands racism, the album, anchored by the nearly nine-minute "White

Privilege II" is a task. Critics panned it, and it sold over a million copies less than Macklemore's previous effort.

You can, in this way, make an argument about Macklemore being the greatest mainstream white rapper of all time, because he was the one most unafraid to sever himself from the comfort of the fame he gained making Black art. Being white and profiting off of rap music has never been about skill as much as it is about what can and can't be sold. If you can both win over white audiences and trick the Black ones for long enough, the formula works. The white rapper joke began when Vanilla Ice was corny enough to be hated but not too corny to sell records, and it has evolved to rest at the feet of Macklemore. The ultimate white rapper joke is the white rapper who never wanted to be as famous as he ended up being, but couldn't help having it happen due to his country's endless desire for a white face to save everything, even one of the last genres to not be stolen from the people who built it, despite attempts from all angles. What Macklemore didn't embrace was the thing that Eminem embraced before him: if you are in a system that will propel you to the top off of the backs of Black artists who might be better than you are, no one Black is going to be interested in your guilt. It has played out in every genre since the inception of genre, or since the first song was pulled by white hands from wherever a Black person sang it into the air. No one knows what to make of the guilt. Some rap fans would prefer that Macklemore never rap again. Some would prefer that he rap only directly to white people about whiteness, but that seems to make him less of a rapper and more of a pastor with a thinning audience. Not to mention, his political knowledge, while evolving, isn't such that he can lead a movement.

But the joke is this: every white rapper is the whole of the white rappers that came before them, because when there are so few of you, it becomes easy to avoid falling into the same patterns. Macklemore did what I would have hoped he would have done, even if he did it painfully and with a tone of self-congratulation. What no other white rapper was able to do before him. He stopped just apologizing for what he imagined as undeserved fame and instead weaponized it, losing fans in the process. The major function of privilege is that it allows us who hold it in masses to sacrifice something for the greater good of pulling up someone else. Macklemore, whether intentionally or not, decided to use his privilege to cannibalize whiteness, tearing at his own mythology in the process. When I saw him last year at a festival, he performed "White Privilege II" to a captivated white audience. Halfway through the song, he left the stage entirely empty, walking off and making room for two Black poets and a Black drummer to read poems about police violence and gentrification. It was a stunning image, an artist holding the mouth of his audience open and forcing the slick red spoonful of medicine down their throats.

I don't think this is heroic as much as I think it is necessary. But anyway, this was never about heroes. My heroes are the backpack MCs who made a lane for white rappers to hone their skills enough to get record deals, leaving them behind in the process. But you've been waiting for the punchline, and here it is: in a country that wanted more than anything for him to be the man to lead rap into something they imagined to be better, Macklemore chose to instead make himself a man without a country.

And isn't that funny.

On Future And Working Through What Hurts

MY MOTHER DIED AT THE BEGINNING OF SUMMER. What this meant, more than anything, was that I didn't have school or some other youthful labor to distract me from the grieving process, which during the summer felt long, and slow. In past summer months, when I would be home from school, my mother would be the one who would often come home from work first. It took a while, after she died in June, to get used to not hearing her car pull into the driveway, the tires kicking the gravel along the glass windows of the basement, where my friends and I would be camped out, spending time watching TV or shooting on imaginary hoops. She was a naturally loud woman, so her arrivals were often loud, anchored by some warming noise: a laugh, or a shuffling of groceries, or a walk that echoed through the old hallways of our old house. The real grief is silence in a place where there was once noise. Silence is the hard thing to block out, because it hovers, immovable, over whatever it occupies. Noise can be drowned out with more noise, but the right type of silence, even when drowning, can still sit inside of a person, unmoving.

By the time I started high school in the summer after my mother's death, I was so wound up from sitting largely stagnant in my own sadness for three months, I didn't know how to re-enter a world in which I had to sit and face people on a daily basis. I fought, I found myself consistently suspended, I was the student that teachers threw their hands up about, confused. It was very out of character for me, but I was rebelling against the feeling of anything but grief. When you allow something to grow a shadow at your back, anything that distracts you from it is going to need severing. I think, perhaps, that the key is never letting the sadness grow too large.

In 2014, Future began a run of production that rap had rarely seen. Starting with *Honest*, he released three studio albums and five mixtapes in the span of two years. The start of the run coincided with the crumbling of Future's personal life. The first album of the stretch, *Honest*, was released in April of 2014, a month before Future's son was born with singer Ciara, and four months before Ciara called off their engagement, separating Future from his son, also named Future. Allegations of cheating followed, and within months, Ciara was removing a tattoo of Future's initials from her hand, tattoos that the couple had gotten together shortly after falling in love. It was an intense and public collapse, with Ciara and Future both responding subtly, and then not-so-subtly to the relationship's end. Ciara, less than a year after the split, was in a public relationship with Seattle Seahawks quarterback Russell Wilson, while Future, it seemed, was growing increasingly frantic, detached, and brilliantly productive.

The crown jewel of Future's run is 2015's *Dirty Sprite 2*, which serves as the perfect companion to *Honest* and stands as one of rap's darkest breakup albums. On the surface, it's simply haunted and paranoid: the artist stumbling through descriptions of various drug-fueled exploits. The title itself derives from the mix of clear soda and codeine cough syrup, Future's drug of choice. But it is more than simply several odes to a vice; it's a discussion of the vice as a way to undo memory. There is still the boastful Atlanta hustler persona that Future cultivated on his past albums, but there's also an exhaustion present. On the song "Groupies," he groans through a chorus of "now I'm back fucking my groupies" in a way that sounds like he'd rather be anywhere else.

The reason *Dirty Sprite 2* is such a brilliant breakup record is that it doesn't directly confront the failing of a relationship, but intimately details the movements of what that failure turned an artist into. It is misery as I have most frequently seen Black men experiencing their misery, not discussed, pushed into a lens of what will drown it out with the most ferocity. Future, in a year, watched a woman he loved leave him with their child, and then find public joy with someone else, while he wallowed, occasionally tweeting out a small bitter frustration about the newfound distance. There are as many ways to be heartbroken as there are hearts, and it is undeniable that it is exceptionally difficult to be both public-facing and sad. Future's golden run was born out of a desire to bury himself. Rather, a desire to be both seen and unseen.

All of the albums released from 2014–2016 were released to both critical and commercial success, which made the run even more stunning. Future wasn't just creating throwaway works to help forget about his sadness. *Dirty Sprite 2* went platinum. *What A Time To Be Alive*, a 2015 collaborative mixtape where Future outshined Drake at every turn also debuted at #1 on the Billboard chart. 2016's *Evol* also topped the charts. In between, there were the mixtapes: *Beast Mode* and *56 Nights* in 2015, *Purple Reign* in 2016.

All of them ruminated on the same handful of emotions, reveled in the same methods of darkness and escape. I guess, when you work so hard to dodge the long arms of grief, it is impossible to allow all of grief's stages to move through you. It is difficult to talk about Future's run without also talking about what the end looks like, or if it will end. He seems to be reaching toward an inevitable collapse. All of us can only outrun silence for so long before we have no option but to face it. I think of this as I turn the volume up on *Evol* the week after it comes out, an album that deals in all of the various and dangerous forms that love can take. It seems like a small shift in a different direction for Future, who seemed to be sliding back in a more confident, recovering persona. A month after the release of *Evol*, Ciara and Russell Wilson announced their engagement.

What often doesn't get talked about with real and deep heartbreak after a romantic relationship falls apart is that it isn't always just a single moment. It's an accumulation of moments, sometimes spread out over years. It is more than just the person you love leaving; it's also seeing them happy after they've left, seeing them beginning to love someone else, seeing them build a life that you perhaps hoped to build with them. Sometimes it isn't as easy as unfollowing a person on social media to not see these moments. When it is present and unavoidable, there have to be other ways of severing emotion from memory. In a 2016 *Rolling Stone* interview, Future tells the interviewer that he spends most of his days in a dark recording studio, hours with codeine and a notebook, until he loses track of time. It walks a line between punishment and survival, like so many tools of escape do. So many of Future's songs since Ciara left him are about how much excess he can absorb until everything around him rings hollow, and I suppose this is maybe a better option than albums directly attacking Ciara's new life. It strikes me as Future understanding that, in some ways, he deserves where he ended up, and the work, the codeine-fueled brilliance, is how he is paying his penance while also trying to never be caught by any single emotion.

It is easy to think of anything that makes you feel better as medication, even if it only makes you feel better briefly, or even if it will make you feel worse in the long run. In my high school years, after my mother was gone, I watched my father run himself into the ground. In part, due to necessity: two high school-aged children, active in sports, caused him, as a single parent, to be in several places at once. But he was (and is) also, by nature, someone who takes immense pride in labor, and this heightened when he seemed to be coping with the death of his wife. At a traffic light on the way home from a soccer practice in 1999, two years after my mother died, my father fell asleep in the driver's seat of the car. The light turned green, and cars behind us honked, eventually jarring him awake. I remember staring at him, the glow of the red light bleeding into the car and resting on his briefly sleeping face. I remember thinking that, instead of waking him up, I should let him rest. That maybe, what we see when we close our eyes is better than anything the living world could offer us in our waking hours. I imagine this is why Future has become obsessed with losing track of time. It is hard to keep missing someone when there's no way to tell how long you've been without them. When everything blurs into a singular and brilliant darkness.

POSTSCRIPT:

It is February 2017 and I am crying in the John Glenn Columbus International Airport in my hometown of Columbus, Ohio. It could be the lack of sleep. I just got off of a plane from San Francisco, a city I flew out of at midnight after flying in less than 24 hours earlier. I am back in Columbus for less than 24 hours to do a reading, and then I am flying back to Los Angeles. It is a wretched schedule, one that has caused many of my friends to put their hands on my face and ask me if I'm doing okay, and I am not really, but I smile and shrug and tell them I'll see them soon. I'm holding a newspaper with my face on it. It is the *Columbus Dispatch*, my hometown's biggest newspaper. I learned to love reading at the feet of this newspaper. As a child, I would unravel it on Sundays and hand my brother the comic section while I read the ads, the obituaries, the box scores. I am in it because I answered questions to a kind interviewer about a book of poems I wrote. It seems almost impossible to measure the amount of work (and luck, and certainly privilege) that allowed me to end up here, but that isn't the entire reason that I'm crying. It is my mother's birthday. If she were living, she'd be celebrating 64 years today, and I am in an airport holding something in my hands that she might have been proud of, and I can't take it to her and place it in her living hands and say *look. look at what I did with the path you made for me.* And states away, someone still living has decided that they aren't in love with me anymore, and so I am flying thousands of miles for weeks at a time and staying up staring at computer screens until there is nothing rattling in my brain but a slow static to ride into dreams on.

Headphones are around my neck as I cry in this airport newspaper shop, blaring the second of Future's two new albums, released in consecutive weeks: *Future* on one Friday, and *HNDRXX* on the next. *HNDRXX* is startling in approach and execution. It is Future both unapologetic and unimpressed with himself, all at once. For the first time, he seems truly sad, made plain. It's an album of broken crooning, finally slowing down enough to undo the vast nesting doll of grief. From denial to acceptance, and everything in between. It seems like this may be the album that ends Future's run. Both are projected to go #1 on the charts, making Billboard history. *HNDRXX* is the logical bookend to *Honest*, which started his run in 2014. *Honest*, with its performed depth, offered nothing of emotional substance. *HNDRXX* ends on "Sorry," a nearly eight-minute song where everything comes apart. It's Hendrix apologizing for Future, or

Future apologizing for himself, or regret piling on top of regret until the whole building collapses. At the opening of verse two is the line, "It can get scary when you're legendary," delivered in Future's signature throaty drone. The endless work, the hiding from that which hurts, maybe leads to some unforeseen success. And the funny thing about that is how it won't make any of us feel less alone. That's how running into one thing to escape another works. Distance has a wide mouth, and I haven't slept in a bed in 48 hours, and the people who miss me are not always the people I want to be missed by, and the last time I stood over my mother's grave, the weeds had grown around her name so I picked at them with my bare hands for a while before giving up and sitting down inside of them instead. Still, I am in a paper because I chose work over feeling sad for three months, and now I don't have the energy to feel anything but sad. The woman who works at the newsstand taps me on the shoulder, and asks me if I can turn down the music in my headphones because it's distracting other customers. She walks away, never saying anything about the fact that I was crying in the middle of her store.

November 22, 2014

BELIEVE IT OR NOT, THERE ARE PLACES IN OHIO where boys load guns on the laps of their fathers and walk out into the slow-arriving winter air for the hunt. Believe it or not, there are places the hunt is about the feeling of pulling on a trigger and the rich vibration it sends through the shoulder. The joy in watching a body fall. I say believe it or not for myself, really. You likely already know this, or have a corner of a place you're from that feels familiar to it. My parents wouldn't let any of their children make their fingers into a gun, even while playing. My oldest brother, the first and most eager to push back against their rules, decided to buy a Super Soaker water gun. In the '90s, they were all the rage. Bright, splashed in fluorescent colors, and large enough to hold nearly a gallon of water. My brother kept it under his bed in a case, taking it out only for the occasional neighborhood water fight. During one such bit of revelry, after he'd gone off to college in the late '90s and left his water gun treasure behind, I remember a boy spraying an occupied police car with a brief and sharp blast of water. The police, outraged, burst from their car and began running, a small gathering of Black children scattering like ants, laughing their way into never being caught.

I am in one of Ohio's corners where animals die by the bullet and pile up in fields, or hide in tall stalks of unharvested land. It is southern Ohio, the part that rubs up close to Kentucky and considers itself a part of the Grand American South. This section of Ohio is interesting due to the aesthetics of the South it aspires to, and fails to reach. People hang confederate flags from trucks and anchor their words in a drawl. It is the South crafted by someone who only understands the South through movie stereotypes. A few days away from Thanksgiving, I am sitting at the table with a man who certainly has fired a gun, both for survival and for sport. On the news, there is another story about gun control and the man growls. We all have a right to protect our families, he says, looking out into the vast land through the window. And I think I agree with him, at least on the surface. So I nod slowly, lowly offer a small sound of affirmation. We all have a right to keep the people we love safe.

The reason my parents gave for their hard stance on toys explicitly molded after weapons was that they didn't want their children to fall victim to the world's obsession with violence at such a young age. What's funny about my corner of Ohio and the corner of Ohio that I am spending Thanksgiving in is that both of the populations, though of vastly different demographics, can tell the difference between a gunshot and fireworks. This knowledge is essential if you are Black and a child in a house with big windows, perhaps dreaming of the outside world and all of its possibilities. The key is in the echo. A gunshot, generally, is a brief burst and then a brief echo. A firework, on the other hand, explodes and echoes back, back, back. It swallows and keeps swallowing. Even if the light never touches a sky you can see, the echo is what to listen for. I don't remember how young I was when I learned this, or if I will teach it to any children I may one day have to look after. We all have a right to keep the people we love safe.

My family doesn't celebrate Thanksgiving, but my partner's family does. So I make my way with her down to Buford, Ohio, each year, and this year is no different except for we don't live in the state anymore, so the trip is longer. I'm generally the only Black person here for miles, which is mostly fine because there aren't enough people in the town to stare at me with confusion. Once, last year, I went out on my own to find a gas station, or perhaps a coffee shop. And when I got to the counter to pay, I reached rapidly for my wallet in my front pocket, and the white man behind the counter jumped ever so slightly. It's one of those things you notice after you spend a lifetime as an object of various levels of fear. After that, I decided that if I go out here, someone else should pay for anything I need. But I mostly stay inside. I am sitting on the couch with my partner's father, who I like because he is much like my father. An Army man, with uncompromising principles and varied politics, who speaks firmly and endlessly, but with good intentions. I like watching the news with him, even when our politics don't align, because he is a curious observer of the world, something that can't be said for every white man his age. In a way, we have a relationship that revolves around us using each other: with all of his children moved on and largely out of the house, I'm the son he can sit with and know that I'll listen to him ramble when no one else will. And for me, he's a small thing that reminds me enough of home to feel safe. I told him, when I was last here, about my encounter with the fearful cashier, and he turned red with anger and embarrassment. He wanted to know where it was, who the cashier was. It was a small town, and he wanted to know who to see about the issue at hand. It was slightly endearing, done with no performance in mind, just a genuine reaction to what he imagined as a simple injustice.

On the news, an anchor is discussing Ferguson. In a few days, a grand jury is going to decide whether or not to indict Darren Wilson, the police officer who shot unarmed Black teenager Michael Brown a few months earlier. I was on a plane when it happened, I remember, landing to a wave of news that got worse with each minute. When I tell my partner's father that I think the police officer is going to get off without an indictment, he shrugs lightly. He was just doing his job, he says. And then, without looking away from the television, he says: I hope those people don't riot in that city.

It occurs to me that for some, emotional distance is what it takes to equalize race. A white man fights in the army next to Black men and so he learns what it is to die for those particular Black men. A white man grows old and a young Black man comes into his life that could be his son's age, and he learns what it is to want to fight for him, as well. We all do this, I think. It's how we learn to work through our various disconnects. Still, without anything chopping at the root of our souls, we're still imagining the individual only, and not the system that surrounds them, that makes them feared. The cashier in Buford, Ohio, who jumped at my attempt for my wallet, didn't know me as an individual. He simply knew fear learned from a system, played on loop to him for an entire life.

We are different and then also not, the people of my temporary Thanksgiving geography and I. We both want to survive through another year. Still, they were taught to run toward guns for survival, and I was taught to run from them, or even the illusion of them. Soon, I will retreat to the kitchen and chop something large into something smaller with the sharp blade of a knife that I would never carry outside of this home, for fear of what the land and the people in it would make of me.

The things we work to unlearn are funny, in that way. In my first year of high school, I snuck my brother's Super Soaker onto school grounds. It was a foolish moment of youthful exuberance. A water balloon fight had broken out in the school's parking lot earlier in the week. It was nearing the end of the school year, and everyone was restless and eager to be finished. During the lunch period, I pulled out the bright, fluorescent water gun and sprayed it at a crowd in the hallway for a few short seconds before the school's security guard snatched the water gun from my hands, dragging me to the school's office. I got reprimanded by both the principal and my father, who took me home, took the water gun, and hid it somewhere. I haven't seen it since.

I didn't, in that moment, understand that what makes a gun real or fake in the imagination ransacked by fear isn't always the color of it, or the shape of it. Sometimes, it is the body of the person holding it, or the direction that they choose to point it in. What my parents were trying to teach wasn't a lesson about weapons, but a lesson of the body and the threats it carries. We all have a right to keep the people we love safe.

In Buford, on a couch in the afternoon near Thanksgiving, I watch old footage of Ferguson, Missouri, on fire a few months before, protesters clogging its streets and chanting for justice. I watch my partner's father shake his head slowly as the bodies of protesters began to clash with heavily armed police. There are sometimes wide and splitting paths that take us away from the people we aspire to love, even if we know they are loving us in the best way they can, with all of the worldview that their world has afforded them. As the sound on the television dies down before bleeding into a commercial, I hear a popping sound coming from somewhere north I wait to count the echoes. I look, briefly, to see if there is any light in the sky.

Surviving On Small Joys

WHEN PEOPLE IN AMERICA ARE FACED WITH CON-
fronting and accepting the evolving landscape of human gender
and sexuality, one of the earliest cries often heard is *How will
I explain this to my children?* People become so caught up in a
child's understanding of a world much larger than their own, one
that, I imagine, they are in no great rush to understand. I think
of these people, eager to burden their children with their own
discomforts, every time there is a mass shooting. Their question
is often posed as *How will I explain this person in the bathroom
to my child?* or *How will I explain those two people kissing to my
child?* but rarely *How will I explain to my child that people die and
we do nothing?* How do we explain to a child that children have
been buried and we were sad but could not let go of our principles and our history and the violence that is born and reborn
from it—that we clung to our guns, those small deadly gods,
more tightly than to our neighbors?

During weeks, months, years like 2016, I remember how
urgent it is for the child to stay a child, or for the joy of that
child to be an entity with its own body, for as long as possible. I
spent the Sunday morning after the mass shooting at the Pulse
nightclub in Orlando underneath a swath of blankets, scrolling
through any website providing news, knowing that the news, in
these cases, rarely gets better as more unfolds. I checked in with
friends and allowed myself to be swallowed by my own anger.
I sent tweets and deleted them just as quickly. I cursed politicians, the ones who were silent and the ones who were saying
the wrong things. Eventually, I was pulled out of bed by a small

chorus of yells and laughter creeping in through my kitchen window. Below, in the parking lot behind my apartment, boys on their bikes were riding in circles, pulling their front wheels up and trying to balance themselves. Falling, laughing, and getting right back up. This small bit of joy, for no reason other than because it is summertime and they're with their friends and they're outside and free. I do not know what they knew of death, or if they knew that a world outside of their own free world was mourning. Or if they knew and, even in knowing, saw clouds blowing in from the south and decided to not let whatever sunshine remained go to waste on a hot summer day to be followed by another hot summer day to be followed by months where the entire land was theirs. The city, a sacred playground with no room for grief.

For poets, the elegy is a type of currency. So many of us are, especially now, speaking to the dead, or asking the dead to speak again, or apologizing to the dead for the lives we still have. Particularly for poets of color, queer and trans poets, the contemporary elegy often exists as half-memorial, half-statement of existence. Something that says *You have taken so much from us, but we are still here.* As we are being asked to come to terms with death, again and again, I consider the elegy and how empowering it can be. Even then, though, I think of my own work, and of how rarely I find myself speaking to the living. How rarely I am asking readers to imagine a world in which I am surrounded by my many living friends, family, and my deepest loves. And yes, rare is the soul who first ran to poetry because they were overwhelmed with happiness. Still, even with a notebook full of ghosts, I have begun to ask myself what these times demand of me, as a writer working to balance grief over the departed and praise for the still living. It becomes urgent, I think, to do more. The people I love are Black. The people I love are Muslim and queer. The people I love can't get people to use their proper pronouns. The people I love are all afraid, and because these are my people, I am afraid with them. I work, in times as urgent as these, to unlock the small pockets of joy that have kept us all surviving for so long. The small and silly things that aren't death. I get on Twitter and make jokes about basketball, or I send a friend a video of a panda that we both remember laughing at once. I text the words "I love you" to people to whom I've owed phone calls. I spend a whole day writing poems in which no one dies.

I want to be immensely clear about the fact that we need *more* than love and joy. Love and joy alone will not rid America of its multilayered history of violence that has existed for longer than any of us have been alive. That violent culture, no matter the amount of prayers and grief we throw at it, remains unshakable. It is rooted so firmly into the machinery of America that it has its hands around our decision-making processes, the language we use for endurance and survival. The violence is, in some ways, inescapable. It isn't always done with a gun, and is sometimes done with a pen. Joy alone will not grant anyone safety. It can, however, act as a small bit of fuel when the work of resistance becomes too much. My activism is at its best when it takes time to laugh over FaceTime with a beloved friend on the morning after people were murdered, because it allows me, even briefly, to imagine a world where that happiness can still freely and comfortably exist. Joy, in these moments, is the sweetest meal that we keep chasing the perfect recipe for, among a world trying to gather all of the ingredients for itself. I need it to rest on my tongue especially when I am angry, especially when I am afraid, especially when nothing makes sense other than the fact that joy has been, and will always be, the thing that first pulls me from underneath the covers when nothing else will. It is the only part of me that I have to keep accessible at all times, because I never know what will come. The only thing promised in this world is that it will, oftentimes, be something that makes living seem impossible. And I hope, then, that a child who blessedly knows less of the world's evils decides to laugh with his friends in a place that reaches your ears. I hope it carries you back to the fight, as it has done for me. Joy, in this way, can be a weapon— that which carries us forward when we have been beaten back for days, or months, or years.

And what a year 2016 was. Oh, friends, those of you who are still with us, what a year we survived together. We are not done burying our heroes before we are asked to bury our friends. Our mourning is eclipsed by a greater mourning. I know nothing that will get us through this beyond whatever small pockets of happiness we make for each other in between the rage and the eulogies and the marching and the protesting and the demanding to be seen and accounted for. I know nothing except that this grief is a river carrying us to another new grief, and along the way, let us hold a space for a bad joke or a good memory. Something that will allow us to hold our breath under the water for a little bit longer. Let the children have their world. Their miraculous, impossible world where nothing hurts long enough to stop time. Let them have it for as long as it will hold them. When that world falls to pieces, maybe we can use whatever is left to build a better one for ourselves.

VI.

After finishing, Marvin Gaye bowed lightly to thunderous applause before walking slowly from center court. Almost a year later, Marvin's fading body was resting in his brother Frankie's arms after being shot by his father. Before dying, he told Frankie, "It's good. I ran my race. I've got nothing left to give."

Frankie told police that he didn't get to his brother's side quicker because he thought the sound of the shots from his father's gun were fireworks.

Bonus Tracks

On Summer Crushing

FRIENDS AND HEARTTHROBS OF THE PAST, FU-
ture, and present: where I am now, the temperature has begun
its slow climb, and summer is preparing its eviction notice for
all the gentle breezes and drives with windows down and the
incessant, joyful choir of birds. We will soon have to settle for
less pleasing aesthetics of romance. Sweat becomes romantic
because it will happen whether or not I want it to, and I've got to
make the best of it. During summer in Ohio, the storms come
briefly, but violently, and seemingly out of nowhere. The sun
will be out as you make your way to the car, but by the time you
arrive at your destination, you're trapped in a parking lot with
torrents of rainwater collapsing on your windshield. I think I
would like to call this moment romantic, too, for all the times
I've sat outside of a grocery store, or a bar, or an ice cream
shop, turning up a song that reminded me of someone in hopes
that the music and the memory might intersect and silence the
downpour.

It is a privilege to have seasons. Sometimes, in Columbus,
Ohio, we don't get much of spring. Winter digs its claws in and
then it's suddenly eighty-five degrees with suffocating humidity.
The planet, of course, may not afford me many more years like
this one. One where I've been blessed with a distinct turning
over from one season to the next. I like it this way, being gently
shepherded through, as opposed to dropped in the middle of a
landscape already in progress. It is hard to create longing without the reminder of what we're longing for.

Speaking of longing, I am here to once again consider the moment in the pre-chorus of "How Will I Know," which creeps underneath the song's ecstatic and bombastic uncertainty. Whether intended in the original message or not, this was the first song that most clearly articulated the anatomy and anxiety and secret pleasures of a crush. While Whitney drags out the words of the song's central question as only Whitney can, the backup vocals trickle in with "don't trust your feelings," which is the moment that feels the most true to the real-life conundrum. A person, shaky, but fantasizing toward confidence while, underneath, their friends try to whisper them back to reality.

It is not true that all people get crushes and it is not true that all people want to be someone's crush. And it is definitely not true that these things happen in equal measure for everyone. But for the people who do crush and want to be a crush, I think that desire can rise and dissipate with the movement of seasons. I always found that my hopes of having a crush existed most eagerly in the early months of a year, as winter faded away. Those hopes peaked in the middle of summer, when I would strive to be romantically unattached so that my heart could be tugged in any direction it pleased. I would guess this seasonal relationship might have to do with the structure of my life when I first discovered what crushes were. Which is to say, when I was in school, especially when I was in school but before my friends and I could drive, when even if a person was romantically linked to someone else, they would most likely part ways before the school year ended. Or pretend that they were going to give it a try over the summer if they lived in neighborhoods that were close enough. But, in the end, the seemingly never-ending possibilities of summer won out. In summer, small relationships or imagined relationships banished the larger relationship to the locker bays of the high school. At Warped Tour, a crush would accelerate into a daylong fling because time was fleeting, and there was none of it to be wasted hand-wringing over maybes. And so, summer, even as an adult, is the time when I allow myself to be most susceptible to crushing on someone. Then, as the fall arrives and the cold begins to circle back around, I want to be indoors, preferably with a person I've had a crush on in the previous months. Your timeline may vary, of course.

There are many approaches to having a crush, and significantly fewer approaches to being someone's crush. For the latter, some may be interested in knowing who has a crush on them and why, and I do see a lot of value in having that information. But for the former, I am too anxious for any interest in reality. Whitney Houston seems to be the questioning type, though none of us can say how long she'd been mulling over the questions before they spilled out. I can hold a crush longer than most of my friends can hold a grudge. I don't really need or even want to know whether a person shares my affection. I'm content just letting the situation play itself out at its own pace. I get that for most people, this seems agonizing. But, for all of the agony, what you get in return is the imagined person and not the actual person. Or, if you're lucky, you get to hold off on the actual person for a little bit longer, until you get to be with the actual person. Whitney's agony seems more urgent, it ticks my heart rate up a notch when I listen to the song. Which, it must be said, is one of the most perfect songs ever crafted. Whitney is saying prayers! She is picking up the phone and dialing some numbers but then hanging up again! It is all too much! Though I'm not one to judge the manifestation of anyone else's desires—particularly if those desires have been bubbling up to the surface with an unsustainable ferocity!

But where Whitney and I meet is this: the idea of falling in love over and over again within an endless loop of uncertainty. Sometimes, it isn't even the person you're falling in love with, just the uncertainty itself. I have been known to take everything as a sign, even if I am lying to myself. That's part of the fun. It's the idea of certainty that drains me. Sure, someone saying they don't dig you like you dig them doesn't stop a crush dead in its tracks, but it does make the emotional journey more finite. I don't know much about love, and I don't wish to know any more than I already do. Like Hayden at the end of the poem "Those Winter Sundays," where the reader can almost hear him, frantic and throwing up his hands:

What did I know, what did I know
of love's austere and lonely offices?

I give in to that question. There's no satisfactory answer. And maybe there isn't an answer to Whitney's questions, either. I have cursed myself for misreading all my crushs' signals, but I have still felt thankful for the time those signals were there for me to read in the first place. To have a crush can be joyous labor, and can also be anguish, and can also be something that will vanish in a day or an hour and never be revived again. While out with my friends now, we'll see an old acquaintance from afar and we might exclaim, "I can't believe I ever had a crush on that person!" and we'll laugh at the foolish desires of our past selves. And I like that part, too. Even if it is played up for effect. To crush now may mean to stay up well past your comfortable waking hours, gently scrolling through rows of old Instagram photos and attempting to not accidentally like one of them, despite your fingers quaking with excitement. There's this old Kevin Durant tweet I love from 2010. It reads: "#uever wake up n the middle of da night and think about a girl u like or startin to like and sit at da edge of the bed n say damn i want her."

And yes, surely that is one of the inescapable parts of a crush, too. The things that keep you awake, or send you to the edge of a bed, speaking out loud to no one but yourself and the world you've built with a person who—if you are one of the lucky ones—might be at the edge of their own bed, thinking of you.

Whitney's tune doesn't end with resolution. It ends with desire piling on top of more desire. She was always better at that than she got credit for. Whitney's voice and the singular stamp she made on ballads is memorable, of course. But so is the way that she set a blueprint in pop music for how to unfold desire without resolving it. I hear it now in Carly Rae Jepsen, in Robyn, in so many others. "How Will I Know" ends with an accumulation of the words *how will I know* sung repeatedly. Nothing promised except another rotation of the question. On the end of the third and fifth rotation, the background singers chime back in. First with *I say a prayer*. And then, *I fall in love*. It is hard to hear because it comes as the song fades away, but it's there.

Falling in love can be an isolating act, even if another person is present while it is happening. It's all so interior, based on many moving parts and internalized messiness. It isn't always like this, of course. But when it has been like that for me, I've come out of it happily exhausted, wondering why anyone would want to do this more than once in a lifetime. But, of course, when whatever love I've claimed fades, I find myself renewed, in search of the feeling once again. I have found ways to renew it even while still in love. Last fall, there was a point where I had a crush on the leaves, for all their twirling and kaleidoscopic showing off. I have a crush on the first few days of daylight saving time in either direction, when the sun does a real generosity and tricks me into staying out longer and later. Or, when it abruptly exits early, reminding me to bow to my true self. I have a crush on the way the familiar buildings of Columbus, Ohio, poke their faces through a puffy wall of clouds when I descend into the city after being away for too long, and it is always too long. I have a crush on too many sentences in too many books by too many people to name. Since I have already decided that sweat is romantic, friends, let me say that I also have a crush on the feeling of night air cooling the sweat off skin when a body pours out of a hot and packed space. I am beginning to have a crush on crystals, I think. Definitely obsidian, but perhaps a few of the others that look like miniature caves. And, yes, I have a crush on memories that were surely not as beautiful as I have made them out to be. Because that's the whole trick. I've had crushes on all my friends, and if they don't have one back on me that's fine because I'm still going to text them at unfortunate and odd hours of the day with some useless miracle that I couldn't possibly keep to myself. So few of my crushes speak back. I am cultivating my comfort with unanswered desires, and it is going well. I have room for so much more. I say a prayer. I fall in love.

Carly Rae Jepsen And The Kingdom Of Desire

ENTERING CANADA AT THE NEW YORK/ONTARIO border, near the edge of Buffalo, a Black border guard asks me if I'm good. It's the first question he asks after taking my passport from me—not why I'm crossing into Canada, or where I'm coming from. At first I wonder if a fairly routine five-hour drive has taken that much of a toll on me before remembering that I am, in fact, not good. After the verdict in Philando Castile's murder came down the night before, acquitting police officer Jeronimo Yanez on all charges, I didn't sleep much.

I have routines for this feeling now—the feeling that comes with a particular set of injustices that you live a life knowing you might fall victim to. I clean my apartment, even if it doesn't need cleaning. I put a record on my record player and let it play all the way through, even the songs I can't tolerate. I call my people and say, "What a world, oh, what a world this is." I do anything to avoid the endless scroll of a social media timeline that would tell me, directly, how much people I know and care for are hurting.

And yet, this is how the night always ends: with me, underneath the covers, staring into an abyss of familiar haunting.

I tell the border guard that I'm good, though I'm not. I think often about the way Black people respond to each other in public in the moments after it can feel like being in public itself is a daunting task. I tell the border guard that I'm good because I don't want to assume that he's checking in on me, even though I imagine he might be checking in on me, in the same way that the older Black woman at a gas station in Cleveland seemed to check in on the group of teenage Black boys who were in line ahead of me. I don't know what side of the border this border guard calls home, or if he feels safer there than I have felt, at times, in the past 12 hours. There are cars snaking behind us, and now is, perhaps, not the time for a discussion of the interior design of our anxieties. He asks why I'm coming into Canada, and I tell him for a concert. He doesn't ask much beyond that, hands me my passport, and tells me to stay safe.

I was coming into Canada for pop songs, which is what this is about. This is about pop songs, but beyond, it is about a search for a small mercy—another window out of some unexpected wretchedness for whatever hours your time, body, and money can afford. How to recharge yourself briefly in order to keep finding your way in a place that loves what you perform, but perhaps doesn't like you all that much.

Onstage at Roy Thomson Hall in downtown Toronto, Carly Rae Jepsen looks nervous. There is a lot at stake here: Jepsen hasn't headlined a full show in her home country in years, skipping over Canada entirely on *E•MO•TION*'s Gimmie Love Tour. There is also the looming presence of the Toronto Symphony Orchestra at her back, shrinking the large stage and cutting just a small corner at the front for her to fit into. It is a homecoming with a lot on the table. After conductor Lucas Waldin introduces her—intentionally drawing out the introduction to raise the anticipation, as any good conductor would—Jepsen peeks out from behind an offstage door, walks out waving sheepishly, and in one sweeping motion the crowd rises to its feet.

The thing with any Carly Rae Jepsen show is that she can be a bit of a slow starter when taking on a full set. Not a bad starter by any means, but it seems to take her at least two songs to work the nerves out. This seems built into her artistic DNA, and perhaps it's related to her particular type of pop stardom: big enough of a star to have an active, caring, and committed fan base that is, at least for now, small enough for her to not want to let them down. There's a difference in playing to 1,000 people and playing to 10,000 people if you traffic in the work of singular and specific emotional connection. And so, after glancing up at Waldin as the signature horn entered, Carly Rae Jepsen kicked into "Run Away With Me," and she was home again.

To counter the point about her slow-starting tendencies, it must be said that when Jepsen is on, warmed up, and comfortable, she operates at a level of onstage confidence that is often stunning. For every moment of breathless nervousness that might take place for a fan at the start of the show, there are at least twice as many moments where you find yourself wondering if this is among the greatest shows you've ever seen.

After playing through a few songs, Jepsen left the stage and allowed the orchestra to play a small solo set. When she returned, still glowing in a golden dress that drank in the fractured light falling on it, she seemed renewed. Some singers can do their best work stationary—standing behind a microphone, moving an arm from time to time. Jepsen is best when she can twist the mic from its cage and make use of the space she has, even if it's limited.

In her second set, she played a delightful and charming rendition of "Tug of War," a single from her 2008 album of the same name, now considered somewhat of a deep cut in the post-*E•MO•TION* Jepsen catalog. She invited Waldin, who claimed to "not normally be a singer," to sing backup, and he made a show of it all, taking off his jacket and rolling up his sleeves. Later in the show, during "Let's Get Lost," Jepsen bounced to the edge of the stage, held both of her palms outward, and beckoned the audience to get out of their seats. It was a gesture both logical and large. To that point, even in the concert's best moments most of us had remained seated, bouncing along in our chairs so as to not break some imagined decorum of the space. Not many of us in the audience had shown up in our Sunday best, but early on, the space and the show both seemed too magical to defile with our raucous energy. But there, at the edge of the stage, was Carly Rae Jepsen, reminding a crowd that there is no space too pure to pour dancing into. Telling everyone to make good use of the space, and the bodies that carried them to it, like any good conductor would.

"This next song is about being stuck in the friend zone. Which I… uhhh… write about a lot. So… I guess… make of that what you will."

Carly Rae Jepsen said this before playing "Your Type," one of *E•MO•TION*'s signature songs, and one that most explicitly speaks to the larger project that is the Carly Rae Jepsen Narrative: close, but not close enough; loved, but not in love. "Your Type" is the bull's-eye from which all other songs on *E•MO•TION* echo outward. The song's introduction was one of only a handful of words Jepsen said all night. As I found when I saw her in New York in 2016, she isn't much for swelling, overflowing onstage banter. When she does speak, it's often to give brief, one-line summaries of a song before playing it, as if she's nervously pitching them to a room of strangers. It's an endearing and refreshing habit. It seems as if she knows the answers are inside the music itself, without any additional language needed to pick apart what will already be clear to those who know the feeling.

It goes without saying that the concept of the friend zone, as it is most popularly known in current discourse, is flawed at best, and entirely garbage at worst. When it is presented as an idea of punishment—something handed down by someone who might love you, but not in the way that you love them—the concept falls apart, swamped in entitlement. But "Your Type" doesn't really sit in that particular place of platonic and romantic tension. It's a song that, more than anything, is about Jepsen's struggle with unworthiness—facing herself, and not the object of her romantic interests. It is more sad than scathing, more self-reflective and melancholy than bitter or resentful. It takes the trope and fashions it into a newer, better weapon.

There are many lenses through which *E•MO•TION*'s central theme can be read, but the one that makes the most sense, as I heard the songs from it in this patient, orchestral context, is the one that I haven't been able to shake for the past several months: that it's an album about falling in love with a friend gradually, and all of the agonizing within. This is made plain in "Your Type," but it can be read all over the album in more subtle ways, and in the moment, I found myself wanting to unravel this part of the story.

When an artist who normally isn't backed by an orchestra suddenly gets backed by an orchestra, their songs can come to life in a manner that isn't afforded by slick production or heavy guitars and backup vocalists. Onstage at Roy Thomson Hall, it was just Jepsen, staying afloat while an entire production came to life behind her. You could see the movements in each of the songs, as if there was a film being pieced together at her back. It takes a special kind of artist not to drown in that.

Speaking of film: when someone realizes they are in love with their friend onscreen, in a movie or television show, the ending is usually happy. There is a small glimpse at some interior tension, but it is of the romantic flavor—a person enjoying their brief agony before the inevitable romance commences. Platonic love is vital, essential, and perhaps the one thing left in this wretched landscape that could save us all for a little bit longer than we deserve. I love my friends even when I don't tell them enough. I have crawled from the wreckage of enough heartbreak to know who will still be standing when I emerge and who won't, and I hold those still standing close to me.

The distance between affections is short and often linear. The distance often hangs on circumstance—a brief moment or a song or two hands brushing against each other in a movie theater. This is, of course, not to feed into the myth that two people of attracting romantic interests can't be friends. Rather, it's an acknowledgment of what the onscreen element of this type of friendship gets incorrect: falling in love with someone you love deeply as a friend isn't necessarily romantic torment... if you truly care for the person, that is. More often than not, it can be a series of value judgments cloaked in an endless longing, until it isn't.

The music of *E•MO•TION*, in one understanding of it, lives in this space. "Gimmie Love" as a grand plea for attention from someone who might have eyes elsewhere. "When I Needed You" as the internal monologue of a relationship speeding off a cliff. "Let's Get Lost" as the ode to stretching out a night beyond what seems possible—the most potent of the album's many motions. The idea of trying to extend an inevitable ending on a dark highway heading toward separation from someone who you might wish to be your someone. You hope for a storm that would force you to pull over, or a traffic jam. *E•MO•TION*, especially heard through a gentle lens of swelling strings and gentle horns, plays out like an archive of the space between platonic and sometimes-not. A relationship with a hundred ways in, but no clear way out.

It has been said that pop music desires a body—a single, focused human form as an object of interest. *E•MO•TION* fails in this, I suppose, because its primary characters are desire and distance. Want may be a machine that lurches us toward a newer, more eager want, but the idea alone, pointing at nothing specific, doesn't sell records. This is one theory as to why Carly Rae Jepsen, despite her ability to home in on a feeling and make it flourish, isn't the biggest pop star in the world. But I'm not really interested anymore in why *E•MO•TION* didn't sell a million copies, because I don't care about how an album sells as much as I care about how an album lives. And if that sounds overwrought or too emotional then by all means keep your numbers, and I'll keep my small escapes into a place a slight touch better than the actual place I'm in.

E•MO•TION is an album that still, even more than a year after its release, makes you feel good. When Carly Rae Jepsen launches into "Boy Problems," complete with her mostly shoulders dance moves, people spill out of their seats in the front row, dancing close to the stage while she points at them and grins. When she plays the inevitable "Call Me Maybe," which, even though I'm weary of it, sounds incredible with the string arrangement crafted to hold it, her own voice is drowned out by the teeming masses howling out each line.

It is not easy to create a feeling consistently. I'm talking about creating across an entire emotional spectrum, so vividly that it draws even the most reserved and casual fans out of their brief darkness. This is a statement of intent—an artistic and creative decision. When people talk about Carly Rae Jepsen's music as if it just arrives as-is—or when it gets discussed as something about or meant solely for youth—it does a real disservice to the work that must go into being able to make people feel everything, all at once. Doing this requires the full investment of an audience willing to consider a type of spatial intimacy coupled with a type of emotional grandeur. That Jepsen's music is not the kind of pop music that relentlessly desires a body means that desire itself is the body. Desire is the living thing at the end of the tunnel, waiting with open arms, and to some, I imagine that isn't a happy ending. Wanting leading into more wanting isn't exactly a neatly tied ribbon, but it is a certainty. I will surely wake tomorrow with a desire for something I cannot have, and even if I can have it, I will chase the idea of not being able to have it until I find something else fleeting. For all of the memes and jokes that circulate among her dedicated fans, it's a discredit to Jepsen's abilities to speak of the feelings she brings forth without at least imagining the idea that she knows exactly what she's doing in her creative process. That she's figured out the simple math: once you've caught that which you desire, the story is less interesting. She gives us, instead, a never-ending chase where the only thing to fall in love with is the idea of falling in love.

At the end of the night, Jepsen, hand in hand with Waldin, took her final bows. She closed the night with an encore of "I Really Like You," the great first single from E•MO•TION that has, for me, somehow become so buried underneath all of the album's other songs that I found myself struggling to keep up as she sang. The show was, by almost any measure, a triumph, as a homecoming and as an establishment of risk—the uncertain places an artist will go in the name of whatever work they believe in.

For all the talk about what she represents and what her aims are or aren't, I won't lose sight of the fact that Carly Rae Jepsen is a pop singer, and a good one. To hear her voice competing with less noise than it was on her previous tour was refreshing. She was, in some ways, built for this show. There is a trick about raising the intensity in your voice without raising its volume, which is Jepsen's greatest strength as a singer. Her best moments come in the quietest spaces of the night: nearly whispering

"I don't want to work it out" over just a few strings in "When I Needed You," or in the spare moments at the opening of "All That." During the latter, I found myself leaning forward in my seat, and noticed a few people around me doing the same. How funny, to have someone draw you closer just so you can hear them sing about that which is far away.

It might not be this one, but there is certainly a small and brief world in which Carly Rae Jepsen is the biggest pop star there is. And everyone there loves someone they can't have, or has someone they can't love. And everyone is all right nonetheless, because everything is fleeting. You can't feel everything at once, until you can. And I can't live in that world but for a few hours here and there, before I drive into another darkness with no one else in the car to get stuck in traffic with. Before I go back to weighing whether it is better to be liked or loved, but never weighing what it might be like to be both. And in Carly Rae Jepsen's fleeting, brilliant world, it feels like there is nothing outside that might try to steal what joy you've managed to accumulate, in spite of the odds.

And there, of course, is the mercy I was looking for.

On Seatbelts And Sunsets

And Damn It / We Are Gonna Figure Something Out / If It
Takes Me / All Night
—Julien Baker, "Hurt Less"

I WAS BORN TO A WOMAN WHO DIED BECAUSE SHE
took medicine that was supposed to make her less sad, but instead it forced a hive to swell in her throat while she slept. And
I guess that's an act of God.

We buried her in the summer and the sun stayed out for
weeks after, sitting wide and low over the blacktop, so that it
was the only unforgettable presence the city could claim, and
that was an act of God.

Once, someone built a boat out of sinkable materials and
told the world it was impossible to sink, and that was an act of
Man.

The ship was so massive that it couldn't steer out of the way
of an iceberg which tore through the ship's hull, sinking it and
claiming the lives of over 1,500 of its passengers, and I am sorry,
but that was probably an act of God.

The Julien Baker song "Hurt Less" is about loving someone
so much that they make you want to stay alive on whatever corner of Earth you figured was wretched and unbearable before
you met them. And, look, it ain't nobody's job to keep any of
us alive other than ourselves, and I get that. But I've been to the
funerals, and I've held friends on the cold tile of their apartments with pills spilled out at their feet, and I've washed bed

sheets three times in a row to get blood out of them, and I have been both the arms reaching and the arms pulling back. And so it's all a matter of perspective is what I'm saying. On "Hurt Less" Julien Baker opens with a statement about how she never wore seatbelts in her car because she maybe wanted to be alive, but not enough to stop herself from dying if she happened to be thrown from a car. This is a small measure, in some ways: the choices we make to stay alive or not are sometimes a matter of the smallest circumstance. To unbuckle a seatbelt on a highway and to take a knife to your own skin aren't equal measures. One action, once taken, forces a darkness to descend, and the other is taken to not prevent the darkness from descending once it arrives. But what Julien Baker wants a listener to hear is that life was something she was willing to opt out of.

I haven't always wanted to be alive, but the only time I ever thought I might actually die was in an airplane over what I will remember as somewhere in the middle of the country. There was an unnatural turbulence—the kind that even rattles the pilots, when you can hear in their voices that they themselves aren't sure the plane is going to descend safely. Turbulence isn't something that often causes planes to crash, but it's easy to forget that when wrapped in the arms of it, tossing a plane from side to side. I remember, in the moment, running my hands along the frayed edges of my seatbelt's thin fabric and wondering if it would hold me in place while the plane broke apart over a field, or became swallowed by a river. The thing about Otis Redding's plane crash is that he died because when the plane crashed into the lake, his seatbelt trapped him in his rapidly sinking seat. No one ever talks about that part. How that which protects us can also be our undoing. And so sometimes it's our saviors that do us in. I have played the card of God on the table so that I can say I think sometimes there is a God who wants us to arrive earlier than we normally would, because the party has gotten boring up there. I was on a plane that felt like it was being stretched to its limits. I think life flashing before your eyes is a cliché. I remember, instead, the future parading itself in front of me. All of the things I wanted to do, but hadn't yet. Death is a bed of unkept promises, and in the moment I thought I might die, I got to see all of them, and how happy I would perhaps be reveling in them. And then, like that, the plane steadied. I had unbuckled my seatbelt without even realizing it.

Once, I was in Ohio, in the middle of a summer where it rained so violently and consistently that I spent what felt like hours at a time in the driver's seat of my parked car, watching the water gather and then cascade down my windshield outside of the grocery store or the post office or the bar where my friends sat inside laughing, waiting for me. And I could convince myself, briefly, that the world outside was flooding and I would be carried away to anywhere else. And I've read enough of The Book to know that floods and sickness are both acts of God.

In that same Once, I lived in Columbus, Ohio, and liked a woman from miles away, a woman who was almost an entire country away from where her father became sick, and laughed at her jokes on Twitter and read and re-read her poems, and we sent each other copies of small books we wrote and then the only plane she could take that would get her back to her sick father in time had a long layover in Columbus, Ohio. And nothing else makes sense but for that to be an act of God.

And in that same Once, I sat in my car on a day it didn't rain. And I held a bag on my lap. And inside the bag was a nervously written letter, and some candy, and a few books. And on the bag I scrawled the name of a woman who was flying back home to care for her sick father and I sat outside of the airport because in a message, she'd told me that she was flying in, that she had hours to be stuck in an airport terminal, and she'd first asked if there was anything fun to do, and then asked if I could maybe stop by and say hello, and I am saying now that I know a sick father and a worried daughter is not a landscape upon which to prop up a monument to romantics and I think now that when I say act of God I am really saying who will suffer so that I might be able to wrap my hands around the neck of some fleeting blessing.

Despite what I knew in that moment, what I know and have known forever is that the people you dream of standing across from don't just drift to you on accident, and they may never drift to you again, and so I grabbed the bag and left my car and went to stand at the exit to the Southwest Terminal in the Columbus airport, and I will call that an act of faith.

Today, months beyond the summer where it felt like Columbus, Ohio, might flood and be carried away, the father is healthy again. And on a couch in her city which is far from my city, the woman who flew home to him laughs at a joke on television. When she laughs, she covers her face with both of her hands, so that all that can be seen are her eyes, small slivers of themselves. Her body trembles from the shoulders down. She is the kind of person who laughs as if she knows joy has an expiration date. You can see it vibrate through her entire body before exiting. She drops her palms from her face, and smiles, satisfied. I suppose the mundane things a person does that we imagine as art are subjective, usually tied to how in love we are with the person carrying out the action. I do not know what it is called when watching a person laugh for a brief moment is the thing you want to capture in a bottle. I think you realize that you love a person when they do something they would consider forgettable, but you see it every time you close your eyes. I don't know what this is an act of, but it is an act of something I don't imagine myself deserving.

There is a very particular hour in a very particular season in Columbus, and it's not always the same time. Some moment, where the end of spring pulls its fingers through the start of summer before finally letting go. The college students filling the town go back to their corners of Ohio, and the thick humidity hasn't settled over the city yet, and the season hasn't yet turned to a violent coughing of storms along the neighborhoods. The sun stays out late, and really fights to go down, making a mess of colors on its way out. It's the type of weather that invites open windows before air conditioning.

The central refrain in "Hurt Less" is more of a plea than anything else. With intensity growing after each rotation of it, Julien Baker sings, twice:

Oh, Leave The Car Running
I'm Not Ready To Go
And It Doesn't Matter Where
I Just Don't Want To Be Alone
And As Long As You're Not Tired Yet
Of Talking, It Helps To Make It Hurt Less

Interstate 270 is an outerbelt that circles entirely around Columbus in a continuous loop, taking a driver through the heart of the city, and through its sleepy suburbs, and past the airport where, if you time the drive correctly, you can see a plane pushing into the sky, scraping past the descending sun and the final living moments of its miraculous painting. You can drive past the clutter of chain businesses at the edge of Sawmill Road and see the signs pushing high into the air: Applebee's, Speedway, an inflatable car from the Toyota dealership. You can get a glimpse of downtown from two different angles, and then do it all over again. It is the only freeway in the city that doesn't end by taking you somewhere outside of the city. If you were young and had little money but a full tank of gas and a person you wanted to spend time with in the golden hours when day turned to night, you might get a couple of shakes from United Dairy Farmers and circle the city with that person who looked perfect first in the sunlight and then the streetlight, and you would get to watch the city from all of its angles, in all of its light and darkness. And sometimes you'd talk, or sometimes you'd listen to a single song on repeat, or sometimes you'd roll down the windows and let the wind rush in and kiss every corner of silence built up in the car while the skyline echoes in a rearview mirror. It can take about an hour to traverse the entire outerbelt, and there are times I miss it, even with money in my pocket, I miss the intimacy that financial restraints could grant me. When I first moved back to Columbus, I would miss my exits on 270 on purpose, just to remember the romance of aimlessness.

Few things know loneliness like a highway, for all of the people going to places they don't want to go, or driving away from people they don't want to be driving away from. I most love the refrain of "Hurt Less" because it's begging for a simplicity. Sit with me in this car, and we don't need to have a destination other than a place where we are next to each other in our shared sadness, which seems a little less impossible in a moving car, with only one other person who is there because they want to be there with you, no matter what you both are moving toward.

My first car was a 1994 Nissan Maxima, and it was a hideous shade of brown. The car had automatic seatbelts. In 1996, when front airbags were about to become mandatory, most vehicle companies did away with the automatic seatbelt. The automatic seatbelt was a hassle, but its main function was to exist in a way that made safety something a driver didn't think about. When you opened the door, the mechanical seatbelt would jerk forward, inviting you to sit down. When you closed the door, it would retract, clasping around your body. They were faulty though—if your car underwent any impact, there was no telling how they'd react. Some of them would stick, trapping people inside. My car was the last Nissan model that had the automatic seatbelt. I would often forget my seatbelt until it briefly malfunctioned, staying stuck to my body when I opened the door, or staying still when I closed the door. In a car with a loud muffler and a broken car alarm that would go off at will, the seatbelts were the least of my problems.

In 2004, my car was stolen from the apartment complex parking lot it was in. Because I didn't trust my car alarm, I had no idea it was taken until I went to go grocery shopping and saw my spot empty. Having a car stolen is one of those things which creates an absence that doesn't seem real, where you stare at a space where something familiar lived and try to will the familiar thing back to you.

Two nights later, a friend called me and told me to turn on the news. There was my car, flipped upside down on I-270, surrounded by the flashing lights of police cars. The person who'd stolen my car got into a high-speed chase with police, but he made the mistake of thinking he could get out of the city by getting on I-270. I never found out how long the chase lasted, but I imagine long enough for the culprit to realize that the freeway would only take him in a circle. In a panic, he attempted to swerve off of an exit ramp to avoid a police car, and the car flipped over and rolled three times. With the car upside down, the airbag deployed, trapping the car thief's neck around the spiral of the automatic seatbelt, which had tightened, due to impact. While police officers drew their guns and cautiously approached my car, he was strangled to death. That's the thing about something holding you so close that it actually becomes a part of your body. You can forget about it until it consumes you entirely.

The thing about being in love with someone who does not live where you live is that the two of you have to think of new and inventive ways to see each other, sometimes based around a shared hectic travel schedule. And so, through the winding roads of New Hampshire, cloaked by ice, I am driving to a place where someone I love is, because I could afford the few days, even if they will skip by quicker than I'd like. There are several churches, all of their signs offering advice, or statements:

To Be Almost Saved Is To Be Totally Lost

Start Your Week In The Arms Of The Lord

Don't Worry About The Things You Have No Control Over

And God, if you are listening, I do worry. God, if you are listening, I count the miles between my body and the body of the person I love and I worry about each of them. God, I worry about the planes we take to each other and the sky that might not hold them. God, I wear seatbelts and visit the graves of my friends in spring to kick away the dirt from winter. God, it is just us talking now, and I worry about everything I can't control. God, can you tell me how much longer I'll get to be alive and in love. God, I am sorry for the times I didn't want to stick around. God, there is a scroll of things I have taken for granted in order to survive this long, and it is endless. And it is maybe too late to want to live forever after everything I've seen and done. But there are freeways between me and the person I love, God. And I don't have enough time to travel all of them. I worry that I can't bend them all into a giant circle from where I begin to where she begins. God, I don't know what I believe in except the shrinking of distance. God, do you worry about the things you can control? I am enough in love to worry about everything that might cast a shadow over it. God, I have touched the living face of a person I love with the same hands I have touched the dying face of someone I love and none of that seems fair. God, I am enough in love that I want to make everything about it an endless circle, with a sunset at the top of every hour. I know this is all too much, God. But as long as you're not tired yet of talking, it helps.

Julien Baker sings the last lines of "Hurt Less" with nothing but a faint piano, growing fainter as she squeezes each syllable for all it is worth:

This Year I've Started Wearing Safety Belts
When I'm Driving
Because When I'm With You
I Don't Have To Think About Myself
And It Hurts Less

That's the thing about something holding you so close that it actually becomes a part of your body.

Afterword

The first time I heard the contralto of Tracy Chapman, it was cutting through the tiny motor of an old pair of Wahl hair clippers. My father, and default barber, was attempting a mohawk for the first time, not because he thought I should have one—he actually couldn't care less—but because I wanted one. I asked for it. Because whatever was good for Mr. T. was good for me, and a neck full of gold chains wasn't an option.

At my house, haircuts always happened in the basement accompanied by anything other than Rakim or Slick Rick, which is what my older brother was blasting in his room upstairs. For my father, hair-cutting music was Howlin' Wolf, a little Hall and Oats, some James Brown. But on this night, the night of the mohawk, my father pushed a new tape into the deck of the old tabletop radio which lived on an end table peppered with my mother's religious and superstitious tchotchkes, prayers of protection for the children occupying the barber chair. Perhaps my father wanted to listen to something new in hopes it would give him the necessary juju to do what he had not been trained to do, but what his six-year-old had been begging him for.

The opening measures of the strummed guitar weren't enough to prick my ears, but once I heard her voice, that voice that seemed to somehow bellow with brightness, I knew my father would ruin my mohawk. Because I knew he'd heard it too. *Don't you know, they're talking about a revolution?* she sang, and I had no idea what any of it meant but I was certain that slight vibrato had caused a tremor in me—in us—and that we would experience it during every forthcoming haircut because my father would play the album for a year straight.

Of course, I can do a mohawk, son. Ain't nothing but a rainbow on your head.

I don't remember the first time I heard the voice of Hanif Abdurraqib. If I had to guess, I'd say it was at some sort of poetry thing. Some event where twenty-somethings were gnashing their teeth, raging on about whatever version of revolution was ours to claim. Whatever iteration of it involved irony and performance and, occasionally, a score. However, I do remember the first time I read Hanif. I was thirty-three, and while I'm trying not to reference the obvious cliché, I had grown hair of wool due to the fact I'd sworn off haircuts for well over a decade. A friend of mine had a copy of Hanif's new collection of essays, the cerulean cover overlaid with a stark image of a wolf in a track jacket wearing a gold dookie rope around his neck, reminiscent of the ones Mr. T, and Slick Rick, and Rakim wore in the eighties. Intrigued, I split the pages, opening it close to the middle and read, "Defiance, Ohio Is The Name Of A Band," an essay that reads like a stream of consciousness and uses a relationship with a particular band as a way to capture a frenetic form of grieving. Five minutes later, upon finishing the essay, I could feel heat on the back of my neck, a physical cue that my anxiety, the kind rooted in possibility, had been sparked. A heat no different than the way I felt as a kid whenever my father would tie a towel around my neck as a makeshift smock to catch what was falling from my head. The bits of me he'd set free.

I read on. And on. Essay after essay, like liner notes to life as compilation. And over the course of a day or so, once I'd devoured them all, I realized, I, too, could use music as a framework to process my life and the world around me. Use it as a vehicle to explore moments of rebellion, complacency, fear, love, race, death. Each song serving as another layer to my personal palimpsest.

I also realized that Hanif's work, these essays, his considerations and confessions, are also music in and of themselves. That these words are, in fact, instrumental. That they also have a vibrato that causes a tremor in me. That they, too, are meant to inspire someone to try something brave, like cutting a rainbow into your head, or whatever else was supposed to look like a mohawk but now looks like something else, but will have to do for now because the fistful of gold is still just out of reach.

Don't you know, they're talking about a revolution? It sounds like a whisper.

—Jason Reynolds,
August 2022

Acknowledgments

Earlier versions of essays in this book have appeared in *Pitchfork*, *MTV News*, *The New York Times*, *ESPN The Magazine*, and *Pacific Standard*. I appreciate all of those homes and the editors who helped to build them.

This book wouldn't be possible without the belief that Two Dollar Radio showed in this project from the start, back when it was something drifting oceans away from my imagination. Thanks to Eric and Eliza Obenauf, Brett Gregory, and Haley Cowans. Your work on this book and your belief in it pushed me to a comfort that made this book come together.

To my family and friends and the people who are consistently swelling with patience and grace when I, at times, don't have that to offer myself. High thanks as always to my dearest pals from Columbus who don't give a shit how many words I do or don't write: Meaghan, David, Sam, and Stephanie. I'll make infinite time for you all one of these days, I promise.

To Eve L. Ewing, the best sibling in art that anyone could ask for. We'll start the band eventually. Once all of the noise dies down, we'll make new noise.

I hold a deep and loving space for my former *MTV News* colleagues, many of them pushing me in the writing of many of these essays: Doreen St. Felix, Carvell Wallace, Molly Lambert, Shrill, Ira Madison III, Kaleb Horton, Meaghan Garvey, Jamil Smith, Amy Nicholson, Brian Phillips, Hazel Cills, Darcie Wilder, Holly Anderson, Simon Vozick-Levinson (Kelly Clarkson has good songs!) and the rest of the staff at *MTV News*. We built an impossible thing, and this book wouldn't exist without it.

To the poets, always, but especially the ones who saw me through this impossible and insecure time and pulled me out the other side: Sarah Kay, Clint Smith, Anis Mojgani. Angel Nafis / Danez Smith / Cortney Charleston / José Olivarez / Nate Marshall / Safia Elhillo / Elizabeth Acevedo / Sean DesVignes / Desiree Bailey / Nabila Lovelace / Aziza Barnes / Jerriod Avant / Paul Tran / Jeremy Michael Clark / Ish / Jayson Smith. May The Conversation live forever. To the generosity of Kaveh Akbar and Terrance Hayes! Fatimah Asghar and Franny Choi and Mark Cugini (thanks for letting Vintage Sadness rock!) and Julian Randall and Eloisa Amezcua. To the encouragement from the poet who writes the long poem and calls it an essay or writes the essay and breaks it into so many pieces that it becomes a poem! I am a poet first and foremost, and second I am whatever comes after.

To Tabia Yapp, who is patient with my ever hectic unfolding life. Thank you, this is also possible because of you.

The Columbus poetry and writing community which has fostered my work from day one, when I was showing up to open mics with poems on wrinkled paper in my back pockets. Special thanks to Writing Wrongs and Writer's Block poetry nights. Will Evans, Scott Woods, Rose Smith, Steve Abbott, Rachel Wiley, Maggie Smith, Hannah Stephenson, Barb Fant, Kim Leddy, Aaron Alsop, Izetta Thomas, Xavier Smith, Joe Atticus Inch, Fayce Hammond, and of course of course Karen Scott.

I owe Jessica Hopper's vision a great deal—not just her vision for criticism and approaching music seriously, but also her vision for what the critical space could look like, and who it could include. Thanks for believing in me, Jessica. It is impossible to measure and express what that means. Can't wait until we figure out something else cool to do together.

I am a student of many critics and thinkers, living and not: Lester Bangs, Greil Marcus, Jon Caramanica (writing this in retro jordans, fam), Justin Charity, Ann Powers, Sasha Frere-Jones, Rembert Browne, Roxane Gay, Brittany Spanos, Ta-Nehisi Coates, Jeff Weiss, Kelsey McKinney, Rachel Kaadzi Ghansah. Steven Hyden, Kelefa Sanneh, Vann Newkirk. Baldwin. Hurston. Walker. Josephine, always. Whitney. Michael. All of the people who still write things on the internet.

Thanks to Dan Campbell. Your music has helped keep my friends alive, and now we're all old and trying to make this fleeting life interesting.

Kiese, you teach me so much and your words of support mean everything.

This book is dedicated to the memory of Marshawn McCarrel and the memory of Bill Hurley.

Thank you, reader, for sharing a small corner of this brief and sometimes fantastic life with me.

PHOTO BY ADAM CENSI

Hanif Abdurraqib—a 2021 MacArthur 'Genius' Grant Recipient—is a poet, essayist, and cultural critic from Columbus, Ohio. His poetry has been published in *Muzzle, Vinyl,* PEN American, and various other journals. His essays and music criticism have been published in *The FADER, Pitchfork, The New Yorker,* and *The New York Times.* He is the author of the poetry collections *The Crown Ain't Worth Much,* a finalist for the Eric Hoffer Book Prize, and *A Fortune For Your Disaster,* which won the 2020 Lenore Marshall Prize, and the essay collections *They Can't Kill Us Until They Kill Us,* named a best book of the year by *Buzzfeed, Esquire, NPR, Oprah Magazine, Paste, CBC, The Los Angeles Review, Pitchfork,* and *The Chicago Tribune,* among others; *Go Ahead In The Rain: Notes To A Tribe Called Quest,* a *New York Times Bestseller,* a finalist for the Kirkus Prize, and longlisted for the National Book Award; and *A Little Devil In America,* which was shortlisted for the National Book Award. He is a graduate of Beechcroft High School.

PHOTO BY MERCEDES ZAPATA

Eve L. Ewing is the award-winning author of several books, including the poetry collections *Electric Arches* and *1919*, the nonfiction work *Ghosts in the Schoolyard: Racism and School Closings on Chicago's South Side*, and a novel for young readers, *Maya and the Robot*. She is the co-author (with Nate Marshall) of the play *No Blue Memories: The Life of Gwendolyn Brooks*. She has also written several comics for Marvel Comics, most notably the *Ironheart* series. Dr. Ewing co-wrote a story with Janelle Monáe as a contributor to the collection of Black queer Afrofuturist fiction *The Memory Librarian*, and she also co-wrote the young adult graphic novel *Change the Game* with Colin Kaepernick. She was born in Chicago, where she lives and teaches.

PHOTO BY ADEDAYO "DAYO" KOSOKO

Jason Reynolds is a #1 *New York Times* bestselling author of more than a dozen books for young people, including *Look Both Ways: A Tale Told in Ten Blocks*, *All American Boys* (with Brendan Kiely), *Long Way Down*, *Stamped: Racism, Antiracism, and You* (with Ibram X. Kendi), *Stuntboy, in the Meantime* (illustrated by Raúl the Third), and *Ain't Burned All the Bright* (with artwork by Jason Griffin). The recipient of a Newbery Honor, a Printz Honor, an NAACP Image Award, and multiple Coretta Scott King honors, Reynolds is also the current National Ambassador for Young People's Literature and has appeared on *The Late Show with Stephen Colbert*, *The Daily Show with Trevor Noah*, *Late Night with Seth Meyers*, *CBS This Morning*, and *Good Morning America*. He is on faculty at Lesley University, for the Writing for Young People MFA Program and lives in Washington, DC. You can find his ramblings at JasonWritesBooks.com.